What Reviewers Say Ab

Simmins's award-winning essays explore a v
harrowing to the lyrical. Her fearless truth i
shortcomings, makes her a memoirist we car
intimate, often unguarded, but always big-hea..... And frequently funny.
  – Harry Thurston, *The Chronicle Herald*, Nova Scotia.

... a down-to-earth and heartwarming memoir; it talks about mature people living real lives.
  – Lynne Van Luven, *Coastal Spectator*, Victoria, British Columbia

I wanted to love this book, and ... I did. Simmins writes with wit, with a great eye for the telling detail, and with emotional intelligence.
  – Marq de Villiers, *The Antigonish Review*, Nova Scotia

With that mix of care, insight and honesty, Simmins has crafted a touching and beautiful memoir. She describes the difficulty of leaving a place she loved so deeply for the Atlantic Coast, where even the ocean smells different, and she's often reminded that she's a come-from-away. It's honest, warm and at times raw. She's an energetic and joyful person, which sparkles off every page, even – and especially – when her story (as life stories so often do) take darker and sadder turns. You should read this book – it's hopeful, inspiring, and just plain good writing.
  – Trevor Adams, *Halifax Magazine*

Journalist and writing instructor Marjorie Simmins' memoir Coastal Lives is framed as a love story, the coming together from Canada's opposite coasts of two writers: Simmins and the prolific Silver Donald Cameron. But her work shines brightest when it's about the geographically fractured nature of modern families.
  – Chris Benjamin, *Ottawa Citizen*

Simmins has a down-to-earth honesty that should be the envy of any writer. There is an intimacy shared with the reader whether she is writing about addiction, loss, a kitchen ceilidh, riding horses or walking her dogs in Point Pleasant Park [in Halifax].
  – John Gillis, *The Oran*, Inverness, Cape Breton

Our lives are made up of stories: tales we tell to others and ourselves. We're born into a narrative, ever-evolving from generation to generation. Author and journalist Marjorie Simmins believes in the power of writing it down. She's a born memoirist.
  – Shannon Webb-Campbell, *Saltscapes Magazine*

Year of the Horse

A Journey of Healing and Adventure

Marjorie Simmins

Pottersfield Press, Lawrencetown Beach, Nova Scotia, Canada

Library and Archives Canada Cataloguing in Publication

Simmins, Marjorie, author
 Year of the horse : a journey of healing and adventure
/ Marjorie Simmins.
ISBN 978-1-897426-90-6 (paperback)
1. Simmins, Marjorie. 2. Horsemanship. 3. Journalists--Canada--Biography.
4. Horsemen and horsewomen--Canada--Biography. I. Title.
PN4913.S495A3 2016   070.92   C2016-902941-7

Cover design: Gail LeBlanc

Pottersfield Press acknowledges the financial support of the Government of Canada for our publishing activities. We acknowledge the support of the Canada Council for the Arts. We are pleased to work in partnership with the Province of Nova Scotia to develop and promote our creative industries for the benefit of all Nova Scotians.

Pottersfield Press
83 Leslie Road
East Lawrencetown, Nova Scotia, Canada, B2Z 1P8
Website: www.PottersfieldPress.com
To order, phone 1-800-NIMBUS9 (1-800-646-2879) www.nimbus.ns.ca

Printed in Canada

This book is a work of nonfiction. Unless otherwise noted, the author and publisher make no explicit guarantees as to the accuracy of the information contained in this book and in some cases, names of people and places have been altered to protect their privacy.

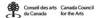 

For Adrienne and Scott Smith,
and for
Helen and Neil Morley:
gratitude as big as Kelly's Mountain.

With deep thanks to
my new horse communities in Nova Scotia,
and my lifelong horse community at Southlands,
in Vancouver, British Columbia.

For Don: once and always.

"I discovered that the horse is life itself, a metaphor but also an example of life's mystery and unpredictability, of life's generosity and beauty, a worthy object of repeated and ever-changing contemplation."

– Jane Smiley, author of *Horse Heaven*

"... we must never forget, every time we sit on a horse, what an extraordinary privilege it is: to be able to unite one's body with that of another sentient being, one that is stronger, faster and more agile by far than we are, and at the same time, brave, generous, and uncommonly forgiving."

– William Steinkraus, Olympic equestrian

CONTENTS

Introduction
Southlands, Vancouver, B.C., June 1972, 11:45 p.m.

The night is even softer than I'd hoped. I have a light jacket on, but I don't bother zipping it up as I bomb down Blenheim on my ten-speed. My windbreaker streams out behind me and the kind air presses against my face and chest. I barely pause at the stop sign at Southwest Marine Drive. There are no cars out at this time of night. I have to get to the barn. I push the word *hurry, hurry* into my hard-pedalling feet.

I am a horse owner. At least I was after school, when I rode this same bicycle to the Calders' place, where our half-Arabian is stabled. Here I am again, the same day, only minutes before midnight. We have owned our horse for six months now, and every day, every night, I can barely take in the dream that is my life. Tonight I couldn't sleep at all, could only think, *To see is to believe.*

I reach Blenheim and 53rd Avenue. I am a half-block from the barn. I swing wide at 53rd and turn east. Past the Mills' place now, then, wheel wobbling, I ride onto the chunky hog-fuel pathway adjacent to the field. I dismount, lean my bike against the fence, find my way to the second stall from the left in the shed-row barn of four stalls.

"Coqeyn," I whisper. Kokane is how that word is pronounced – not Coquin, as some people say. His name sounds exactly like another word, cocaine, the illegal drug, which, of course, people have teased us about, or even, in their ignorance, presumed to censor. Someone else said, laughing, "Don't worry about it. In fact, be proud. There was a famous stunt horse named Cocaine once, in Hollywood." Even still, Kokane is how I see it in my mind.

Sometimes we call him –

"Coqer."

I cross my arms on the flat ledge of the Dutch door. The top half is latched back.

"Coqer," I whisper again. "It's me."

And suddenly, from out of the dark depths of the stall, the chestnut gelding's face emerges inches from my own. In the dark night world I can mostly only see the white on his forehead, face, and nose. He moves closer yet. I turn my cheek and he presses his nose delicately into it, then rests. *Velvet.* It is the most memorable horse kiss I will ever receive, though I do not know it then.

"How did you ever find me?" As though in response, and still against my cheek, his lips start to move. It tickles. I can't help it, I have to laugh. I do this into my sleeve, making barely any sound. I was quieter yet when I snuck out of my house up on 43rd and Dunbar. Mum would have had a fit if she'd caught me up – *and out* – at this hour, on a school night to boot. But if the barn owners find me here, I'll be in big trouble. There are thefts at the barns all around here sometimes – even the horses, taken for dangerous joyrides around the area's bracketing golf courses and sand dunes. Must be quiet. Besides, I wouldn't know how to explain that I … just had to check that Coqeyn was real – that a source for such mountainous joy could reliably exist in the world for a thirteen-year-old girl who only six months ago was earthbound ordinary, didn't even imagine that she could call to a horse and have one appear from the silky summer darkness, as her own. Would I always feel this connection to horses? Or would I change as I grew older? Perhaps life would do the changing, push horses deeper into my past, not permit them in my present or future. *No, unimaginable.*

Year of the Horse is a true story about my experiences with horses over a lifetime. I am not a professional rider, or a coach or instructor, or horse expert of any kind. I offer you one horsewoman's story – about horses, healing, and improbable dreams. Whether you ride horses or not, whether your own adventures involve the other sacred elements – earth, water, or fire, not air – this book is intended to give you the best seat in the house, atop one of the world's most elegant and swift creatures. Eyes up and heels down – the pace is about to pick up.

1
YEAR OF THE HORSE

I am arcing through the air headed toward the ground, but there are heartbeats enough to think before I hit. Tuck 'n roll, they taught us as kids. So I will tuck and I will –

Smash. Heartbeats aplenty now, and that sickening feeling of I am hurt, I am really hurt, followed by, This is bad. I don't move an eyelash, then a wash of electric current travels from my right seat-bone to the tip of my right second toe. It is the nastiest funny-bone zap since ever the world spun, and it's happening underneath my body, where it lies in the dirt of an indoor riding arena. Now water is collecting under me. It must be water because whatever the liquid is, it's cold – so what else could it be? Could it be blood? Does blood feel cold when you're lying down hurt? It's a cold spring day. Maybe I landed in a puddle. But there are no puddles in here. That's just silly. I close my eyes for a second as the funny-bone current bangs against the end of my toe, regroups, and is now speeding back up my leg. I could puke for the power of its forceful malevolence. I've fallen off horses countless times, but I've never felt this assaulted, this damaged.

"Help! Help me!" I have only just enough air in my lungs to shout. I think someone said, I'm coming!, or maybe, Horse first, then you, or even, Are you all right?

Help did come. They did indeed put the horse away in its stall first. And I was decidedly not all right. It's three years later – and I am still not all right.

But I am plotting.

It's 2014, Year of the Horse, according to Chinese astrology. This year, the Chinese New Year will be ushered in on January 31. Grandly, it is a year that promises to be "thrilling" for all. I find these facts online, but really, all I care about is the phrase *Year of the Horse,* which I keep hearing over and over, even here in Halifax, Nova Scotia, where there is a relatively small Asian community. Maybe I hear it because I have an ear and spirit tuned to the Chinese New Year. In Vancouver, British Columbia, where I lived most of my life, the celebrations for the new year will be joyous and well-attended, covered by all the mainstream media and enjoyed by the majority of its residents, Asian or otherwise, even if just for the "dancing dragons" and other parade characters who throng through the main streets of Chinatown, seen in person or on television.

Year of the Horse. I explore the phrase silently, behind my eyes, and aloud, in a whisper, where the syllables filter deep down into my heart and guts. I feel a quickened pulse at the base of my throat. Involuntarily, I lift that right foot of mine. The insole still tingles, is dysfunctional. I shake it, reposition it on the edge of the carpet: heel down, toes up, just as the foot would be positioned in a stirrup. Just as it was positioned, that last time ...

May 2, 2011, the day I flew without wings, then crash-landed. I did a lot of damage to my sciatic nerve that day, which is the longest and largest nerve in the human body, spanning from the lower back to the foot, and about the thickness of a person's thumb. The condition of sciatica is caused by the compression or irritation of a nerve root in the lumbar spine. *Thump!* When my body hit the ground, the impact compressed my spine. Skeletal damage was only part of the picture. Overall, my body's "soft tissue" was thrashed. This included my tendons, ligaments, fascia, skin, fibrous tissues, fat and synovial membranes (connective tissue), and muscles, nerves, and blood vessels (which are not connective tissue). The right-hand side of my body took the brunt of the fall, and the left side was terribly jarred and injured as well. My gluteal muscles, a group of three muscles that make up the buttocks, were as bashed and bruised as if I'd landed on cobblestones. Why was this fall so bad? Distance of the trajectory, velocity of the impact, hardness of the ground, and how I landed, I can only guess.

Similarly, I think, but do not know, that it was the sciatic nerve, leading directly from the centre of my right buttock down my leg to my second toe, that used to make me feel I'd stuck a wet finger in an electrical outlet. Every day, throughout the day, that nerve "came alive," punching and twisting its way down the length of my body, and most reliably, if I tried to stand. It no longer spasms along that whole long route, jerking me off my feet or even off the toilet seat with its laser-blue intensity. Occasionally I get a shortened muscle spasm, or "Charley horse," which aches its way down the back of my thigh, then viciously curls and bites down my calf. I repeatedly bash, then press my heel against the hardwood floors in our bedroom – the spasms almost always occur while stretching in bed or rising from it – which somehow uncurls the muscle. Often, I am able to stop the pain.

Mostly the nerve path hovers and taunts – like a negative, recurring thought you'd rather not have. If you could see it on the outside, I think it would look like a seamed stocking. Inside, I envision it as a grey ghost, its gauzy arms wrapped around my tendons, ligaments, and muscles. My right calf is always tight; the muscles healed completely, but short, from so much inactivity. Three months in bed, then teaching myself to walk again, wobbly as a blind kitten. Radiating pain like I never knew existed and over two years of profound disability, which deeply shocked me, changed my understanding of the world forever. Changed my body forever, too.

There are the able-bodied, and there are the others – the ones the uninjured honk their horns at, when they walk with a child's steps through a crosswalk or across a parking lot. The people you sigh at, mightily, when they shuffle before you at the grocery store, impeding your darting progress down the food aisle. The ones who walk with canes or push those portable, wheeled seats. The ones who sit in wheelchairs. Those people I stared at, covertly, as never before: *I could have been you. Forgive me, I don't want to be you.*

The fact that I had even the shallowest understanding of a life where you couldn't walk scared me to my deepest interior. I gritted my teeth and kept on with the physiotherapy that alleviated pain some days, and on other days, simply spread it around. My seventy-three-year-old husband, fit and well-able, as the Irish say, bought me a cane to use. Two revolutions of the small upstairs area of our house, and I was exhausted, couldn't wait to get back to bed. With my balance so poor, I was wary of the long staircase to the main floor, frightened I would tumble down it. I gave it as wide a berth as I could. Even still, I could look down the staircase and think about the life that waited for me to resume it, down there: my office, the kitchen and fireplace room, and the bright dining and living rooms, both with generous windows looking out over the ocean waters of the Northwest Arm, which lead in turn to Halifax harbour and the open Atlantic.

Then, only just back on my feet, I paddled and bobbed my way through a summer of hydrotherapy. My lower back was numb and still is, to a substantial degree. It also still puffs up when I exercise or stand too long. And it still feels – different than it did. Weak some days, cranky others.

I don't know how to explain the fury I felt, after the event, because even as I travelled through the air, shot high and far from a horse that bolted, then deked sideways, I was sure I was going to be all right, would be banged up, but not grossly injured. *Tuck and roll,* all our instructors drilled into us, and I thought – I was so sure! – that I *had* tucked, and *would* roll, that the landing wouldn't be too bad. Ten minutes later, shock settling in nicely, I even laughed when I tried to stand, and collapsed onto my right shoulder and side again. "Call the ambulance," I said to the woman who had come to help me, helping her instead, to make the necessary decision. "I'm not walking anywhere." I remember feeling glad I wasn't crying and being difficult to deal with; I even directed another young woman how to find my cell phone and ring my husband, to tell him what had happened.

I also remember, within minutes of landing, wiggling my legs, toes, and last and gingerly, my head. *I wasn't paralyzed.* Nor was I in terrible pain, I decided. I didn't know that the full pain had not yet descended – had no idea what lay ahead for me.

Even recalling these memories has that ghostly nerve path complaining, and I'm just sitting here at my desk, not moving a muscle. Up and around come those wispy grey bits, looking for nerve endings to shake and enliven, striking pay dirt when they do get a spark and I gasp out loud, more in remembered fear now than with acute pain.

Pain – you think you know pain? says the voice of memory. *Don't you remember –*

Yes, I do. She was one of the people at the Rehabilitation Centre, in my hydrotherapy group. None of us exchanged names. There were six of us, and she was by far the cheeriest. She was at least seventy, I would guess, but carried a nice trim weight and did not seem frail. "Good morning," she'd say warmly. "Another lovely day, isn't it?" Yes, I'd reply – almost completely unaware of the physical world in those days – a fine one indeed. We'd chat about the water temperature, which was hot enough for a Japanese public bath, and in the way of women, admired one another's bathing suits, knowing how hellishly hard it is to find one that fits and flatters. Her face was open and gently creased, and she walked slowly, on a slight tilt to the right.

But I didn't see this woman from the back until several sessions along. Or perhaps she had on a different, more revealing bathing suit. I was still using the cane to walk beside the pool and we were both working our way along to the top right corner, where the steps descended. She walked in front of me. I was concentrating on my feet, nervous to slip on the tiles, obsessed with fear of falling. Then I looked up.

Her back was a maze of train-track scars, thick and ugly. The scars were both old and white, and new and pink. I couldn't guess how many surgeries they represented. I had never seen a body cry *wounded!* to that degree. I was nauseated and fascinated, could barely look away. It was reminiscent of the feelings I had soon after the accident, when I looked at people in wheelchairs: pity and relief. This time, though, I also felt respect for the woman's fighting and effervescent spirit. I continued to watch her as she stepped steadily down the stairs, easing into the water. The scars were out of sight now. But her smile was evident.

"The best yet," she called to me, from ten feet out. "You'll see."

She was right, the water was fine that day. So was the reverberating shot of courage she gave me, two and a half slow-moving years ago.

You know, I had the overall idea right, to return to the world of barns and horses I've known almost all my life, and to get strong and bold again. That right leg is still pesky, and the back is not what it should be, but there's nothing wrong with my left leg, or my arms or hands or anything else that I need to ride again. Nothing wrong with my heart, either, and as the title of the pop song goes, "The Heart Wants What It Wants." As for the horse who dumped me, I forgave him long ago. He was just being a horse, bolting at the sound of a violent wind gust, as it smacked the roof above us, then turning a nimble 180, to return to the safety of his barn. If I had been stronger, I could have sat *down*, and pulled him up, before he dodged sideways. *If I had been stronger* ... my heart keeps time to the phrase, and the other, more insistent one, *Year of the Horse* ... Bring them *on*. Or is that, bring them *back*? Again. After all, I was never supposed to quit. I was supposed to ride all my life. That was the way I'd always imagined it. I even remember when I first had that thought.

I was fourteen. I spoke to her for a few minutes forty years ago, and never forgot what she said or the way she looked that day. I still trust the goal she inspired in me.

I don't know why I remember her so vividly. At Southlands, a rurally zoned equestrian area in southwest Vancouver, there were many older women who had ridden horses all their lives and remained limber and fit. This woman was merely one of these, though rumour had it she'd won the Western Pan American Trials in individual dressage in 1967, and had then gone on to win a Team Bronze, so in a place of many fine riders, she might have been exceptional. She certainly had the competitive rider's assurance, in or out of a saddle, and the confident tall woman's magnetism, also in or out of a saddle. I don't even remember her name. I was just a teenager when she was well into her middle years. She was also rich, a barn owner, and I was a middle-class kid whose divorced mother worked two jobs to pay for our horse's feed and board, and that at a rundown "do-it-yourselfer" barn where my sister and I did the feeding and mucking out for our own horse. The woman had silver hair cut in a smart bob and was thin as a Danish cracker. She also owned Pomeranians, round-eyed peach fluff-balls on which she doted. It was because of the Poms I spoke to her – once and once only, walking back to my barn, after watching a friend's jumping lesson at Southlands Riding Club.

"The coyotes are everywhere now," she said, scooping her two dogs up from the quiet road in front of her house. "They even have a den on the hunt course at the club." I guess she spoke to me because I was right there in the middle of the road walking toward her, and smiled at her squirming dogs. I think I said something such as, Really? That's awful.

"They're getting the chickens at our neighbour's place," she continued, the dogs now wilted and quiet under her firm grip, "and they're into everyone's garbage, of course." Her attractive, lined face hardened. "Last week, two of them tried to take my dogs right out of my arms – right here, in this very spot where I'm standing." What did you do, I asked. "I kicked at them, yelled, then turned around and walked away. You can't run, you know. They'll get you if you do. Damn things, they're feeding their pups now." She turned away from me, started heading back to her house. She stopped for one last comment: "There's hardly a cat left in the area – all killed and eaten by the coyotes. Small dogs, too. That's it, no more outside time for my dogs. Not without me nearby, anyway."

I suppose I should have been frightened or at least wary as I continued on my way. But the hunt course was well behind me now and I'd never seen coyotes over by my barn, three blocks away. Wrapped in these flimsy comforts I banished any worries and kept walking. Her words lingered, though, and I couldn't help wondering: How do you save yourself, and the two cherished heartbeats pressed tight in your arms, if slashing teeth set upon you?

But it hadn't happened. She didn't let it happen. She shouted them down before they rose, and turned that resolute spire of a body and its attached cargo away from hungry eyes. She wasn't scared in the moment, of that I am certain, any more than I was hearing about it days later. Her words are clear, even now, but what I remember clearest of all is the woman's face, form, and spirit, all of which I admired. I could never be that tall or that straight-lined; that's just not the way I came to this world. But I would and did get older, and I always hoped to resemble her in essence, fit and comfortable with her own well-tuned, strong body, and maybe, when times demanded it, that determined and defiant, even scornful of danger.

Keep riding, said a voice inside fourteen-year-old me – *just keep riding.*

And I did, but with long spaces between. Too long. My thirties might even have been my best riding decade – to date – my forties were sketchy, and I'd just started back again, in my fifties, when that scared old schooling horse bolted, deked, and dumped me, causing me those two hellish years of pain and dysfunction.

"Soft-tissue damage," the ER doctor had said, shaking her head. "Complex and long-lasting. You're gonna wish you'd broken your back. That would heal a lot faster." In fact, I just wished I hadn't gone to the barn that day, hadn't heard that gale-force slam of wind against the roof of the indoor arena, hadn't felt that sickening surge of power beneath me and hadn't thought, I can bring him back, *I can.* And didn't. You feel oddly ashamed, when you fail at something as elemental as looking after your own physical placement on the earth. Human bodies are not built for air travel. And even earth feels like a cliff-face, given enough force when you hit it.

Why go back? ask non-riding friends, gently but uncomprehendingly. You could have ended up paralyzed – or worse. Don't you worry it could happen again?

Because./Yes./And yes again. All those years of joy, physical and spiritual, from age twelve on. All that hard work, to make the gains I did make; God knows I was never a "jock," never even particularly limber or strong, certainly without riding in my life. I am not getting stronger now, either. I don't want to be a frail older woman. I don't want to look at people decades younger than me and some few decades older, see their slim, trim frames and know that my choices pushed fitness and health out of my life. And I would miss horses, elementally.

But perhaps another sport, the friends (and husband, at first) persist. Something less dangerous?

Isn't every sport dangerous to some degree? And at the risk of employing specious argument, doesn't taking up an entirely new sport in my fifties have more than a generous chance of injury involved in it?

Listen, I say finally, knowing no argument will really hold water, because it's just so hard to see someone you love hurt badly – riding horses was never just something I did. *It's who I am.* I love the whole world of horses, want it in my life now, and as I get older. I want it for my body, and for my mind and spirit. As it makes sense and as circumstances demand, the manifestations of horse life may change in coming years. Maybe I'll end up "grounded," working around horses, not riding on them. I'll accept those changes as they come along.

But not now. I do not accept a non-riding life now.

I am fifty-four years old, fifty-five in February. To me, with the moves and changes in my life over the years, it seems as though I have lost and regained my riding seat three times. Did I wait too long to go back this time? Have I finally and completely "lost my seat"?

It's a peculiar phrase – to "lose your seat." The image that comes to mind is of a person with no backside. Doesn't a middle-aged woman wish for that! Well, perhaps not no bottom at all, but a smaller one, certainly, would be fine. Or perhaps the phrase makes you think you've "lost your seat" as you might in a child's game of musical chairs. But no, it is neither of these things.

A "seat," when used in the context of riding horses, means your basic rider body position, which you strive to maintain while in the saddle. The seat, or the rider's balance, is one of the natural "aids" used to control the horse's direction, gait, and speed. Other natural aids include the rider's hands, voice, and legs. Artificial aids include bits, reins, saddles, and spurs. The seat is the foundation of all aids, and the primary one to control rhythm, speed, length of stride and downward "transitions," or changes of gait (canter to trot, trot to walk, and so on).

In all horseback riding disciplines, riders find it amusing when non-riders refer to the horse "doing all the work." No, we do not just sit there. I wish. You use almost every muscle in your body. If you are not fit, those muscles will be talking to you after each ride, loud and long.

Having a good seat is all about lines and angles, grace and strength. And, as with all sports, it's also about breathing. A sketch of a rider exhibiting good "form" or posture would show a straight line running down from her ear, shoulder, hip, and heel. The idea is to keep your centre of gravity over your hips. New riders, struggling with the large and unfamiliar movements of the horse, tend to fold over at the waist and grab onto the reins for balance. When I was learning to ride in the 1970s, we used to call this "the fetal position."

When you tip forward, disaster beckons. First you've jabbed the horse in the mouth when you pulled on the reins and bit, which annoys and hurts the animal, then you've lost your balance, and can easily be unseated. Someone with a good seat can actually ride without reins or stirrups. The closest I came to this was what I called "bareback toodles" – no saddle or bareback pad (both of which have stirrups), no bridle, only a halter and a lead-shank, the rope run through the halter rings to make reins of sorts. You must trust the horse with heart and soul for this kind of riding, and even then, accidents can happen. Fight or flight, it is what horses do in so many circumstances, with flight being the far-preferred choice and the obvious physical gift.

With so much to think about when you are on a horse, it can be difficult to relax. But learning or relearning the sport, you must aid relaxation of mind and body by breathing regularly and deeply. The entire back must be upright but fluid, to maintain effective posture. The hips, too, need to be loose and "giving," to flow with horse's movement. At the same time, the body's core muscles (stomach and backside) are engaged, keeping the rider stable.

Then there are the rider's feet. The ball, not the sole, of your foot is positioned in the stirrup, which allows for "weight" (pressure downwards) to fall into your heel. "Heels down" is a phrase a rider will hear directed to her by instructors throughout her life. Heels are lazy, and prefer to stay level or better yet go up – anywhere but down, leg and foot muscles engaged.

Action by action, riding sounds strange and unnatural. In some ways it is. But in other ways, it's a natural domino-effect. You start at the top and work down. Head up, shoulders level, back straight, arms bent, hands soft but grip firm, knees close, calves closer, legs long, heel deep. Easy as pie.

Not. At least not for many years. You know the way when you watch a fabulously skilled figure skater whirl about and your heart thinks – not your head – That's not so hard, I could do that! And of course that's nonsense, but there's a stubborn bit of that pounding heart of yours that loves the circling, leaping beauty before you so much it just seems it should be yours, *gratis.*

I don't know for sure, because I never skated well or even competently, but I'd guess that to lose that way of skimming over ice would be heartbreaking. I feel heartsick myself, from having lost my riding seat. I love to look at horses as much as most people. But it is that glorious close contact – warm, soft coat under your hands, locomotion under you, a curl of coarse mane under two fingers as you lift to the sky over a jump – which horse people want more than anything else. Like the skaters, we can fly. Unlike the individual skaters, there is another heartbeat in the equation, another personality and temperament to deal with, apart from your own. In the upper echelons of horsemanship, there are two talents working together – human and animal – and both will have good days and bad. They'll even have good and bad days together, or at odds. The complications are numerous. No matter how trained the horse or rider is, if one or both of the pair does not acknowledge the basic partnership aspect of riding, not much enjoyment will be had, nor progressions made.

The fact that a human ever took it into his head to jump on a horse, grab the mane, and gallop away – well, I would have gloried to have seen that first caveman cover ground. I wonder how long he stayed on, and how he had the guts to try again, after he was thrown. Maybe he didn't, and *she* did.

And the fact is, I haven't actually lost my riding seat – I've merely misplaced it. I know what to do, and muscle memory and a lifetime of riding experiences will support my efforts to ride well again. Once all my muscles are working and engaged again – legs, stomach, back, and arms, even my hands, I suppose – then everything will feel, and look, right. It takes time. Lots of it. And belief. After all, I owned a horse once, and rode many other horses at the barns we boarded at. Then I leased a half-dozen different horses over the long-term, in my twenties and thirties. It was my forties that were sketchiest – and small wonder there, after moving from Vancouver to Cape Breton, and not knowing anyone period, let alone anyone in the horse communities. Then, just into my fifties, and after a move to Halifax, I found a schooling barn near the city. Before the accident, I was making excellent strides (so to speak) on getting my seat back – though there were days I was gasping as I rode. Every day was better, though. Then every day was hell. That was then, this is now. Somewhere inside me is a confident rider who knows how to do this.

Memories help.

THE HORSE WHO ALWAYS WHICKERED –
REMEMBERING KABER

I'd never known a horse who whickered much, but one year I found myself leasing one who whickered every time he saw me. Up came that regal grey head from grazing, or poked out, ears alert, from his stall, then the rounded lips would start to tremble. A cascading rumble sounded, the warmest equine welcome ever: *Hello! It's you!* As though it was a miracle I'd come back to the barn again, even though he saw me twice a week, and had for a year by then. Didn't matter – Kaber the half-Arabian was always happy to see me. He even came to me from the furthest corner of the field and dipped his head into the halter. I felt so lucky, so singled out by his friendship. I flattered myself in believing that he wasn't so interactive with everyone.

"Kaber can be hot – be careful," said one of the other young women who had leased the athletic gelding before me. "His shies are sky-high and his bolts are legendary. You pay attention and hang on."

I didn't tell her that I sometimes rode him bareback, with only a halter and a lead line. We'd jog around the neighbourhood and canter down some of the soft hog-fuel paths that ran alongside the properties at Southlands, in southwest Vancouver. I rode English, but Kaber also had a perfect, slow-motion Western lope. No matter what was asked of him, or where we hacked, he gave me an honest, cheerful ride. He was just as content trotting alongside the river paths as he was walking deep inside the coastal forest, where the Douglas firs soared to uneven peaks and broken light dappled the trails.

One sweltering summer day I didn't see him in the field or in the barn. I exited the barn headed to the paddocks behind. I wore jeans and a cotton shirt and was thinking it was definitely a bareback day. What a season it had been for sun and no rain. Even the horses had sunburned noses.

Whicker-whicker – two in a row, his usual, but I couldn't see him. Where was he?

In the furthest paddock Kaber was lying down the way a cat would, with his forelegs drawn up and back legs close to the body too. His head was low. My heartbeat spiked with worry – then I smiled. He was sleeping. I slipped into the paddock. He didn't move. As quietly as I could, I sat down beside him. The earth was warm and there was a scattering of starchy, heat-scented hay near to us. I pulled out a red-skinned apple from my shirt pocket and took a bite. Kaber's head rose at the crunch, his dark eyes fastening on the fruit. I bit off a piece and offered it to him. The politest lips took it from my outstretched hand. *For your kindness, Kaber.* I took one more small piece for myself, then gave him the meaty core, which he chewed with gusto. *For your friendship.* Our snack gone, we sat in silence with a buttercup sun above us – until the shadows lengthened. There was no ride that day, not even a grooming. Just two dusty friends sharing space and time on a summer day.

2
The World Before Coqeyn

I was a horse owner once – and it is a whole other way of life. Taking lessons or leasing other people's horses is a privilege and pleasure, but being entirely responsible for another creature-soul and heartbeat in this world is a sobering and at times overwhelming experience. The joys are equally intense.

It's hard to remember there ever was a world before our horse, Coqeyn, but there was, of course. He came into our lives in 1972, in January. In the autumn of 1971, I was twelve years old and in grade six attending "the Big School," Kerrisdale Elementary in Vancouver, B.C. It was a big school, on an immense property, facing Carnarvon Street, and bordered by 41st Avenue on the south, and 39th Avenue on the north. Some of us had come up from tiny Kerrisdale Annex on West 43rd Avenue, for grades one through three – and were intimidated by the size of our new school, at least in our first year there. Two years on, most of us were thriving.

Voluble or silently lost in my imaginings, I was as content playing with friends as I was reading alone in the "Girls' Basement," or indoor play area, where my mother dropped me off each morning shortly before 8:00 on her way to teach high school in Richmond. I snugged myself into a corner by the door, and piped, *Good morning* to all the teachers who came in after me, barely looking up from my book. Like my three older siblings, Zoë, Geoffrey, and Karin, I was working my way through the school and local library. At the time, I was reading fairy tales and fantasy literature of every sort. I was caught up with the idea of being a witch, but definitely a "white," or good, witch. There were no politics of colour in my consciousness then. I just wanted to be someone with some power in her life, but nice, biddable, too. I was a girl of my times.

Our big house on 43rd and Dunbar was a complicated one. Not always – we listened to music and played guitars; we sang, played card games, and read ever-replenished piles of books; and conversations around the supper table were lively and wide-ranging. In my teenage years, no friend was ever turned away for a meal or a mug of tea, but in the early '70s our home was a serious place with hard-working residents. I wished there was something I could do to make things easier for my family. Especially my mother. She laboured long hours, in and out of the house, and had too many worries about money, and raising four children on her own. One child had already meted out more than a lifetime's share of misery and pain.

Sometimes I stole flowers from the neighbours' rock gardens as I walked home from school. Mum's face lit with happiness when I handed over the posies – "Knicky-knicky knack, which hand do you tack?" – and we both pretended the flowers were birthed in my hands.

Autumn, 1971. I lie down in the middle of the pebbled lane and look up at the dusky-indigo sky. At least the ground's dry, still warm, actually, from a hot day. Late summer in Vancouver and a dry one at that.

"What are you doing?" whispers my friend, eyes wide. A moment ago she said she didn't believe me, when I said I was a witch. Got to do something a bit dramatic to change her mind.

"Reading the stars," I say. "Wanna know your future?"

"I don't know" – despite the silence, she checks over her shoulder for any cars coming along – "maybe." She is tempted, one Dr. Scholl's sandaled toe bumping another, but surprised, too, and decides to barter for time. "Do you mean my future right now, or years from now?"

"Whatever you want." There's a warm bubble of tar under my right wrist. Other little tar-drops, under my back-side and calves, are soaking into my jeans. I will hide the soiled clothes at the bottom of the laundry basket. *Sorry, Mum. Witchy business, you understand.*

A small *ahem*, then, "Will I get married?" asks my friend. We are twelve years old. We read *True Romance* and talk endlessly about breasts ("two fried eggs"), our periods (I have mine, she doesn't), kissing (she has, I haven't), and boys (noisy, fidgety creatures, who often smell bad and eat glue). We gush the phrase *he's cute* all the time, but week to week, someone else is always *way* cuter.

"Married?" I echo. My parents are divorced, her parents are divorced; it's one of the reasons we're comfortable in our friendship: we are different from our classmates, and they make sure we know it. Maybe they're scared it's catching.

My friend nods at me, resolute in her desire to know. I think you get strong that way, when you have a stepdad who whacks you when you're "cheeky," as my friend does. She actually calls him by his given name, *Ron*, with exaggerated politeness. As in, Did my chores, *Ron*, or Supper is ready, *Ron*. Sure made me blink at first, made me think she and her brothers lived with a stranger. Which they do. But then I guess "Dad" is already taken – even if he's not around to be called that. I don't know where he is. Vanished – banished? Nameless, anyway. At least I can visit my dad. And call him Dad. My friend doesn't talk much about her real father.

She clears her throat again, impatiently. This is a gift,

really; she's more boy-crazy than I am – of course she'll get married.

"I see a tall, dark-haired man" – just like the comics – "who loves you big as" – look high above – "all the stars in the sky." Both our households sweat for money, so I decide to add in a practical detail. I lift my tar-spotted right arm, point to the biggest star I see. "Right there, says he's rich as a prince."

"But is he *nice?*" All this good news I give her, and she just wants more. I barely hear her, though. Her head's down, stars forgotten.

"Nice?" One of those non-words, but with so many meanings. Nice – your dad buys you a kitten to take home on the bus, when you visit him downtown, just yesterday. With three cats and a dog in the house already, Mum *loved* that. "Make yourselves scarce," she said through tight lips, and me and the kitty did just that, hoofing it up the staircase to my bedroom. I just love that orange kitten, called him Pumpkin. Nice – your dad makes you a "salad supper" (not hot, he explains) of soft-boiled eggs, cheese, rye bread, and pickles, which you both eat seated at the low wicker table from Chinatown. That was really nice – simple but good food and no fights or heart-folding silences as there were at the supper table at home, before he left the house. Nicest yet – we walked together along Denman, then the beach at English Bay and he explained that it's all right, that bottle of wine I saw in the refrigerator, well, it's for a *lady friend*, not him. Truth-nice that was, like him taking a lump of granite off my chest and the relief making me gulp in air through my mouth like a Fraser River bullhead, flopping in a boy's hand. *He's gonna make it* – without us – but he's gonna be all right. *Lady friend.* But no booze. We can all live with that.

The pebbles are getting to me.

"Nice," I say, readjusting my shoulders to a less poky place, "sure, we can find a nice one for you. It's all up there, in the stars. Witch's honour." My friend is smiling down at me now, scrawny arms on slim hips, head on a tilt. "Why should I believe any of this? Where'd you get your witchy papers, anyway?" We laugh, me sitting up, one hand rubbing at the back of my skull. My friend *is* cheeky, no getting around it, and with two older brothers thumping on her a lot, she's tough, too. I like that, like to see her give them hell when they get too rough. *Sorry,* they say, and thump on one another, like boys should do. Mostly, they are kind and caring brothers. And they don't like *Ron* either.

Standing now, I give it one more try. If she believes me then I believe me. It would just make things easier now, for both of us. Perk us right up.

"There's no harm in believing you can do special things," I say. *See? Look now – my friend is happy, the tears gone. I helped a bit with that.* "You know the way you love to dance – the way you're so good at it?" I am jealous of her grace, but I also enjoy it, pretend it shakes a bit over me, when I watch her. "Well, who gave you your dancing papers? You just gave them to yourself, right?" I can see that for the sake of friendship, she's considering my argument.

"But a witch," she says, eyebrows high over sea-blue eyes, "potions and spells and knowing the future – you really think you can do all that?"

"Not all of that, yet," I hedge, voice still firm. "One thing at a time." I will not plead. But I am hoping. This is so much more important than boys. Even princes. *We can make our own magic, my graceful, dancing friend – throughout our lives. Just by believing in it.*

"Hmmm," says my friend – smiling. About as good as I'll get tonight.

It's getting cool. More importantly, it's getting close to curfew time.

"If I'm late again," says my friend, "Ron will ground me for two weeks, not just one. I just came out of a grounding!" When I'm late, my mum just gets this anxious crease between her eyebrows, says, "I was worried. Don't be late again." I rarely am. Her worry puts that granite back on my chest.

Suddenly we're running and laughing and here's a little magic: chubby me is keeping up to my slim friend and even passing her, just as we get to my house. "School starts Monday!" I shout as she continues on past me up Dunbar. "Come get me," she shouts back. "We'll walk together."

A new school year. We will be in grade seven, turning thirteen after January. I bash open the back door, which is never locked. Lorenzo the German shepherd runs to me, tail wagging, his kind black and blond face raised for stroking. My own brother, almost fifteen and reading a book in the kitchen nook, calls out, "Noisy, or what? Close the door." He thumps on me sometimes, too – unfortunately, he doesn't have another brother to pick on – but I've learned some fine tricks to deal with that. Bent-back thumbs are about the best. Gotta be quick, though, when you're small. Otherwise, you'll need more than magic to get out of a headlock. *Boys.*

"Mum?" I ask him.

"Upstairs, reading."

"Hi, honey." The room is small, the bed set right by the door. Mum loves it when I tuck my head around the corner of her bedroom door and start reading her book from above.

"A good one?"

"A good one." Mum chooses her books carefully, as she's taught us to do, so they are all "good ones." One adult and four kids and we all read each day as though the libraries will be locked forever, starting tomorrow. *Best magic ever.*

A small, orangey movement occurs down by Mum's feet. "That Pumpkin?" I ask. Mum looks embarrassed. "Yes," she says. "She's a nice little kitten, isn't she?" Nice, I repeat – *I must not laugh* – yeah, she's sweet. After twenty-four hours, Mum is incapable of disliking an animal. Dad knew that.

Men.

"Sometimes the unexpected things are best, aren't they?" says Mum.

I nod. I want this to be true for Mum, more than any of us. *Witch's honour.*

* * *

Buying a horse was completely unexpected. It flooded both magic and turmoil into our lives.

3
NIZZEYN'S COQEYN

Incredibly, I do not remember the first time I saw him, that inaugural trip to the Calders' barn at 53rd Avenue and Balaclava Street and looking into his stall and saying (I must have), "Hello, Coqeyn – hello, you wonderful horse. You belong to us now." I remember writing in my journal, "Over the weekend we bought a horse; Karin and I will be looking after him," which sounds so flat and unexcited. I know I was gut-tied worried, as I was so frequently in those growing up years, and worried particularly that Mum could afford this miracle for us. She already literally worked night and day, teaching both day school and night school, while looking after four kids on her own.

What my mother wanted, of course, was a larger miracle, and that was to help my older sister Karin, then seventeen, stay off the hard drugs she'd used heavily but intermittently since she was thirteen. We were only just starting to understand the depths of her mental illness, parts of which were induced and exacerbated by the combined use of heroin and barbiturates. "Drug-induced schizophrenia," her doctors said grimly; that was the main condition Karin and we were dealing with. But there were other mental illnesses troubling Karin, as well, ones that left her impervious to the pain of others, and intent on getting her own way, no matter what the cost, again, to others. While our mother researched and worked unceasingly to find the right therapies, doctors, and support for our sister, I, the youngest sibling, mostly thought drugs were the root of Karin's violence and conniving, heartless ways. They were, and they weren't. Many days she was a stranger in our midst, beautiful in form, frightening in action. Sober or high, she always wanted *more* – of everything. She was the greediest soul I've ever known. And yet, she was loved by all of us, and could be charming and fun.

Part of her dynamic nature was encouraged by the freshness and colour of the 1960s and '70s. My sister was born in 1954, and christened Karen Francesca Simmins. In her teens, she changed the spelling of her first name, becoming Karin, with an "i." Lots of teenagers of the time changed the spelling of their names to assert their independence, and "i" was a curiously popular vowel. Karin asked all the family if we would respect her choice to change the spelling of her name from Karen to Karin. It seemed a small enough request to me, and I did it.

During our horse years, Karin and I were inseparable. I will always be grateful for the unstinting time she gave to me, and her enjoyment of my company. She loved me. I believe she loved us all. She just got lost in her search for *more.*

Only three years. It contained three lifetimes of experiences.

When I think now of the burden we instantly placed on those slim equine chestnut shoulders, my heart constricts in pain. Coqeyn was just a small, willing, "green-broke" or newly saddled pony, who'd been trucked down to Vancouver from Kelowna, and was looking for a forever home. He deserved better than what he got. *Be fair!* comes the voice that pulls me through the darkest memories. *You were devoted to*

Coqeyn from earliest days. Both of you. Neither you nor Karin could imagine then how you would fail him later. Don't let the bad times dominate the sweet ones. So many sweet ones.

Yes, well. I try.

I can tell you he was stunning – from that first sighting buried deep in memory, and he stays stunning evermore, at the forefront of memory now. A golden-red chestnut, almost a sorrel, his summer coat gleamed and his mane and tail were sunbleached, long and silky. No dished Arabian face, but finely chiselled all the same, with a star, strip, and snip white markings adding interest, and his cocoa-dark eyes bright with intelligence and life vigour. He had one white "sock," white hairs up to the bulb of his fetlock, which made that hind hoof partly white, too.

Coqeyn was well-bred. His dam's name was Little Coquette and his sire's name was Nizzeyn's Comar. A Welsh pony mare and an Arabian stallion, which meant that their offspring, Nizzeyn's Coqeyn, was referred to as a half-Arabian, because only some horse breeds register their half-breeds, among these Arabians. Coqeyn, then, was a registered half-Arab (the more common diminutive). He was also a pony. Although we told everyone we were "buying a horse," Coqeyn actually stood only 14 hands high (HH), which made him a pony. Horse-height starts at 14 hands, 3 inches (14.3 HH). One "hand" is equal to four inches high, or the equivalent of a man's palm, the original method of measurement. The Welsh blood gave Coqeyn part of his compact beauty and well-shaped, strong legs. But he was all Arabian when it came to his high tail carriage and locomotive speed. His "takeoffs" – zero to flat-out gallop – were frequent and terrifying, especially to my sister and me, who were new riders.

Horses vault into a gallop when they are startled or scared, and depending on breed and temperament, they can often be that way. Some breeds are simply more reactive than others. Half-Arabian Coqeyn was among these.

September 1972

As I turn down the long side of the ring, I see with surprise that someone has left open the wide gate at the far end: this is not done. We only open that gate to let the tractor in to groom the ring's sands. Otherwise, we enter and depart from the small side gate.

The ring is wide open to the street beyond. Then, out of sight, the tractor engine starts up, the driver goosing the engine to a whiny roar. They must not have seen me, thought the ring was empty. The whine builds, then the tractor lumbers into sight. Coqeyn's head jerks left to watch the emerging vehicle. I don't have to look behind to know that his tail is rising.

Oh no, not again –

I have time for a gasp of air before Coqeyn leaps forward. He is a chestnut bullet, his cylinder-hard body roaring straight ahead. His head is stretched up and back, the bit far back in his teeth. Speed is the only factor in the world, fear the only feeling. I am staying on, barely. First I was pulled back in the saddle, now I am leaning too far forward. My feet are also too far forward in the stirrups, and my reins too long for any control. I am completely unbalanced. But determined to stay on.

We've covered the ground from the ring to the street. There's only one thing that can happen next –

Left, of course. He always goes left. It's his preferred lead. And now there's air all around me.

The asphalt greets my body, a leaping brick wall. I can hear his hooves thunder-clacking down the road to the east. *Where is my sister Karin?* She'd gone to muck out Coqeyn's stall and must be done by now.

"Maggie, I'm here. I'm right here."

"But Coqeyn –"

"Someone's gone to get him."

"I don't think I can stand, Karin. It hurts too much."

"It's all right, just stay where you are." Her hands rest on my arm. She squeezes gently. "You're going to be okay."

I was – but I could barely tie my own shoelaces for three months. I was back riding in a week.

* * *

We tried everything to work with Coqeyn's bolts. Hot green horse, with two "green" or new riders. It was not an easy way to learn to ride, for any of us. The bits got stronger and stronger (the metal or synthetic part of the bridle, which is placed in the horse's mouth, and rests on the bars of the mouth in the area where there are no teeth). We settled on a pelham bit, customarily used with two sets of reins – again, fussy business for new riders – and with a leather "converter," which required only one set of reins. We also used a mechanical hackamore, which is a bitless bridle with long shanks. These provide leverage, just as the cheek-pieces or shanks on a pelham bit do. Unlike a bit, which applies pressure inside the mouth, the hackamore places pressure over the nose. There is a domino effect of sorts with this bridle: pull the reins and the crown of the bridle pulls down against the horse's poll (the part of the head right behind or between the ears), the nose-piece pulls against the horse's nose, and the chin strap applies pressure against the chin. This all sounds much harder on the horse than it is. Most times, horses "hack" (light exercise) very happily with bitless bridles. Simply knowing the pressure lurks and can be applied with alacrity is enough to make most horses quiet.

The hackamore was a godsend "up trails," which is what we called the then-narrow paths alongside the Fraser River. Along with the city of Vancouver, these are part of the traditional lands of the Musqueam First Nation. The trails passed at the edge of the Musqueam Reserve, and then led into a maze of trails inside the forest lands near the University of British Columbia. Cutting across these, the trails spilled out onto the beaches running along Vancouver harbour. Those rides to the beach were rare, but once we got there – me riding Coqeyn, Karin on a borrowed horse, or vice versa – we could finally gallop safely. That horse of ours ran like mercury down a cliffside ...

Slowly, the bolts lessened in frequency, and we got better at stopping him. The safest method was to "get him" in the first three or four strides. After that you were pretty much toast. In a ring, with lots of room, we'd grab his mane with one hand and use our free hand to pull his head in a circle. Up trails, where circles were often impossible, we'd do a "pulley-rein stop," planting one hand on Coqeyn's neck and pulling the other hand straight back and up. Coqeyn bolted less, and we got stronger. We also rode other more tractable ponies and horses at the various barns at which we boarded or took lessons. Altogether, our confidence and fitness grew.

Coqeyn, we discovered to our amazement, could do it all. We trained our attractive pony to hack safely for hours on end, and to jump any object under his nose. We played mock polo, glad for the mount who turned as deftly as a sailboat with a fin keel, and sprang like a dolphin over the waves. Once I even jumped him over an immense Douglas fir log on Spanish Banks, heard a shriek, and looked back to see a couple who had been lying down, entwined in one another's arms on the other side of the log. We'd landed adjacent to them, ten feet to the right. Not close enough for harm, but close enough for the shriek, and pounding hearts. Karin and I laughed all the way home again.

In the largely hunter-jumper Southlands horse community of the times, we even took a summer of dressage lessons. Sleep was for those unfortunates without a horse. We hand-galloped (a slower, controlled gallop) around the riding club's half-mile track on opal-skied summer mornings, so early not another horse and rider was there. We entered in schooling shows, where the objective is to school the inexperienced rider and/or horse, and then one Equine Canada recognized show, which brought in serious competitors from around the province. Borrowing Western tack from the kind barn owners who first owned the big barn at 55th Avenue and Blenheim Street, Karin won a ribbon in a Western Pleasure class. I cheered my sister on, she cheered me on. Every day was new knowledge and insights. Every year saw gains to our strength and flexibility. I knew it then, I know it now: I was impossibly fortunate, blessed. Then the world changed.

Karin died at age twenty, in December 1974, from an overdose of drugs. I had been hiding the horse from her for months prior, squirrelled away in a dark, low-ceilinged barn, across the street from the nicer one we'd been asked to leave, after Karin's behaviour became too violent with me and with Coqeyn. I missed our dear little do-it-yourselfer, which was a part of a larger, expensive barn complex, and together, was a friendly and supportive community. Our five-stall barn, modest though it was, had an array of different and interesting horses, and caring, experienced horse people in it. I loathed the new barn, which was old and cramped.

When I wasn't scared Karin would find us and possibly hurt Coqeyn, I was suffering from acute humiliation at our circumstances. *I hadn't done anything wrong. Coqeyn hadn't done anything wrong.* I missed my friends and the second set of barn owners across the street, most of whom, understandably, melted away from my life. "I do understand," the wife of the couple had said with rare sympathy to me and my mother. "People we know have these challenges, too. But you just can't stay here."

And so we moved horse, tack, and belongings two hundred or so feet to the south, to a tiny barn beside the larger, much-despised rental stable. I think our barn may have been a part of the rental business, either then or earlier. It's hard to remember. It may have just been owned by the same man, who at one point, ludicrously, had a senior position on the board of the SPCA. One thing for sure, no matter how often I mucked out Coqeyn's wretchedly small corner stall, it stank permanently of urine and old sweat. Our handsome, high-stepping pony, who smelled like marigolds and sea salt, who did every task we ever asked of him, with horse-sized heart and then some, was now stuck in an old rental horse barn, in a stall with rotten floors. I wept rivers for him, and for myself. I didn't know anyone, and no one talked to me. But at least we were safe.

So there we were, hiding in plain sight, only a stone's toss from our old barn, with everyone at both barns sworn to silence if Karin ever showed up. To my knowledge, she never did. The horse-riding heart had gone out of my strong, star-crossed sister. As it would for me, for about seven years.

Maggie, I am here. I am right here.

I know, Karin. That used to be the hardest part.

SAYING GOODBYE
FOR COQEYN, SUMMER 1975

It was a stolen afternoon in early June. No airless high-school classrooms after lunchtime on that Friday. I rode my Peugeot with the royal purple frame down to the barn, long hair streaming out behind me. I loved the new private family barn, on Balaclava, near 51st Avenue, the fourth and last one Coqeyn and I would share in our four years together and a Hilton, compared to our last one. It was only a couple of years old, the exterior finished with grey-blond shingles. All the stalls were big and had high ceilings, deeply bedded with light curls of resin-tangy wood chips. In each, automatic water cups refilled with fresh water with the press of a horse's nose. No more ugly green plastic garbage buckets of water for my majestic pony. Now he could slurp like a king

– like King of the Wind, the Godolphin Arabian, read in a dark school basement, years ago – the water cold, never stale.

The tack room was a dream. Tiers of saddle racks and rows of matching tack boxes, everything new, the air that heady blend of pine and leather. Affixed to each tack box, a brass tag with the owner's name on it. *"Marjorie Simmins, Nizzeyn's Coqeyn"* – that was the one I was supposed to have, but didn't, because we'd only been there a short time. The no-name tack box I did have was just as nice as the others, though. Inside, there might have been only one leather-backed body brush – a gift, I can't remember from whom – alongside the other, more ordinary wooden-backed dandy brushes, and rubber and plastic curries, but I had everything I needed. I owned expensive English tack now, too, which had taken years to accumulate: a Stübben all-purpose saddle, a Stübben rolled leather bridle, braided reins on our every-day bridle, a handsome breast-plate, two martingales, and the long-desired "numnah," or fluffy, sheepskin saddle-pad. Coqeyn deserved the best, we'd always said.

Coqeyn himself had never looked better. To afford this lovely barn, my mother and I were leasing him to a slim but strong junior. Terry was daffy for him, and rode him every day, when her busy schedule permitted. "Are you sure?" she asked. "Is it really all right if I ride every day?" She was polite but also ambitious, and delighted with Coqeyn's abilities. Sure, I said, he loves the attention, and he's really fit now. Just don't jump him every day, and leave me Fridays – I'd like Fridays to be mine. Terry nodded with enthusiasm, her round, cornflower blue eyes bright with happiness. She would go on to take the Pony Jumper Championship with Coqeyn that summer of 1975, at the Pacific National Exhibition. Coqeyn easily cleared the five-foot jump-off fence. I did not watch – I couldn't. If I couldn't share the suspense and victory with Karin, I wouldn't know how to cheer, either. I was sixteen, only one year older than Terry – and felt centuries older.

Karin had been dead for six months now.

I reached for the saddle, then decided against it. Warm, with a blossom-scented breeze, it was a bareback day if ever there was one. I returned to Coqeyn's stall, took his halter from the nearby rack.

Coqeyn was in a paddock by himself, stablemates on either side of him in their own paddocks, all three working on flakes of summer-fat timothy. Only Coqeyn raised his head from his hay as I approached with a halter and lead line.

"Hey, sweet pony, how are you?" Coqeyn didn't whicker much – a low, whuffing sound – but he did occasionally nicker, which is a louder, clearer, mid-range sound that is not quite a whinny. Today he nickered, the top note fluted with surprise. He didn't often see me this time of day; I'd skipped out of school, something I'd started to do a lot. I slipped on Coqeyn's halter and led him to the cross-ties outside his stall.

His coat was heated from the sun. I groomed him longer than usual, resting my hands on his glossy coat, every hair-whorl and every muscle-curve memorized long ago. His whiskers were long that day, some white, some black, and the bridle path between his ears needed trimming, too. But there were no shows coming up. Summertime shaggy was fine. Especially when his coat was nearly reflective with all-round good health. I'd even "strapped" him, as my dressage instructor, trained in the U.K., had shown me how to do, using a soft shammy to smack-smooth against his coat, thus releasing the body oils.

I'd done all right in the past six months, when it came to his care. Better than all right. For myself, I didn't know if my hair was brushed or if I'd showered/ gone to school/ or spent more time with that self-absorbed first boyfriend, who never once said – *I am sorry for your loss.* Instead, he turned the sadness around, made it his loss, his drama, said Karin was troubled by her unrequited love for ... him. *You,*

I wanted to say – *you? Karin never gave you two thoughts, except to think it might be nice if you were nicer to me. How do I know what she thought? It was in the journal she left behind, that's how. She didn't give a toss about you.* Numb, I moved in tight, grey circles for those first two interminable months after Karin died. Then it was February 1975: *Happy birthday, sweet sixteen …*

June now, and I pressed my nose against his shoulder: *marigolds and sea salt* – no other horse I ever knew smelled this way. I pressed the scent deep into memory. *Perhaps, perhaps, another time, another place.*

I had a favourite grazing corner for Coqeyn on The Flats – the nickname we used for Southlands, which is under sea level and is indeed quite flat. The corner was at 55th Avenue and Carnarvon Street, just a few blocks from our current barn, and the boulevard grass there didn't seem to get mowed very often. Long and lush, the grass was perfect for making a whistle. You'd pluck one long strand, press it between the plump pads below your thumbs, and then blow against the reed with your mouth. *Vareeeeck,* came the sound, if you'd done it well, pads pressed tight together, then *eeeek, eeek, eek,* as the sound faded off with each new and less powerful blow. The vibrating grass would tickle my mouth, make me smile. I'd rub my hand across my mouth to take the tickle away. One clear bleat was all I needed to "win" the grass game, though it didn't always happen. That day, the grass blade was a bugle. I really smiled then. Coqeyn and I could have been charging to battle, invincible, untouchable.

Instead, we were quiet warriors. No saddle, no bridle, just bareback transit, me sitting tall astride my shining chestnut pony. When we arrived at the corner, I slacked the lead line so Coqeyn could choose his grazing spot. We moved from world to different world in measurements of inches. A tilt to the left – and my hands were dappled by the leaves above. One step to the right – and half my face was in the sun. As he cropped the grass, he flicked his tail back and forth; the flies enjoyed the way his coat smelled as much as I did. Dragonflies whirred past us in turquoise-silver blurs. Barn swallows and starlings crossed over us, streaks of brown and blue on the sky-page above. Bees buzzed. My pulse slowed. Utterly trusting, I even crossed my right leg over his left shoulder, as though I were riding sidesaddle. It was a surprisingly comfortable position, and totally vulnerable to a slip to the ground, if Coqeyn were to move suddenly. But there would be no fall on that day, I was sure, as never before or since.

I felt one strong beat of a mended heart – and knew at the same time I'd be mending all my life. But Coqeyn gave me more than that moment of peace. Deep understanding was in that kind June air. *I did no wrong, nor did you – it wasn't our fault.* He dipped his head, then pushed it one world ahead, to a sweeter clump of grass. *And all that sadness, all that loss – we couldn't change it, couldn't hold it back, not even for a day – could we?* He shook his head, getting the flies out of his eyes. We moved into full sun. Two was one/ was always/was summer/was every season and every creature who ever cared about anything or anyone, and ever tried to take earth and skies of pain away, to see the path ahead. We pulled deep centaur-breaths, heartbeats slow.

The horizon reached up for the sun; the air turned cool.

I pulled my right leg back over his shoulder. Coqeyn raised his head and turning west, we walked away.

I do not remember the last day I latched his stall door shut, or whether I pressed my cheek against the talc-soft spot between his nostrils, one last time.

How Do They Get Those Tails So High?
1973, McCleery's Golf Course Clubhouse, Vancouver, B.C.

We are fourteen, sixteen, and nineteen – and we all think older-than-us Gwen is about the coolest horsewoman ever to set foot in our barn. Coolest woman, period. She has a lovely bay Anglo-Arab mare, Redwing – that's half-Arabian and half-Thoroughbred – who's as flashy as she is, and every bit as high-steppingly feminine. It's the '70s, so the whole world, it seems, smokes cigarettes, but without any particular style, or panache. Not Gwen. She uses a long black and gold filter with her cigarettes, and draws upon them like a movie star of old. It's easy to forget about smoking ourselves, and just watch her elegant intakes and outtakes, chin tilted up, creamy throat exposed. As riveting to us are Gwen's eyes – dark brown, glinting with humour and intelligence. Best of all, you just *never* know what she's going to say –

"I used to own and show Tennessee Walkers," she tells us, tucking a thick strand of her silver-blonde hair, worn in a bob, behind one ear. "They give the smoothest ride of all the gaited horses, I think."

"What's gaited mean?" I ask. We are sitting at our favourite corner table in McCleery's Golf Course coffee shop, the corner one by the windows, overlooking the pond. The shallow green waters are covered in lily pads and profuse pink blooms. I point to the sugar bowl, filled with paper-wrapped cubes. "K'I have the sugar, please?" Gwen slides it over towards my tea mug. I slip two in my pocket, for Coqeyn, and stir a small Dairyland milk cup into my tea.

"Those are horses that have been selectively bred for natural gaited tendencies. They have smooth, four-beat gaits," says Gwen, pulling the sugar bowl over to her own coffee mug. "Sometimes they call these 'ambling gaits' – *capiche?*"

I don't know that last word, but I followed most of the preceding ones. "Sure," I say. "I get it. Like Standardbreds, right?"

"Yes and no," says Gwen. "The American Standard-breds have special under-saddle shows, same as the Tennessee Walkers. The riders wear tails, top hats, white gloves, and all. But most Standardbreds are used for harness racing – those are the pacers or the trotters. A trotter uses a diagonal gait, moving his left front leg with the same motion of the right hind leg and the right front leg with the left hind."

We are quiet a moment, summoning this image to mind, then, as riders do, counting it – *one, two, one, two* – right, a two-beat trot, the sound our own horses make. Gwen continues: "A pacer, on the other hand, moves both legs on the same side at the same time." A longer pause, while we digest this odd image. This would make for a *lateral* two-beat gait – which would feel very odd – though God knows at the fevered rate they go, they cover ground.

"Can you ride them normally?" someone asks. Walk, normal trot, canter, and *gallop*, we mean.

"Sure," says Gwen. "Depends how long they've been off the track. They make great saddle horses, if you train 'em up. But Tennessee Walkers are the only ones with the 'running walk' – a walk so smooth it's a waterfall with no bottom, just water and motion running on down forever." She lifts her appealing, almond-shaped face and shakes some platinum hair across one eye, à la Veronica Lake: "And on the track or in the show ring, there's not a horse I can think of that can match the Tennessee Walker, in the looks department."

They are certainly flashy. Karin and I can't gobble down enough horse magazines and have seen lots of photos of the Walkers, which, like the American Standardbreds, under saddle have epically proud and erect carriage, however artificially produced. But the Walkers come in many more colour variations: palomino, roan, grey, sorrel, not just bay, black, and brown. I remember reading that they grow the hooves of Walker show horses longer, weight the shoes, too, then laboriously train them to exaggerate their steps, to have highest-of-the-high "high action." There was something else odd about the gaited horses, too, Walkers among them, and that was their tail carriage, governed by the dock, or tail vertebrae, raised almost straight up, so the long tail hairs flowed outwards. I have no idea how they make them hold their tails so high …

"Walkers were bred first to work, not for show," says Gwen. "They started out as saddle horses on plantations in the American South. The overseers rode them, to monitor the work of the slaves in the cotton fields. Those plantations were big, so they'd be in the saddle all day. The horses had to cover ground fast and comfortably." Unaccountably, she starts chuckling.

"That's not exactly funny, Gwen," says the sixteen-year-old, who reliably speaks up against the casual racism in our white-bread Vancouver world. She and her family are Caucasian, and immigrated from the southern United States themselves several years ago. Canadians, she says, are much slyer about their racism. She defiantly states that she sometimes misses the out-front racism she grew up with. You know exactly when to stand tall against it, she says.

"No, no –" Gwen's sputtering and coughing now, the long filter resting against the ashtray in the centre of the table. "I'm not laughing about the black Americans on the plantations – good God, no! I'm laughing about something else." The three of us are skeptical, our eyes demanding an explanation for the oddly timed merriment.

"It's the horses' tails!" she squeals. "Don't you want to know why they hold their tails that strange way? I sure did!"

"Aren't they broken in half?" asks Karin. "I read that somewhere."

"No," says Gwen, smirking. "Though they do nick two muscles in the dock sometimes" – she sighs heavily – "which allows a break-over of the tail. Other manual contrivances, too. Nasty, all of them. Well, not all." She's grinning again.

"Out with it!" I holler. "How do they the get the tails so high?"

But she's going to make us suffer. "Now, you all know I wouldn't do anything to my horses that I wouldn't do to myself, don't you?"

We nod. It's true. Gwen's crazy not just for her horses, but all horses, all animals, for that matter. She gets wild at the merest whiff of creature abuse or neglect.

"So, repeat after me, if I was told to do something to my horse, and I didn't know what it felt like, first-hand, I probably wouldn't do it, would I?"

Three pairs of eyes do not blink.

"Ginger!" she shrieks. "They use ginger!"

The manager of the clubhouse, a sunny, Scottish-born man, calls out, "Everything all right over there?"

Three of the youngest faces turn to nod to him, and turn back again. Then someone in the trio waves a dismissive arm behind her head: *All's well.* This coffee shop is as much the riders' watering-hole as the golfers'. And the manager might even prefer the horse people, given that his jockey-sized son is a talented hunter-jumper. There's even talk of him becoming a real jockey out at Exhibition Park.

Three intent faces refocus on Gwen, as though uninterrupted: "Ginger?" Then Karin demands, "What do you *mean*, ginger?"

"Put it up my rectum. Took a piece of fresh ginger, peeled it, and put it up my bum."

You'd guess that we cracked up laughing. Or that one of us did, making two of us, then three of us crack up laughing even harder. Instead, we remained daisy-eyed, even shocked now, incomprehension spreading like a whole bowlful of spilled Dairyland milk tubs on the table.

"Ginger?" asks someone. "Up your *bum*?"

It was the deliciously unexpected bum word, of course, repeated in a public venue that got everyone near to peeing themselves. *Whywhywhywhywhy* – would anyone ever put ginger up their bum? We laugh, we choke, we collapse on to the table, heads on our crossed arms or backs pushed into our chairs, arms against our stomachs – gasping, quiet, then starting up all over again.

"I wanted to know what it felt like – before I did it to my horse," repeats Gwen, straight-faced, loving every saucy bit of bravado and fun of this moment, and of all her life. Nothing daunted Gwen, we knew that, loved that.

"Hot!" howls someone. "It must have been bitchy hot."

"Ah, no," smiles a Cheshire-cat Gwen. "It was any-thing but hot."

If it wasn't hot – we'd finally stopped laughing – what could it *possibly* be?

"Cold! The goddamned thing was icy. And it makes the horses –"

"Raise their tails!" we shout. "It makes them raise their tails like flags!" The table falls silent. For a moment.

"Son of a gun," says the sixteen-year-old.

"Son of a bitch," says the nineteen-year-old.

"Are you serious, Gwen?" I say. "Did you really, *really* –"

She picks up her cigarette filter, removes the old butt, and inserts a fresh white tube of tobacco. The silver lighter flashes white-gold and she pulls on the cigarette with pretty rouged lips. Wispy blued smoke emerges from her mouth, along with a lazy, oval smoke ring.

"Sure as hell did. And I never felt bad about gittin' that tail up again, either."

4
OUTDOORS AGAIN
JULY 2011, HALIFAX, N.S.

Have I mentioned that I am claustrophobic? No? That in my regular, uninjured life I have to get out of the house at least once a day or I feel twitchy? While my work as a freelance journalist keeps me at home, in front of my computer the majority of the time, I can always think of a reason to run a few household errands after lunch. My husband and I have a brilliant Shetland sheepdog named MacTavish, as well. We walk with him each afternoon. Well, Don does, right now. But it's easy to remember how good it feels to stretch chair-cramped legs and stiff backs, and breathe fresh air. Perhaps I was a prairie girl in another life, lived in big sky country and never felt hemmed in, even inside a house.

With the exceptions of being carried or assisted to the nearby bathroom, or some short, hobbling revolutions through Don's office, also on the second floor of our house, I have been a prisoner in this small bedroom of ours since May 2, 2011. I could scream for the sameness of the days. Once I made it halfway down the staircase to the main floor – stepping down backwards, because for some reason that was much easier on my legs and back – and then I stopped and turned around properly, facing the other half of the staircase and the front hallway below. *And just what do you think you're going to do when you get downstairs?* I asked myself. *Bake a bloody cake? Sit at your desk and put in a full day's work, perhaps?* No, I couldn't do any of those things. Before self-pity could descend I felt a heart-skip of fear. *And what if you can't get back up the stairs? What will you do then?* My body didn't scuttle up those stairs – it couldn't. But my psyche did, just like a crab at the beach, when a predator's shadow falls over it. Back in bed, I felt relieved and ashamed.

It's been one of the darkest springs I can remember on the East Coast, maybe the darkest in all the fourteen years I've lived here. Drawing the curtains in the morning makes little difference to the light in the room. It's like going from night to twilight. Day after day.

"If I were you," writes an editor friend of mine, in an email, "I'd be mighty sick of the decor in my bedroom by now." He's a witty guy and I usually enjoy his humour. Usually. It's hard not to dislike everything in this room, and that includes can't-put-on-her-own-underwear me, maybe most of all. *Why couldn't I have been strong enough to pull that damn horse back? Why did I say to myself, Just one more lope around the ring? If I'd quit even a few minutes earlier, I could have been safely inside the main barn again, when that wind gust shook the roof of the indoor arena, with the horse back in his own stall.*

I am able to use my laptop computer in bed now. I prop it up on the old wooden tray-table we used when we were sick as kids, my older siblings and me. The table legs unfold with a satisfying *thwhack* of wood on wood. I am fine to work on my computer in bed, propped up by pillows. As long as I don't move too much. Move at all, really. Then the spasms in my legs start, and the unspeakable pain follows. Which is why I have muscle-relaxant painkillers. Nervous about the mental effects of drugs – I hate not feeling clear-headed – I use them sparingly. But not today; today I took two. For insurance. I am higher than a Georgia pine and not the least perturbed about that. This event *will* happen.

"I think we're about ready to go," says Don. "It's even clearing out there. It's going to be a lovely day." We have gone nowhere and done nothing yet and it's already a great day. In just a few minutes I am going to be outside.

No walls.

I still can't ride in the car, which is so low to the ground, and requires me to bend my knees and back. My back doesn't really bend at this point. Or it can, but it hurts, six kinds of crazy. But I can step up into the truck, and then use the grab-handle to pull myself onto the seat. I can even put on my own seat belt. Finally, doing some things for myself, not the perennial *sooky baby*, as they say here in the Maritimes, a sooky baby waiting for help. *Fight your own battles*, my mother used to say, or, other times, *Paddle your own canoe*. Believe me, I am trying, Mum.

"All set?"

I give him the biggest smile he's seen in months. "Yes."

The whole world is sun and blossom. Rhododendrons, azaleas, hydrangeas, and abundant green growth everywhere. We pass one of my favourite houses on the street, one where cats live.

"Oh, look, there's the neighbour's cat with stripey legs – so beautiful. I think I gotta have a cat again one of these years. Siamese again, for sure. That would be best. Not now, though, I want a second dog now. The flowers! They're everywhere! So many cars. We're turning here? Oh, yes, of course. Up Herring Cove Road. Turn, turn, we're away. That was fun – ouch, kind of. I can't believe the sky. So blue and no clouds. Look! Another dog. A beautiful dog. Just a mutt, but who cares? Look how happy those two are, just walking along in the sun. I love mutts, don't you? I love you, Don, and I love this truck. It's so kind to me. You're so kind to me." A deep breath and I resume: "Amazing, isn't it? We're driving on a road in the big wide world. *Ow, owwww* – I don't know what to do with this back of mine – whether to sit away from the seat or sit back or what. Oh, God, I am in the *world* again."

Finally, I am silent. The back is not happy, but I am hummingly ecstatic. We've turned to the left again, this time on to Purcell's Cove Road. We pass the Armdale Yacht Club, with its high-on-a-hill clubhouse, stunningly sited to look southeast, out the Northwest Arm towards the open Atlantic. This is one of two yacht clubs on this road, the more affordable one, the one we were members of for several years, when we were still sailing regularly. That was before Don and I got very busy making enough money to live in the city, and I came to the point where I just had to have horses back in my life. I love sailing. I just love horses more. I think I still do, anyway. I try not to think about horses right now. My heart is too conflicted.

The Armdale Yacht Club is a big property; even in the car it takes some time to pass by the ocean mooring fields and then the club's land. It's also a busy and socially active club. Every Wednesday evening throughout the summer the club members race in the Arm. The sailboats' hulls, mostly fibreglass, make me think of Lifesaver candies: red, yellow, green, and blue, the primary colours intensified against the billowing white mainsails, jibs, and spinnakers. Some of the boat designs are achingly elegant; "feathers on the water," Don calls one of these, the Roue 20s. They were designed by the same naval architect who designed the *Bluenose* – the first one, the famous twentieth-century racing schooner, which started life as a fishing vessel and whose image finally graced our Canadian ten-cent pieces.

I never saw a schooner growing up in Vancouver. But I never tire of seeing them here. Sometimes I still have to double-check the rig: fore and aft sails, raised on two or more masts. The old ones all have wooden hulls, of course.

They sail right out of Atlantic Canada's salty, bloodthirsty colonial past, and claim their respected place in the current sailing world, by right of their beauty and longevity. But even here in Nova Scotia, schooners are rare now. We see one at anchor at the club's inner mooring field. It's an urban pirate's dream.

Also on club property is a nineteenth-century prison, which once housed French prisoners and now stores the club members' sails and gear. These lockers were cells first, and they are small. With arms outstretched I am sure a big man could touch both walls. Enough length to take four or five strides, maybe. A tiny barred window on each door, but no lights in those cells all those years ago. Only night and twilight, like the spring I've had – except for years on end. For the prisoners, two or three times a day, perhaps, a bright stab of sunlight when the doors at the front of the building opened, and the guards stepped in to distribute food and water. Then dullness again, when the door banged shut. I've never felt more sympathy for the imprisoned.

We pass the Royal Nova Scotia Yacht Squadron, which is 177 years old, and costs thousands of dollars a year to be a member.

We drive on towards the ocean-nestled community of Purcell's Cove. As we have all the way along, we see modest fifty- or even one-hundred-year-old homes, and the vulgar, vast new homes of the *nouveau riche*. Those face the water, always, on big chunks of razed land with many expensive vehicles in the driveways. *You live on the water, too, missy.* Yes, but our home was built in 1937 and it is not fancy. Quite frankly, it is a struggle for two writers to keep this house, even with a rental suite supplementing our income. No getting around it, coming to a big mortgage late in life is challenging. That's exactly what happened when we moved to Halifax from Cape Breton in 2006, where Don had lived since 1971. We'd love to have the money to do an extensive renovation at our city home; we have ideas galore, most of them practical, not extravagant, such as a foyer at the second-floor entrance, or a proper porch with a roof at the main entrance. This won't happen. It doesn't matter. To us the house is priceless for its old-fashioned and warm character and its million-dollar view. We'll keep it for as long as it makes sense for us to keep it.

At last we come to the charming harbour-cleft of Herring Cove. Here, too, are working-class homes and working vessels, and architect-designed homes and sleek yachts, all moored at the homes' private wharves. Some of these are sturdy and restored; some are rickety. Together, somehow, it all works, has great visual appeal and interest.

Nova Scotia does these sorts of contrasts very well. I've always enjoyed that. Be rich, be poor, be somewhere in between – but don't talk too much about any of that. Just live your life with verve and gratitude, and be a proud East Coaster. I am a proud East Coaster. I just say it quietly most of the time, as born-aways must. Atlantic Canada is a close-knit family. Strangers have to prove themselves for a good long while before they're shown to a seat by the fireplace. Fair enough, b'y, says I. Loyalty is one of my favourite words ever and I have a good measure of it, for the two coasts I am privileged to know and love. Some of my old friends understand this now. Some just think I fell off a cliff somewhere galaxies out of sight. I've been surprised at how few of my old friends have visited me here. That said, travelling is expensive, work and family commitments are numerous, and sometimes it's hard to see beyond those Rocky Mountains. This is also one immense country to come to know well, and care about. I have lots of missing bits myself, too. I hope I can see more of Canada in years to come.

And not just viewed from a car, either.

"How are you doing?" asks Don. We're at the end of Herring Cove, have parked the truck in the parking lot by the government wharf. This is the cove's mouth; beyond it, the cobalt Atlantic Ocean. Next stop, Ireland. Or you could tack starboard and sail on to the Caribbean. I love the way Halifax opens to the world.

"Did you hear me?" he asks again gently. "How are you –?"

"Good," I interrupt. "I am beyond good." It's true, I am. I am also exhausted, but I don't want to say so.

"Time to go home maybe," says Don, reading my face as much as my mind, I am sure. "We don't want to over-do it your first time out." He holds my gaze and smiles. I turn my pale face and lilac-shadowed eyes away from him. "If *you* would like to go home now," I say deliberately, "that would be all right. We could have tea." I am already think-ing of tea in bed, and how my back is craving the support of a pillow behind it. I don't have one here in the car. But next time we go out, I will have one. The painkillers are wearing off. Only fatigue left. We drive home lost in our own thoughts, while the dark clouds roll in again to cover the sun.

THE CHERISHED ONES

I tried not to think about horses during that gloomy spring, but it didn't really work. Sometimes a memory would come to me and I'd bat it away as though it were a deer fly, ready to chomp down on any exposed flesh it saw. Other times I'd just sink into the memory-film and know there'd be no blood-letting there, only images that made me feel safe and happy. Those memories entertained me over the long, immobile weeks of recuperation. I'd trot them out purely to push the day along. Slowly, the kinder memories crowded the centre-stage. It was physics, really. There were more of them.

The Cherished Ones: *Kaber; Boo; Ryan; Cliquot; Fritz; Madonna.*

Allow me to introduce you to the horses I leased and

rode throughout the 1980s and 1990s. A decade's worth of regular riding, on horses I leased two or three days a week, for goodly long stretches. Half-Arabian, Appaloosa, Hanoverian, Thoroughbred, Morgan, Half-Appaloosa. Small, medium and head-touches-the-sky. That was Hanoverian Ryan, at 17.1 hands high – that's 69 inches to the top of the withers, or base of the neck. Collectively, these horses were green-broke, schooled some, well-schooled, and multischooled. Some had come from the country or the suburbs to live at Southlands, the ultra-convenient, expensive horse enclave in the southwestern heart of the city. Others came to Southlands via Hastings Park track, by the Pacific National Exhibition in East Vancouver, where they'd changed owners after running a "claiming race," which is a race in which every young Thoroughbred in it is for sale at a stipulated price. They may have run well, in their short careers, but not well enough to be consistently "in the money" at the ticket windows. Once sold, they began new careers as saddle and show horses.

With only one skill – galloping hard on the left lead, as races always proceed to the left around the track – not all these two- and three-year-old horses flourished at their new homes. As well, galloped on tender, still-growing bones and tendons, some of them were intermittently "unsound," or permanently lame, pin-fired legs and all. Pin-firing, also known as thermocautery, is the treatment of an injury to a horse's leg by burning, freezing, or dousing it with acid or with acid and caustic chemicals. The aim was to induce a counter-irritation and speed and/or to improve healing. This barbaric practice did not work reliably or over the long-term, and is rarely done now. Incredibly, proponents still exist. Pin-firing certainly made the horses' smooth legs ugly, with dotted scars running in lines down the cannons or shins, the part of the leg below the knee, before the bulb of the fetlock.

Pin-fired or not, many young Thoroughbreds from Vancouver's track stayed sound off the track. They went on to find good homes, transitioning successfully to being shown as hunters or jumpers, or three-day eventers. This last sport requires that the horse does dressage, cross-country jumping, and stadium jumping, over the course of three days. It takes monster stamina and talent, for both rider and horse.

For many equine aficionados, there is no horse more breathtakingly beautiful than the sleek, long-legged Thoroughbred. They are also the fastest horse on the planet, over distance, able to maintain speeds of forty-five miles (seventy-two kilometres) per hour for a distance of more than a mile, for races such as the Kentucky Derby, which is a gruelling mile and a quarter (two kilometres). For their radiant good looks and magnificent stout hearts, Thoroughbreds can thank their Arabian forebears. Every registered Thoroughbred can trace its lineage back to three founding Arabian stallions in the eighteenth century. Almost every modern breed of riding horse has Arabian bloodlines. The desert-bred Arabian horse is indefatigable as an endurance horse and excels in many other riding disciplines. With their arched necks, dished faces, enormous dark eyes, and blazing speeds, Arabian horses are romantic and ravishing. And shimmeringly intelligent.

Some of my lease crew were intellectually sparkling, too, and blessed with humour and presence. Others were dull and timid, or sweet and tractable. Yet others were ox-strong and goat-stubborn, determined to have their own way. One was grumpy as hell when I tacked him up, and a protective angel under saddle. Another was just plain mean, on the ground and under saddle. I learned much from all of them.

I am grateful to all the owners, who charged me so little for these half-leases, willing to forgo better money in favour of my reliability and observant good care of their horses. I had many blessings in my young adult life, first as a student at the University of British Columbia, and then, as a self-employed writer living in the Lower Mainland, but great prosperity was not one of them. Since earliest days, though, there were always people like me who, one way or another, found a way to ride at Southlands. We weren't well-off, as many of the area's residents were, along with many of those who lived in other toney Vancouver neighbourhoods but came to Southlands to ride, take lessons, and compete in shows riding their own horses. We were just working- or middle-class, horse-crazy people, women, mostly, looking for safe and affordable opportunities to ride. Some of us shovelled a lot of manure for those opportunities, and didn't really mind. It's all part of horse life.

My darlings in the lease crew were half-Arabian Kaber and big, bold Boo, the Appaloosa.

When I think about Kaber, I think of that soft summer day we shared an apple in his paddock, and, of course, his charming, whickering ways. But almost every memory of Kaber is warming to me. He was the right size for me – 14.3 hands high? hard to remember for sure – and I loved his grey dapples and alert expression. During the time I rode him, Kaber was stabled at two different barns, the second one by far the nicer. A half-block from my first barn with Coqeyn, Kaber's second barn was tidy and airy, with paddocks and a big field for turnouts.

Kaber loved being groomed, and I loved grooming him. I'd rub the dusty centre of his forehead with my palm and he'd freeze on the cross-ties, loving every itch-relieving moment. Then I'd use a soft-bristled brush to shine up that spot, and his whole body. *Thanks for being my hands,* said his dark, extra large eyes, courtesy of his Arabian forebears. *Thanks for being my wings,* I'd answer.

In fact, Kaber and I were an unusually grounded pair. We didn't fly over jumps, either in a ring or up the trails, and we didn't, that I recall, gallop together, either. We rode bareback a lot, ambling down the dirt or sawdust fringes of Southlands' roads and along the river trails, sometimes to the very end of the estuary basin, where the Fraser River meets the Pacific. Sometimes the waters roiled with pink or sockeye salmon, returning to spawn upriver; sometimes we'd see the hungry, following seals or sea lions rise to the surface, mouths open. There was always something diverting to watch, was our take on things, and our default mental setting was serene. That's what Kaber gave me, companionship and peace.

Boo was a saltier fellow. He had been shown as an open jumper, which is a stadium or outdoor arena event, where horses are judged on how quickly they can complete a course of jumps with the fewest faults, or knock-downs; the jumps start around four feet, with "spreads," or considerable widths, and go well over five and even six feet in the jump-offs. (In Puissance events – the word means power in French – which are the high-jump competitions in the show jumping world, the jumps have exceeded seven feet!) Roany, raw-boned Boo also achieved the Prix St. Georges level in dressage, which is the introductory level for international level dressage competition. At the time, it was not a common achievement for Appaloosas, who are more often shown in Western disciplines. It's still fairly unusual.

Best of all for my interests, Boo loved to hack up the trails, for hours at a time. Every gait he had was round and comfortable. And he really loved to jump. On Boo, I was a Puissance superstar myself, rocketing over fat chunks of deadfall that sometimes blocked the trails ahead of us, having toppled during rollicking Pacific gales. For many months we went out of our way to find every natural jump we could, and pounded toward them, at any gait the footing allowed, until one day, one of Boo's owners casually remarked that due to his worsening cataracts, she hadn't jumped him in over a year.

"It's just too dangerous at this point," Tash said cheerfully. "But I told you this, right?" Heart banging in my chest, I nodded. She hadn't said anything to me, not that I remembered. My guess is, she and her sister Letsa thought the situation was obvious enough that I'd figured it out on my own. Boo's lovely big eyes were indeed clouded enough to spell trouble. But he never once tripped or stumbled on our rides, at any gait, and I had no reason to doubt him. Boo thought he was a superstar, and I agreed. So what if he was getting long in the tooth? As far as I knew, he'd never had a lame day in his life. And when it came to jumping, Boo the one-time open jumper rushed his fences as determinedly as he ever had. The impaired vision did, however, explain his early takeoffs, and the extravagantly generous clearances of obstacles, no matter how modest their height …

Boo, bless him, never told on me. We just kept on hacking alongside the river and in the woods, turning around when our path was blocked by deadfall, or a purposely set small log. He didn't mind. Every day out of the barn was a good day for Boo. He made every day with him good, for anyone in his company. We even rode in the pouring rain, for the rains will come to the western rain forests, and mightily so. We returned to the barn semi-drowned rats. I rubbed him all over with a towel – even those big, hairy ears – brushed him and covered him in a toasty blanket. I'd leave the barn to the sound of long teeth grinding grain, walking through the puddled main aisleway, my own hair wet and frizzy. How do you thank a horse like that, who was game for anything, anytime? Even though he snaked his head around, ears flattened, and sneered, a horse from the nether regions when I tightened his girth. "Cinchy," they call that – as in, people had hauled on the girth (English) or cinch (Western) too vigorously over the years, and Boo felt the need to tell them off.

No one's perfect.

Some of the lease crew really were not perfect. Fritz the Morgan was so violent they had to twitch or sedate him when he was shod. A twitch is a device used to restrain horses in situations they find stressful, such as a veterinary treatment. The most common nose twitch has a long wooden handle with a rope or chain loop at the end. The loop is wrapped around the horse's upper lip and slowly tightened. The idea behind it is to release endorphins as pressure is applied on the twitch, not causing the horse any pain. Mostly, I think this supposition is nonsense. But used correctly – slowly and steadily, to distract, not hurt, the horse – I have seen twitches "do their job," and keep horse and human safe.

Some horses have had horribly painful experiences with farriers, the few who don't do their jobs well. When it comes time for a good farrier to tend to them, however, the horses understandably refer to the bad experiences in their past and can cause a lot of trouble. Other horses haven't had hard times with a farrier at all. They're just jerks. The Morgan gave me some good rides over our time together, but he was fairly green (not well trained) and strong as a freight train hurtling brakeless down a mountain pass. I managed to control him – with difficulty. I had the distinct feeling he tolerated me, and then grew to actively dislike me. I moved around his stocky body very carefully on the ground and rode, more often than not, with an elevated pulse.

Our last ride together concluded with a spectacularly agile forehand buck, which sent me over his head onto the hog-fuel path. I landed neatly on my feet, an unexpected and welcome outcome. More astonishing yet, I still had the reins in my hands. I stared back at him, and he stared back at me. He was well pleased with himself. I quit the lease soon after. Nonetheless, I walked away from that lease with stronger arms and legs, and grateful for the riding hours I'd had. Not every date is a keeper, but you learn more about what you want in a relationship. There had to be other horses out there with milder personalities.

Ryan was as mild as warm milk with cinnamon. And if I thought Boo had big ears, Ryan's were twice the size. Ryan's overall frame was immense. Again, at 17.1 hands high, Hanoverian Ryan was 69 inches (five feet, nine inches) at the withers. I am five feet, two inches tall. So the top of Ryan's head was out of sight for me. I used a stool to groom him. Very fit and slim at the time, I could actually mount from the ground. I figured that if I ever came off him up the trails, there wouldn't be a mounting block handy, to re-mount and ride home. Mostly I was just vain about being fit – a feeling I can only just barely remember, being nowhere near fit now, or for some years. It's still a nice memory.

Ryan was owned by a businessman – a lawyer, I think. I never met him. The barn manager set up the lease for me. Apparently the owner, even well-heeled, thought the board fee was too expensive and wanted a half-lease to offset this. As usual, I couldn't afford what he was asking. The barn manager, bless her, suggested a smaller fee, to which he agreed. I didn't know it at the time, but I now believe she wanted someone else riding Ryan, someone who actually liked him.

* * *

A cool autumn day and I arrive at the barn eager to ride. I've met several tough deadlines for fisheries articles, my bread-and-butter "beat," and have spent many hours in-side at my computer. The fresh air is rejuvenating. I could wiggle down my body like a Labrador retriever, I'm that happy to be at the barn. I walk to the paddock where Ryan is usually turned out on a clear day such as this. To my dis-appointment, he's not there. It's a big barn. Not every horse gets out every day, or for the full day.

I find him in his stall. His hindquarters face outward and he doesn't turn around when I greet him. His head is pointed into a corner of the stall, his nose almost touching the sawdust bedding. A thick flake of hay sits undisturbed on the other side of the stall. I have never seen him be-have this way and I am instantly worried. For all their size, weight, and strength, horses are fragile. Is this some strange new manifestation of colic? Colic kills. Maybe the hay is mouldy, has caused gut trouble. I stare harder at the hay. It looks fluffy and fresh.

"Ryan – hey, big guy, you OK?" I haven't stepped in the stall yet. I'm guessing he would not kick me; even still, walking into a stall with a horse's backside facing you is not a safety-oriented move. "Ryan? It's me. You feeling all right?"

"You haven't seen him like this before, have you?" I turn to see the barn manager beside me; she must have been in the close-by tack room, then heard me talking to Ryan.

"No! I've never seen him acting so strange. Do you know what's wrong with him?"

"That's depression you're looking at. Deep, dark depression. Ryan's been like that since the hunt on Saturday." It's Tuesday. That's over three days looking like this.

"The hunt?" I ask, guts starting to clench. This gelding's too out of shape for hunting.

"Yeah, his owner trucks him out to the Fraser Valley each weekend and rides him hard on the hunts they do out there. As we both know, Ryan's not fit, but he gives that guy everything he has. Wait 'til you see the overreach he did this week. His legs are a mess."

I glance down to the front leg I can see from this viewpoint and sure enough, see a nasty gouge on the pastern, between the bulb of the fetlock and the top of the hoof. It is seeping blood. The whole leg is filthy with dried mud. Ryan's entire body is matted with dried mud and sweat.

"The wound's still dirty!" I cry. "Couldn't you have cleaned it for him?"

The mild air goes frosty. "I was hoping you might," she answers. "I've got quite enough to do around here. I can't be interfering with other people's horses. You're the leaser."

"Of course I'll clean it," I say. "Do you have any antibiotic cream?"

She goes in search of this. I still haven't gone in the stall, and Ryan still hasn't moved. The manager returns with cream. "How long has he stood like this?" I ask. "All morning," she answers. She glances at her watch. "And for these two hours after lunch. Really, he hasn't moved much at all since the weekend. And he's not eating worth a damn either. Even the hay out in his paddock."

She goes to walk away – then stops. "I can't interfere with the boarders' horses," she repeats. "But as barn manager, I can call the vet, if I think the horse needs to see one. It's in the boarders' contracts with the stable that I am allowed to do that. You let me know, and I can make that call. It's not necessary this time; that overreach isn't serious. But it might be another time."

I look her full in the eyes, which are sad but resigned. This is nothing new for a barn manager at a big boarding barn to see. There are the treasured horses, and there are the others. But she's on Ryan's side, for sure. He needs all the friends he can get. I nod, say nothing, turn back to Ryan.

"Hey, big guy, I'm coming in." I unlatch the stall door as quietly as I can, uncertain if he's even really heard me and not wanting to startle him. I have been kicked before. Worse than an angry beehive smashed into you with a baseball bat. No movement from the usually towering strawberry roan. I pass behind him, move up on his left side, still a small mountain, heading toward his lowered head. The left eye is unfocused and unblinking. "Hello, Ryan," I whisper. My hand moves as though pulled by a magnet to his long neck. Dried sweat on it, too. He was obviously taken from the trailer to his stall with no stops for grooming or first-aid. He'd galloped his hunt course, done what was required, and was summarily chucked back into this stall. He moves his head the tiniest turn toward me, allows my hands on the flat of his cheek and then up, to his poll and the backs of his ears. I smooth his forelock, pulling an errant piece back from behind his ears. I expect him to raise his head – maybe slowly, but to raise it part or all the way up. He does not.

* * *

You may have heard a person who loves or cares for their horse talk to them, when the horse is ill or injured. It's not so different from one human speaking to another human, one they love or care for. It may be most similar to the sing-song words of a mother to a hurt or frightened child. The voice is low and steady, the words repeated over and over, a comfort-chant intended to soothe and calm the listener. I chanted to Ryan for the longest time. Finally, he raised his head. Not his full, erect carriage, but the head raised enough for me to slip on a halter, and some croonings later, to lead him from his stall to the nearest set of cross-ties.

I found a clean sponge and some mild soap and then boiled water in the kettle in the tack room. I added the soap to a bucket, pouring the boiling water in first, then cold water from the hose until it was the perfect temperature to clean his wound. The vivid pinkness of the flesh cleaved into the hair of the pastern, just above the hoof, made me wince, but at least it was a solid pink, no pus that I could see. I kept on talking to him the whole time I washed down his legs, belly, chest, and haunches. The tangled tail could wait. It was the perspiration and mud on his body I was after.

Ryan stood stoic and still for all of it, even when I went to find a stool, to be able to reach and wash his back, still evidencing the outline of the saddle, and when I washed around his ears and muzzle, where sweat had gathered under the bridle. The hairs were spiky and matted. Several times Ryan leaned into the sponge as I worked on his face. I even dabbed at the corners of his mouth, where foam had dried. Finally, I sorted out the rat's nest that was his tail.

Then I took an old, clean beach towel from my car, meant for swabbing my whippet's paws after a run on the beach, and rubbed Ryan dry from top to bottom. He was fuzzy as an Easter chick, all the sour old sweat gone. His head rose higher and higher, then he lowered it again – and shook all over as a dog would, from stem to stern. My jeans and shirt were soaked from the entire effort. I was very pleased with the results of my labours.

We went for a halter walk that day. We didn't walk far from the barn, just a couple of blocks, searching out the thickest grass on the narrow boulevards that ran alongside the properties. Ryan chomped and I daydreamed. Sometimes I leaned against his clean shoulder, or stood back, giving him all the room he wanted to move from clump to clump of grass. I thought about a man I'd never met, who owned the horse I leased. I'd seen far worse abuse of horses in my time with them. Ryan was more sensitive than many horses, as well. It was the unthinkingness of it all that bothered me, with this man simply going about his self-focused ways with no recognition of consciousness and feelings in The Others, as writer Farley Mowat called members of the animal kingdom. *My* horse, Ryan's owner might think, the same way he'd think *my* car, *my* golf clubs. *Things.*

Of course, these were all my imaginings. I never knew anything for sure about this man; everything came to me second-hand and the rest were guesses. I only knew Ryan was depressed and frightened and became more so, as the weeks went on.

The worst fall I never had was on Ryan. And yes, it would have been worse than the one I did have, in 2011. I don't think I'd be here to write about it.

I never galloped Ryan. He was too easily startled and far too strong for a small woman to pull back from a disaster of any kind. Mistakes made at a gallop can quickly turn lethal. Instead, I rode Ryan very gingerly. He seemed happiest up the trails, wind off the river in his face, free from the confines of stall and ring. Mostly we walked and trotted and in the safest of places, we did a slow canter. With Ryan's immense strides, the canter was a stretched out, floating gait I'd never experienced. Smooth, though, my own magical flying carpet.

Ryan and I often rode up the trails, which run alongside the Musqueam Reserve. Now and again, the Musqueam teenagers or young men would fire BB guns, or maybe .22 rifles, at targets in their yards, I am guessing. I don't know for sure, as we couldn't see the guns being fired, could only hear the shots. My brother had a BB gun in those days, too. It was a boy-toy of the times, even for city kids. Your average horse hates loud noises, and becomes extremely reactive at the sound of a gun going off. As I say, Ryan was more sensitive than most.

Ryan and I were trotting along a straight stretch in the trail where we sometimes loped. I didn't canter that day, because Ryan was too wound up, and I didn't want to fight him to stay steady. *Bang!* After the gunshot, Ryan leapt into a gallop. In less than a heartbeat, his continent of a neck was stretched out as far as he could push it and the only world that existed was pounding motion and sickening fear. Animal transformed into a hurtling comet. Ryan's horseness vanished. He was a death-vehicle and I was on his back, certain to meet my Maker.

I concentrated on two things: staying on, and considering my options. I could bail. Or not. There was a sharp corner coming up. One or both of us wouldn't make it around that corner. Everywhere I looked for a bail spot, I saw broken bones or silence in my future. He was far too firmly into the bolt for me to be able to haul back, saw on the bit, or use the pulley-rein maneuver, one hand braced on the neck, the other pulling back with everything you have. I briefly considered reaching down to grab the ring of his bit to haul backwards on that – but the bit was a universe ahead of me and my short arm, and if I pulled on it, I was just as likely to send myself somersaulting over his head. I was also trying hard to keep my backside in the saddle and not rise up into a full hunt-seat, where I would stand in the stirrups and lean forward, losing even more control and balance in the process. I had only one real option. Voice. I could talk to him. The way I did the day he was hurt.

"*Whoa*, Ryan, whoa. Come on, big guy, *whoaaaa –*" Over and over I crooned these words. I didn't think for a moment it was going to work – until it did. Then it was as natural as an evening wind gusting up and dying down. It simply happened. His full gallop shortened to a hand-gallop, then to a canter, then to a trot, then to a jog. His body was shaking, but his ears were flicking back and forth, back and forth, listening to me, as my chant kept on, and then changed. "Good boy, Ryan, good boy, atta boy, well done, good fellah," over and over again. We passed the sharp corner I never expected to see past – possibly live past – and rode at a prancing jog all the way home, a good mile or so. He couldn't bring himself to walk – the bang-demons might catch him. I figured a jog was fair enough. He'd listened when it really counted.

We mostly rode in the ring after that. His owner continued to hunt him hard on the weekends, and I kept on tidying up the aftermaths. I don't remember how the lease came to an end. Perhaps Ryan moved, perhaps I went from Ryan to a safer lease.

That said, I had many good rides on Ryan, and I've never had a horse come back so quickly from terror to trust, quite the way Ryan did after the gunshot. If ever a horse said *Oh, it's you, I can do this for you,* it was Ryan to me, on that day.

I always felt I earned that reprieve.

And perhaps I earned the easy-heart lease I had with Cliquot the Thoroughbred. As I recall, dainty, slim Cliquot had spent an unbelievable seven years at Hastings Park racetrack. This means he was a fast, steady winner, all those years. As he came off the track mostly sound, it also meant he had legs of iron. Most Thoroughbreds leave the track no later than four years old, more often two or three.

Here was a horse that had spent his whole life galloping, and Cliquot – like Boo, Kaber, and even cantankerous, arthritic Madonna – *never* bolted on me and had no desire to gallop. Considering all my lease crew, I would call him the most polite, even self-effacing. He was sweet and tractable in the ring and on the roads, and quiet and willing up the trails. He was also a relatively small horse, perhaps 15 hands high. It's always easier for me to work around smaller horses. When I think of Cliquot, I remember his ultra-soft, thin coat, a hallmark of Thoroughbreds, and what an attractive bay he was.

In his personality, Cliquot was a gentleman, through and through, and a handsome one at that. His coat was the dark brown you'd find in a forest landscape, or see in delta lands. His "points" – mane, tail, forelock, and lower legs – were shining black. I enjoyed grooming him. His chest was a bit narrow and somehow that made me feel protective, as though he were the "98-pound weakling" that Charles Atlas, the 1950s body-builder, used to deride to sell his body-building program.

But frail though he might first appear, Cliquot was no weakling. His track record proved that. Off the track, he was a dependable and cheerful ride. When I picture his face, it's with his ears pricked forward, all the time. He didn't nicker or whicker, that I remember, but he always seemed pleased to see me, and had lovely "stable manners" as I worked around him or tacked up, either on the cross-ties or in his stall.

Once out on the trails, and similar to Kaber, everything interested cheerful Cliquot: great blue herons fishing in the Fraser River's estuary shallows; barges filled with golden peaks of sawdust, towed with or against the tide by Seaspan tugs with mighty, growling engines; white-bellied airplanes rising into the sky from the Vancouver International Airport, its runways located south, across the North Arm of the river, where we were; other horses and riders; Sunday strollers, throwing sticks for their Labrador retrievers; plaid-clad golfers out on the greens of Point Grey Golf Course and the Musqueam Driving Range. Cliquot watched all this and more with wide eyes, but he never shied or caused me any trouble. Instead, for a little guy, he stretched out into a prairie-eating walk or, when asked, rose promptly to a pert trot or pleasantly contained canter. *Gallop, who me? Not anymore, thanks, anyway.*

Occasionally, passing through boggy bits of the trails or going down hills, Cliquot's back end would slip under him, and I would wonder if his hocks – the rear "elbows" – were trashed. God knows how much pounding those legs and that spine of his took in seven long years at the track. But mostly he just hacked up trails as though he were the luckiest horse ever – no hard track, no mad galloping, no aching legs and back, no tender feet, no whip against his flanks, and no threat of being trucked off to the knacker's – not that he'd know to fear that evil day, bless his stout heart, until he was living it. At seven, it was a tidy miracle someone had claimed him off the track. Life was good as a retired racer. In return, he was good to his owner, and to me.

Madonna was a small country-raised mare who came to the city. She was another red-roany horse, like Boo, but without the lovely spots Boo had, and most Appaloosas do have. Nonetheless, we decided that Madonna was a half-Appaloosa. "Oh, yeah," said the barn's veterinarian one time, when she was at the barn to tube-worm all the horses for parasites, "she's definitely got Appaloosa in her. Look at her thin tail, and that downhill conformation, backside higher than the withers. Appy for sure." (Boo was in my future at that point, or I might have been mightily offended by her insulting summation of the Appaloosa breed, many of whom are jaw-drop gorgeous, and are not in any way configured "downhill.") The owners, when asked, had no clue what Madonna's breeding might have been. It didn't really matter, I was just curious. Among horse people, breeding details aren't usually completely mysterious. But a lot about Madonna was.

All these years later and I want to remember that mare fairly. She was so green that the basic natural "aids" a rider would use with a trained horse while riding – weight, legs, voice, and hands – were mostly confusing to her. She had a short temper, too, once evidenced by cow-kicking me in the gut, the hoof also grazing my eye socket. That was the first time I got carted off in an ambulance due to a horse. I'm still shocked she did that, lifted up that hind hoof and kicked forwards, pasting me as I stood at her shoulder. I stared at the small nick by my right eye for days after the accident, when I washed my face in the morning and at night. So close …

Madonna may not have been well-schooled, but once you pushed past her stubbornness – no small feat – she started to listen and gave a reasonable effort. We ended up looking quite decent on our rides together, and even took occasional lessons from a dressage instructor. It was this instructor who belatedly decided Madonna had arthritis, and some of the athletic things we asked her to do, she simply couldn't do without being in considerable pain. Hence the kick: an emphatic "fuck you" because we had been schooling her too hard. Heaven knows the owners were round-eyed when they learned of the accident. She's always so *good*, they protested. But then, they didn't actually ride Madonna. They just came by the barn to groom once in a while, and visit with her – on the ground. If ever a horse needed a leaser, it was Madonna. Otherwise, she would rarely have left her stall.

In the end I guess I'd have to say the good far outweighed the bad, again. Madonna gave me many enjoyable hours of riding. There's a price we humans pay for not listening to animals, and I paid that price when I trained Madonna as seriously as I did. We had a modest, wary friendship, Madonna and I, especially after the kick. From start to finish, there wasn't one smidgen of the love-fest I shared with Boo and Kaber, or the gentle gratitude and liking Cliquot and I shared. Even still, I progressed as a rider with Madonna, becoming trim and supple the summer and fall of our lease, and refreshing my skills in basic dressage, which I hadn't done since Coqeyn days, many years prior.

Madonna gave me what she was able to, for which I thank her. Each and every one of the lease crew enriched my life.

In the final reckoning, and by the generous, elemental nature of their gifts – giving their bodies as transport, and, rightly or wrongly, sublimating their wills to obey humans' wills – horses will always give us more than we can give them. In my experience, they also provide excellent and spiritually uplifting company.

But some of the most gloriously intimate and triumphant moments come when horse and rider work together, for a common goal, which both of them desire. Open-jumping; fox or mock hunting; steeplechasing; polo; track or barrel-racing; endurance riding; three-day eventing; reining; driving cattle; pulling a stone-boat, carriage, cart, or plow; executing English or Western dressage or equitation – to name but some disciplines, sports, and work that horses and people engage in together. Once you and the horse really believe you are a team, two hearts do become a singular will, a winning drive.

Oh, I would love that! To feel as though I was a team with a horse again! Not me the human and they the horse moving in separate worlds, on the ground or mounted, but instead, the intermingling of spirits and will, when two creatures know there is a binding task ahead that must be done, all for the joy of a skillful execution. That rich, driving feeling of Let's Do It. Let Us Do It, We Two.

Those respectful, resonant moments can't be beaten for heady pleasure on the human's part, and snorting, head-dipping satisfaction on the horse's part. Horses are such proud animals, and every horse is good at something – even if it's making the landscape more beautiful, as writer Alice Walker noted – especially when they are raised and trained with kindness and skill. If two-legged humans are lucky, they form relationships with these four-legged mythical creatures who help them to look wondrously skilled and graceful at their chosen endeavour. Strong and fleet, too.

And yet it is not the human who jumps from the ground over towering structures, small or tall rider atop, or safely carries sled and passengers over icy winter roads, or out-thinks and out-moves darting calves, driving them back to the herd, or heaves into harness to clear an immense stony field – that is only the horse, trusting the people who guide it, and moving ahead with the honed work ethic so many horses can develop. You may be invited to be a team member, but the horse does more, always.

There's no denying the singularly powerful connection some horses can have with some individual humans, either as a competitive unit and/or as companionable or working units. No matter the central circumstances, being simple friends with a horse is always a great surprise and privilege, disregarding as it does language and species barriers to allow two creatures consistent pleasure in one another's company. No lifetime rider ever gets over the miracle of it. I sure didn't.

* * *

Once again it has warmed me to think of all my horse connections over the years, and how much each one gave me. I feel sad now, though, wondering if horses will only ever be my past, not my present and future. How will I ever find the exact right horse that I can "come back" on? I need a horse I can trust completely to cart my battered body and wary heart around safely – and maybe, just maybe, a horse I can grow with as a rider.

That's it – grow with as a rider. What if I surprised the hell out of myself, and really surprised family and friends, just for the thrill of it? Kind of go off the deep end with a crazy-new goal or plan, you know? But what could that something be? It's as though the vision is just around a corner. I run up to see it, but there it goes, slipping around the next corner. All I see is a scarlet flash, a silk scarf at a woman's throat, then nothing, as though the dream loses its lifeblood.

My heart knows what my eyes haven't seen yet. I'll just have to run faster.

My mother, Barbara Simmins, holding Coqeyn, and my sister Karin at Foreshore Beach, Vancouver, B.C., 1973.

Nizzeyn's Coqeyn.

Kaber the Kind, a half-Arabian who loved to whicker.

Cliquot the Mannerly, a Thoroughbred

Bold and brash Boo

Ryan the Hanoverian

5
GOING UP WITH A FIGHT
MAY 2013, HALIFAX, N.S.

All those memories of all the fine horses in my life and that tidal pull of excitement about something new and special, the estuary that will lead to the wider ocean of my new horse life. Now I can't stop thinking about the one horse that's out there, just waiting for me to find him or her.

But who am I kidding? I am so far from the reality of riding – even now, two years after my fall – that it's like longing for a silvered walk high on the moon, when you're actually weighted down on the murkiest bottom of the ocean. Here I am, fashioning dreams of the grandest sort – *and I can't breathe, I cannot breathe, when I think about being near a horse –*

And why should that be surprising? I went back to riding because I wanted to build a good physical life to take onward into my senior years. So far, it's the exact opposite of what I was hoping for; I am far worse off now than I was before I took it into my head to find a schooling barn and resume riding. I never had an enduring back problem in my life. Two years on, I am still in pain, for God's sake. Do I really want to take the chance of being badly harmed again and end up worse yet? I still can't even feel my lower back or right foot. I mean, let's be practical. How would I actually manage to ride? It's not possible. I also need to get back to my freelance writing, maybe even plan to teach a writing course soon.

And yet, and yet ... I'm carrying all those memories in the arms of my heart, keep repeating the names that touch me most.

Coqeyn, once we understood your fevered ways, knew how to sit down and ride you out of a bolt – all was well. I could anticipate then stop a bolt in two footfalls. Kaber, equally hot at times, I have no idea why you were so kind to me – but thank you, dappled boy, thank you, for all those uneventful hacks. Cliquot the mannerly, I cherish the memories of our serene rides under leafy canopies. Boo the beautiful, so tall and roundly muscled, and not one moment of unease riding you in over a year. Ryan the timid, who listened with twitching ears to a 104-pound woman crooning to him when the bang-demons chased him; Ryan the immense, who listened to her earlier, believed she could chant his troubles away, accepted the hands that washed his wounds clean, told him he was a fighter, not to give up.

Told him he was a fighter – not to give up. Is that what I am supposed to remember, most of all?

Maybe. For now I only know one way to build up my courage. Memory-jewels.

Foreshore Beach, Vancouver, B.C. April 1973

Karin's riding Redwing, and I'm riding Coqeyn. It was kind of Gwen to lend Redwing to us, so we could ride together. We hardly ever get to ride together. It can be tiresome to take turns on one horse. Instead, we've been chatting and laughing all day, riding side by side, or, when the trail demanded, single-file. The time shimmered by.

Coqeyn has a mechanical hackamore bridle on, so it's been easy to keep his bolts in check; there's a reason they call those things "brakes." No bit in the mouth, but the reins connect to shanks placed between a noseband and a curb chain. When I pull back, there's a lot of pressure on Coqeyn's nose, chin groove, and poll. Of course, I don't want to hurt him, so I am careful on those reins. But I need to stay safe, too, especially crossing the busy highways and city boulevards that connect up the forest trails from the southwest of the city to the beach lands along Vancouver harbour. It's basically a lot of bridle for a lot of horse on a long and unusual rural/urban/forest/beach ride. The hackamore is a Western bridle, and I'm not too keen on these long, separated reins, but so far, so good – I haven't dropped one yet. Just have to remember to keep them crossed over his neck, then hold them in two hands, as I would a set of English reins, which are joined in the middle, with a buckle.

I suppose Coqeyn looks a bit unusual, with an English saddle and Western bridle. Not that there's anyone around to notice right now, on a quiet weekend day, just before noon. And what's it matter, anyway? The idea was to feel well in control on my long hack, and I have. The gentle Eggbutt snaffle bit we have on our English bridle is like riding with only the suggestion of a bit. Fat and fine for everyday, because we don't want to harden his mouth, but not on the trails.

Half-Arabian, half-Thoroughbred Redwing is nearly as hot in temperament as Coqeyn, and heavier, taller. But Karin is taller and stronger than I am, and she and Redwing get on well, with only the occasional disagreement, when I'm in the lead on a trail. In general, we had an uneventful, relaxed ride down here today. Now we're sitting in our saddles, stirrups kicked out, letting the horses crop the short dry grass at the edge of the beach, waiting for Mum to arrive with a thermos of hot, milky, sugared tea. Silent, we watch the coastal world around us.

Foreshore Beach is a gold and blue gemstone today. The warm-hued sands lead to cerulean waters and across the outer harbour, set high and multi-peaked, the smoky-blue North Shore Mountains, crowned by scudding clouds. Hatless, my ears and cheeks are cold, as are my gloveless hands. The wind is a slicer. Even land-based me knows that it's blowing from the northwest today. Don't need to look at the air-tumbling seagulls to know that. My oldest sister, Zoë, twenty-one, is a commercial fisherman. Zoë talked about the prevailing wind patterns on the West Coast often enough that I have my own recognition of them. Blue skies and seas, cavorting winds and super cold? Nor'westerly. Dark skies, grey waters, blowing sullen and hard, medium-cold? Sou'easterly. Nor'westerly is the ballerina-precise one, the one your heart rises to, even as your hair does the same, then cuts across your face, and your hands start to numb.

I shiver. I'm parched and cold. What I'd give for tea, maybe a snack. I look behind to the road, hoping to see Mum's 1964 gold Chevrolet Bel-Air. How do I know all these identifiers? My brother, Geoffrey; he's not car crazy by any means, but he loves lists and detailed descriptions of any sort, and loves to teach whatever he's learned – needs to teach, in a cheerful, insistent way. I think he likes the stability of facts and figures; unlike family comings and goings, they can be relied on to stay put. I crane my neck each direction, but no dice on the car front.

Even Geoffrey would find it a challenge to count the freighters today, all at anchor, some tucked one before the other, a bow sticking out here, a stern there. More boat talk that I picked up from Zoë. She's always so busy with seriously exciting adventures. Imagine, she and her husband fish over 900 miles north of Vancouver, in the frigid, choppy waters of Hecate Strait, near Prince Rupert. That's near to the "A/B line," as the fishermen call it, referring to Canada and Alaska. Why A/B? Because this imaginary line separates the water of A (Canada) from B (the U.S.). A to B – get it?

Both my sisters are willowy, hippie-beautiful, and smart, though they don't always get along. I just dance between them, grateful as well for a brother, who, at sixteen, is already fairly independent. When Geoffrey's around, it's relaxing to play cards with him and play music on our guitars. I love all my siblings, though am closest to Karin right now. And today, thank God, she's straight. No needles and fix today, not even any pills. I think she's enjoying her outdoor-sharpened senses, feels no need for artificial elevation.

Will I remember this? Will I remember the hard ball of happiness in my gut when I look at her pale face, dusted with only a few freckles, the shining, sober eyes a match for the cobalt ocean on a nor'westerly day? Will I be able to recall her hands, slightly bigger than mine, the nails cut straight across, resting now on the pommel of the saddle? Will I be able to revive this feeling of sacred peace – knowing as I do, somehow, that on this day, there will be no scenes, no shouting or obscenities, no blood or injuries, hers or others', no thugs at our front door, and no tormenting of me, my other siblings, our unflaggingly devoted mother? That cowlick on the right side of your hair-part – it makes me smile. That's the only bona fide curl you have, Karin. Your auburn hair has body, but doesn't frizz up, as my curly light brown hair does. You have the typical redhead's or blonde's translucent fair skin; even the tiny hairs on your face are white-blonde. Don't worry, I'm not staring at you to dissect your looks; I just feel calm watching you in profile as you breathe. Your chest is slowly rising and falling. As slow as mine. Puts me in the dreamiest place ...

Do you remember that time we dialled up Santa – on the radio of "Bluebird," the Ford station wagon we had before Mum's current car? I wasn't sure it could be done, but you said yes, trust me, we can do this – and we did. I was four or five, which made you nine or ten. You knew how much I wanted that plastic, blow-up baby reindeer – the ones they had in the holiday displays at Safeway. I mean I really wanted it. That critter would be my dearest friend, I was certain. Worried and pining, I could barely sleep for the wanting of it. It even had fawn-dots on its back! Oddly, the baby deer also had grown-up antlers, but I didn't mind. Be easier to pick it up by an antler than by its head or ears, surely. And I would be picking it up, traipsing around with it, hugging it all the time, loving it forever and ever, Amen – if I could only get one for a Christmas gift. And then, miracle of miracles, right up there with the birth of the Baby Jesus him-self, to five-year-old me – I did get the plastic blow-up baby rein-deer, complete with spots and antlers on Christmas morning! All because my powerful sister called the North Pole on the family car's radio, spoke to Santa Claus, and ordered us one for deliv-ery on Christmas Eve. Was there anything this astonishing sister couldn't do?

It's a funny story, Karin. I should tell the rest of the family about it, sometime. And really, I still think you could do any-thing you set your mind to …

Coqeyn shifts his weight from one hind leg to the other, leaving one hoof upraised. This makes me unevenly seated in the saddle. I lean the opposite way, and the resting hoof lays flat again. With my feet kicked out of the stirrups, I rotate my sore ankles.

"I'm so tired – are you?"

"Yeah," answers Karin. "But that's OK, it was worth it to get here."

As if pulled by a magnet we look to the surf, each cresting wave a separate story, before their mingling dissolu-tion on the shore.

She's right, it was worth it to get here, sharp winds and all. Her satisfaction makes me look forward to the ride home. The horses were good on the way here – little stars, both of them. I wonder if we'll ever be able to do this ride on two horses again? Or maybe Coqeyn and Redwing again? Why does this feel so defined and singular – once, and once only, for you, my complicated sister, and me?

A thick strand of sunbleached hair has come out of your

elastic hairband. It joins the ballet of a windy day. Somehow I love your face even more with your hair messy. You always smile, tilt your head to the side a little when I tell you I love you. Gooey little sister admiration and affection, for a big sib – I can't help it, you do everything so well. I do my best, and ambitious you are always glad to see that, and kind enough to acknowledge the improvements. But that's not part of this equation. Ever and always, "Love you, too, Maggie," you say in turn. I didn't have to earn this love, improve or work for it; the solidity of it was simply there, from first years.

Today that love is clenching at my heart – maybe it's the relief of not seeing her ugly and stoned; she's such good company when she's straight – so nice to look on. I want to say, No, really, listen ... I love you beyond those far mountains, beyond this day of horses, beyond all the places I'll see/you'll see when we're older, living apart. I can do that, right? Love you when we're older, far apart – maybe even mountains and skies between us? You'd still know I loved you, right?

"There's Mum!" says Karin, pointing to the parking lot. "There's her car." And there indeed is our mother, and the 1964 gold Chevrolet Bel-Air. Sister-love spills over to mother-love. Mum's the best. Holding all our lives together after the divorce, supporting all of us in so many ways. Just being generous Mum, to us and all of our friends. Our house is a lighthouse to people of all ages and backgrounds. Come in, eat, drink tea, laugh, share a story. Smoke? Sure, here's a can of tobacco to roll your own, or if you want, take one of my "tailor-mades." We'd sit at the picnic table in our small kitchen nook, the large window at its end presenting a painter's view of leaves or blossoms from the nearby cherry tree, the two-tiered yard beyond generous and flower-filled – "Dr. Ida Wallace was a fine gardener," our father used to say of the previous owner, for whom we used to receive pieces of mail for at least a decade – and puff on our tobacco, as so many did in the 1960s and '70s.

Mum started smoking when she was eleven, she told

us – mind, that was 1930, she was a decided rebel – and she was still defiant, not one smidgen repentant. She had her own streamlined car at age sixteen, too, posed with one cuffed trouser-leg up on its running board, looking so fresh and sporty, she did, in long-ago London, Ontario, our beside-Lake-Huron-raised mother, able to swim and row well, and who even had her own pony growing up, a stocky little bay called "Tiny," shown in photographs with a tall-standing, growing-out "roached" or shaved mane, which must have wavered back and forth like a fat metronome as they trotted down country lanes. I wonder now what breed he was and how he came to their lives, and exited their lives, too. No doubt he had to be sold after my mother's father was "killed in a hunting accident," said Mum, "by a captain in the army, of all things. He should have known never to fire a gun at someone, unless …" That unless destroyed the Atkinson family, perhaps fourteen-year-old Mum most of all. "Your mother never got over the loss," said our father, with quiet understanding. "She missed him all her life …"

What did you see that day on Foreshore Beach, Mum? Your eyes always sought out your beloved mountains, so I bet you saw them first. Hard to miss the horses next, and there atop them, two of your daughters, waving. Did you toot the car's horn? Or more likely just quickly waved back and parked the car. Five years between Karin and me – I was fourteen, she was nineteen – and while I did look older, even haggard some days, I didn't look nineteen. People still got confused, called us twins – remember? Twinned certainly in our long, thick hair, and in our navy ski jackets, jeans, and knee-high rubber riding boots; twinned in our smiles when we saw you, too. Tell me I vaulted off Coqeyn, handed the reins to Karin, went to meet you, help you with your laden arms. I hope so much I did that. I know the sight of you warmed us both, took the edge right off that driving Pacific gale-wind, long before the proffered plastic cup from the thermos. Another pair of small, soft hands, your eyes North-Shore grey-blue, holding us in your gaze as though all the world was in its right place now, with two of your four-own before you, the other two, on that day, not far away. All of us in that ambered moment doing fine, just fine.

"Take therefore no thought for the morrow (Matthew 6:34): for the morrow shall take thought for the things of itself. Sufficient unto the day is the evil thereof ...," I would think, so many years later, of that contented day and others in my life.

It was the best cup of tea *ever in the world* – before or since. So were the sharp cheddar cheese sandwiches, apples, and crunchy chocolate chip cookies Mum brought us. Such an angled day of colour and vitality all around us, our eyes reflecting those blues, greens, and golds, and such a soft-edged world for we three humans – and two horses – our mouths full of sugar-linger, and our spirits as light and heedless as the wind-tumbled gulls above. The horses got the apples, of course.

* * *

Karen. Karin. Then, six or so years after we lost you, you became "sister-Karin," more often than not. By then there was another family member named Karin and we siblings didn't want to confuse matters when we spoke of you. Sister-Karin. Our blood relationship to you was a fact, could not be altered or diminished by death. But somehow I think you know that.

6

THE MOUNTING BLOCK
JUNE 2013, DUNDEE, CAPE BRETON, N.S.

I'm going to do this. I'm really going to do this.

Can I do this?

Caberfeidh Stables, near Dundee, Cape Breton. I'd forgotten what a nice barn and property this is. Why didn't I build an ongoing relationship with this stable back in the late 1990s and early 2000s, when Don and I still lived full-time in Cape Breton? It's only a half-hour's drive from our small home in the village of D'Escousse, on Isle Madame. I know I rode here a few times several years ago, but somehow Don and I were never in Cape Breton long enough to set up steady lessons or even a part-time lease, if that had worked for all. By 2006, the city of Halifax had claimed us by reinvigorating our working lives and for me, pursuing a long-postponed master's degree. We kept our home on Isle Madame, but time in Cape Breton was hard to bring about.

It's getting easier to do that now, and after so much time in the city, we're craving country time. Summer days in D'Escousse make me think of the long summer days when you were a kid – the middle bit filtered through a soft-focus yellow lens, the hours bracketing this marked by rosy starts and indigo ends. It's mid-morning now, a golden-syrup day, topped with blue. I reluctantly roll up the passenger-side window in the truck. This place smells good, too: nearby, flowers, grass, and horse; on the breeze, muted salt from the Bras d'Or Lakes, an inland sea.

Don and I get out of our truck and walk by the big ring toward the barn. I may have ridden here before, but my dancing guts tell me it's the first time I've ever ridden, at any barn. I refocus on the reassuring barn smells and pin a smile on my face.

I am doing this ... why? My motives are ... exactly what? These are not so much thoughts as they are querying heart-words, thudding in my chest.

You couldn't walk, you couldn't even turn over in bed, you just lay there in leaden agony, week after sullen week – and now you're back in a barn again? These heart-words thud even harder.

"You sure about this?" asks Don quietly. In two more steps we'll be inside the barn. I am struggling to keep the fear off my face – I don't want anyone but Don to see that. He'll support any decision I make. We could simply walk back to the truck, make our apologies to the barn owners later.

"Yes," I say, not looking at him. Maybe I don't want him to see the fear, either. Maybe those concerned hazel eyes will make me more fearful yet.

Unbidden comes the memory of Don telling me, soon after the accident, what his plans were, if I'd lost my mobility permanently: *I got in the car and started driving to the hospital, to meet you and the ambulance there. All the way downtown I was planning how I could change the house, so we could live in it if you were in a wheelchair. I just didn't know what we were dealing with. But I thought, it's all right, we can live on one floor and still make the house work for us.* Our house is sub-road, on a hill overlooking the water. He re-minded me of the ramp we have at street level, leading into the second floor of the house, which had been built by the previous owners, who themselves had "mobility issues." *The ramp was a good start, he continued. But we would have had to put in a kitchen on that top floor, and a new bathroom, both suited for a handicapped person. You weren't going to be coming down the inside staircase, to the front door and main floor of the house. Ever again.*

He didn't say it then, aloud, but we'd both thought the same thing: *even in a wheelchair, you can keep on writing.*

Right, the freelance journalist who goes nowhere, rarely leaves the house, and learns only from a computer screen, not from in-person interviews and site-research. But in fact, he was right. One way or another, I would have kept on learning and writing. Working. It just would have been a very different world. Remembering all of this has me breathing through my mouth. I pull myself into the present moment.

Fake it 'til you make it, fake it 'til you make it. And that heart-chant evokes a genuine smile. It's what my dad used to say – one of a list of useful adages from his many years at Alcoholics Anonymous. My father passed away thirteen years ago. He's still helping me live with backbone.

I take in a good lungful of farm air: wood chips and sawdust, horse manure, sunned earth, and the fevered green growth of early summer in Nova Scotia. There, I'm better now. I'm here to make things right again, to stop letting fear and pain dominate my memories. What comes after that, I don't know, and that's all right. *One day at a time,* right, Dad?

"Hi, Marjorie, hi, Don – good to see you!" Adrienne is grooming one of the horses in the cement aisleway. The horse is secured on cross-ties. He's a big grey quarter horse – with an unusual name, which I can't bring to mind.

"You remember Gofor, don't you?" asks Adrienne helpfully. She loves talking about her horses, who, along with her human family, are the anchor and joy of her life.

"His full registered name is Juanagoforaspin. His dam

was Juanasomesugar, a grey cutting horse from Texas. His sire was Krysum Classified, who was shown as a Western pleasure horse, and at halter, for conformation. Both parents were registered quarter horses." She puts a hand atop Gofor's withers, obviously proud of him. "So that makes Gofor a registered quarter horse, bred to be an athletic pleasure horse, with excellent conformation."

I nod – sure I remember Gofor, if not his name straight away, and there's no doubt about it, he's a distinguished horse. But that's not uppermost in my mind today. What I am thinking about is this gelding's sweet nature, and how he gives a lovely comfortable ride to anyone who climbs aboard, no matter what their level of competency. This might be a tiny, ten-year-old girl, just getting started, or a middle-aged person like me, "coming back" from either an accident or prolonged inactivity. I've ridden Gofor several times. I know I will be well taken care of with him.

I am starting to relax. I wasn't sure who Adrienne would choose for me to ride this first time back. Gofor's the closest I have to an old horse friend here at the barn. He's just what I need.

So's Adrienne. I felt so awkward ringing her at first, explaining my situation. It seemed such a long, convoluted story. But she just stayed quiet and listened. First I explained my hopes for getting strong on horseback again. Then I described unexpectedly finding a popular schooling barn near the city, riding regularly, and making some decent progress over the spring of 2011. Then the accident, then the long, ongoing recovery. Last, the physical parts of me that still aren't working very well. That may never work very well again. And the other parts of me – the emotional parts – that still give me trouble. Two years and a month after I was tossed.

"Can you help me ride again?" I asked finally, that day on the telephone. I got the question out fast, just succeeding in pushing past a fissure in my voice.

Yes, she said, without hesitation. Of course.

A lifelong horse owner and successful competitor, Adrienne knows all about bad falls. As a certified Equine Canada coach, she also knows all the ways you can come back from these life-changing events and build up confidence again. I felt as a child might, when we talked on the telephone, anxious but trusting of the deep healing she may help to orchestrate. I feel that way now, too. The trusting part feels good. The child part does not.

I move closer to Gofor, pat his shoulder, then step back again, and watch Adrienne begin cleaning his hooves with a hoof pick. *Please, I don't know how to be me without horses in my life. Centaur-moments are god-gifts, their effects permanent and strengthening. I can't give that up.*

"Listen, before we get you back in the saddle, let's talk some more," says Adrienne. To my surprise, she puts Gofor back in his stall. I thought we'd tack him up next. She bolts the stall door and turns to face me.

"You've told me about your accident, and about the physical and emotional challenges you're still sorting out, and I know what we need to do. But you haven't really told me what *you* want to do. Have you thought about that?"

What do I want to do? I am not following.

I probably look stricken; I certainly feel worried. Maybe Adrienne thinks I'm not up to the task of riding yet. If she knew how hard it was to even drive here, from our close-by village of D'Escousse. Every pretty country road we passed seemed a better idea to drive down than the equally pretty one that led here. I am here on the idea of courage, not because I feel brave. Is my fear so naked?

"I don't think you understand what I mean," she says. "When I ask you what you want to do, it's not a trick question. Do you want to resume your English riding – or do you want to try something entirely new?"

The hairs on my arms are tingling and I certainly understood this time, I think. "You mean I have a choice?"

"Of course you have a choice. That's what today's all about. Making new choices and seeing how that works out. Might be a good idea to do something really different from that day back in 2011. Even different from your earlier riding years." She pauses, then suggests the obvious: "Want to try Western tack and a Western lesson?"

My heart is so constricted that when it opens – when I quietly but surely pull in big breaths of oxygen – I get a bit dizzy. *What a perfect idea. Have some fun! Don't get all weirded out about perfect English equitation day one. Instead, saddle up Western and learn something new – from one of the best Western coaches anywhere.*

"... and besides," laughs Adrienne, "it's harder to fall off with Western tack! Just grab the horn and stay on!" I missed the whole first part of that sentence. Doesn't matter. It's just Adrienne being lighthearted and kind, and making a joke to push us past an awkward moment. Poor woman, I must resemble a deer in the headlights – her favourite kind of adult student, for sure.

"Yes," I say. "I'll try Western. I'd love to."

This is perfect. We have a plan and it's a good one. Let's grab that Western saddle, pop it on Gofor, and get this cattle drive started.

"On second thought," says Adrienne, "I think you should try riding Winnie today." My heart drops. Who's Winnie?

"Winnie's our palomino quarter horse. She's our daughter Helen's mare, but she's here with us now, and has been for some years. Winnie's so well-schooled, so smooth, just like Gofor. But she's a bit smaller. She'll be just right for you today."

And suddenly there's Winnie in front of me in her stall. Yes, of course I remember her, though I haven't ridden her before. She is the perfect shade for a palomino – "a newly minted gold coin," my childhood books used to say. She has a pert face, the compact, muscular build of the quarter horse breed and their dainty feet. She isn't very tall, either.

"She's only 14.3 hands high – just barely a horse," says Adrienne. Perfect for not-so-tall me to work around.

Her mane and tail are silky white. *And the gold the gold of her coat –*

If I were twelve years old again, I'd cry to be able to ride such a storybook horse. If I were fifty-four years old …

"I'll be right back, Adrienne. Just have to get my hard hat from the truck."

"Sure. I'll tack her up. You're not ready to hoist that heavy Western saddle yet. Soon, but not today."

I smack at my cheeks with the back of my hand, striding back to the truck. *Absurd woman. You're fifty-four and crying for the beauty of the horse you get to ride.* I open the back door of the truck, pull out my riding gear bag. Bang, I shut the door.

No, I'm not silly. I'm hanging on by the skin of my teeth to make this work and I'll take any essential bit of distraction I can get. Fairytale horse, for someone in need of a fairytale ending. Damn right I'll say yes to that. I settle the velvet hard hat on my head, secure the chin-strap. Boy, does Adrienne ever know what she's doing, to suggest a ride on Winnie. What a lift to my spirits. Go with that, keep faking it 'til you make it.

Firm words, followed by a wave of doubt so strong it halts my steps: Now you have to get up there – actually *up* there, on the horse. *Shh, shh, just leave me be* – it's best if I don't think out every part of this. Move, just move with the weight of all my horse years pushing me along. Ignore the cold fear, that press of a steel blade against my throat. I feel so alone.

Maggie, I am here. I am right here.

Son of gun, as we used to say – so you are, Karin. You know, I'm really not sure about any of this, either you being here or this whole horse situation in general –

G'wan – Winnie's a dream. I'd ride her in a wink. You're

lucky. I start walking again. Beneath my feet is a memory-current of how much we laughed together, Karin and me, during those many long and companionable days at the barn, caring for Coqeyn and occasionally other horses, and sometimes just being sisters, baking chocolate chip cookies and drinking strong milky tea. We also *stayed on* a lot of hot and difficult horses. Now that's a strengthening memory. I could ride for both of us, I suppose. That would be all right. G'wan!

Suddenly I am smiling, remembering with deep pleasure the part of Karin's personality that was goofy – a trait widespread in the Simmins family. She would collect up her tabby cat in her arms, cradling it like a baby, and would then mutter into the hair between his ears, her lips touching the top of its head, *"You are in the arms of love"* – using a laughable French accent. *Avec l'accent,* I still use the phrase today, when I collect up my dogs for a hug, and now and again, when we are feeling silly, with Don.

I step into the barn smiling. Don returns the smile. You'll be fine, he whispers. I can see that now.

Eventually, I am. There are moments when mind, heart, and body clash and struggle – even long frozen minutes when the idea of swinging a leg over the cantle of the saddle seems the single most daft and impossible action a person could take. Leg up and over this large hunk of leather – and I would do this how, and why? I stare at the saddle and horn as though they are alien objects, there to trick me or embarrass me. I've seen Western saddles before, of course, and even ridden in them – but that was forty years ago. I look away, then look back. The saddle is still there, and I am still not in it. Somehow my brain can't take this in. The saddle is an abstract idea I can't align with appropriate movement on my part.

Winnie is only incidentally there, too, so steady and quiet as to be not quite real. Perhaps she is a fairytale horse. I can't take her spirit in, and this is troubling me. But truly,

I can only focus on one thing: stepping off the mounting block and settling in the saddle, which seems to be suspended in air, and not on the back of a living animal. *Just do it,* I tell myself.

And still I don't move. There's no getting around it: the saddle is my biggest challenge. It was from it that I was ejected into harm and agony. I always knew the horse didn't mean to hurt me. It was the damn saddle – all along. Malevolent, conniving, *bastard* of a saddle –

"Take your time," says Adrienne, her calm voice banishing the demon-chatter. She stands by Winnie's head, both hands on the bridle. "We're not going anywhere." I want to smile at her, show her I am reassured – but if I break my gaze straight ahead, I'll never do this. I plant my hands on the horn, place my left foot in the stirrup, breathe in, and over goes my leg. *I did it.*

"There," says Adrienne. "Now, how are those stirrups?"

"Big," I say without thinking. We laugh. It's true, Western-style stirrups are a lot bigger than English-style stirrups. They're leather, of all things, not thin arched metal, with the customary rubber foot-rest. I wiggle my feet. "But the length seems fine."

So is the next hour. Better than fine. Once I am in the saddle – and a very comfortable one it is – Winnie becomes flesh and bone real. Now it's the saddle's turn to disappear. Instead, I am aware of the golden mare with the silver-white mane, walking and trotting beneath me. Her spirit is amiable and willing. I am also keenly aware of Adrienne, my focal point of safety and support. She starts our ride with Winnie and me on the lunge line – a long line is attached to the horse's halter, worn under the bridle; the instructor holds the other end, and both she and the rider can control the horse's movements. It is the safest possible re-entry to riding.

After some simple warm-up and stretching exercises, Winnie and I are on our own, walking around the large rectangular ring fringed by forest on the southern side, and country acreages on the others. Adrienne continues to build me up minute by minute, always stressing the positive, no matter how awkward I feel. As I relax more, Adrienne continues with a soothing stream of observations and instructions. These are the words I've heard all my life, from countless instructors, and today, they're cool water down a summer-day throat: *heels down; shoulders back; breathe, don't forget to breathe; chin up; more weight in the heel; bend your elbow; good, good, lift those hands; more inside leg, outside rein* – riding-poetry to my ears.

English or Western-style riding – a good seat is a good seat, and a properly balanced horse needs the same support from its rider. The tack and tasks the horses perform are different between the two styles of riding, and there are different movements and abilities, too. For me today, though, I am simply sitting as tall as I can in a deep, cushy saddle, and trying not to drop one side of the long, split reins, which are certainly quite different from the shorter, buckle-joined English reins. Then there's no thinking at all or talking at all. Just Winnie and I continuing to amble around the ring, me with my feet kicked out of the stirrups and everyone smiling. *Can I ride forever, starting right here and now?*

"That's a long ride for the first time back," says Adrienne. "Let's call it a day."

It was more than that. It was all my riding yesterdays, good and bad, and all my riding tomorrows, beckoning afresh. *You can do this. Again.*

"Got some good photos," smiles Don. "Think you'll like them."

Adrienne opens the gate for me and Winnie and I saunter on a loose rein back beside the barn.

"You can dismount by the door," says Adrienne, catching up to us. Suddenly it's the mounting moment all over again. Dismount? I am just fine "up here," but haven't a clue how to dismount – and don't want to. I feel velcroed to the saddle. This was all I had to do today, right? Get in the saddle, and stay on. Getting off wasn't a part of the agenda.

Slowly, with much coaching from Adrienne, I do finally manage to separate from the leather and get my feet on the ground. My legs are as bowed as a cowgirl's. My ankles ache and my lower back feels so congested and peculiar I don't want to even think about it. My right leg hums with discomfort, the nerve path alive and not well. My right foot is partly numb. I am sweaty and hot. Hungry as a moose in spring.

I feel great.

In the barn, Adrienne lifts off the heavy saddle and I groom Winnie. Then the fairytale mare returns to her stall. I slip in and give her a carrot. She takes it gently. I'm reluctant to take my eyes off her, or leave her. I could live in the warmth of this moment till the sun sets – next week sometime. I had no idea how today might go. But Winnie made it all possible. Not just Winnie. I couldn't have done it without this horse at this barn with this coach, on this exact summer day.

Or without Don's faith in me. *In sickness or in health, as long as you both shall live. ...*

Don drives and I am ecstatically silent for most of the trip home to D'Escousse. We pass the same inviting country roads I imagined turning down on the way to Adrienne's, to avoid showing up, and now I like our main road best. *I am back in the saddle, back at a barn.* My story is large to me and mine, and such a tiny imprint in time. There are so many other stories barns can tell, stories of the hearts and hooves they've cared for, over the generations.

7

RE-ENTRY

Three years after the accident I realize how slow and awkward my re-entry to the world was, in both the social and business spheres. I was gravely injured, and for many days our house was quiet as the deepest, sunless forest, except for when I howled or moaned in pain. There was no laughter, ordinarily the most common sound in our home. Only gentle questions from Don to me, about food, or how to get to the bathroom, or how to actually sit and achieve anything when I got there. My back was so numb, my stomach so flaccid.

Survival. I lay on my back in bed mostly, and prayed to the ceiling and the God beyond it.

For Don, the days were filled with unceasing caretaking and worry. For me, it was like running in place each day, hoping for fitness: exhausting and repetitious, but I could measure the progress by hair's widths by the time the sun went down. At the very first, my goal was simply to experience a pain-free day. Mentally, I fought every day to get back to normal living – to enjoy my tea and food, to take interest in the newscasts and world events, which blathered at me on daytime TV.

Finally, the black fear receded and the crimson anger roared back: *Why couldn't I have stopped that bolt – before he turned so sharply?* I used my raging heart to help resist lethargy and depression. Being pissed-angry really helped me improve physically. Other than gasps, bellows, and involuntary tears of fury, I never once cried after I came home from the hospital. My Irish-origin temper served me well.

To the world at large, I was just a bedridden and then slow-moving woman who obviously didn't work or help to run a household. That said, the cleaning crew Don hired was sympathetic and kind to both of us, and knew damn well I had a life I wanted to resume. They'd make themselves discreetly scarce when Don would lift me out of the bed and set me on the couch in his office. Once I was out in a "public" space, they would talk to me as much as I indicated I wanted. Usually, that wasn't much. The crew would say a few cheery things to me, then scurry about changing the linens. After this, they'd whisk through the entire house to do the housework that Don couldn't do, with my care being so all-consuming of his days. His own writing was for the most part shelved in those first hard months, which meant neither of us was making any money. That stress didn't help, either. I remember sitting on that office couch thinking the five minutes it took the crew to do the bed was about five eternities. I felt elderly and fragile. My back was a throbbing plank that would not bend, never gave me a moment of ease.

For most of our friends, by the time they'd been told I was injured – Don was far too busy looking after me and our abandoned lives to share our misfortunes with the world – things were under control, if not resolved. Some friends brought by food in those early days. Into the house they came, bearing delicious, homemade muffins or casseroles. One friend came over and made the most fragrant and rich mulligatawny soup, enough for days, a kindness I will never forget. Bless you, Michelle Saulnier.

Our families are scattered across the country. They phoned, wrote regular emails and letters, checking in often, with great love and concern.

So, I was healing, but it was hard to tell most days. Four months after the accident, working mostly in bed with my laptop, I started doing research for an article on border collies, a story I'd wanted to do for ages. As the weeks went on, I met and interviewed many fascinating people and slowly, reluctantly disabused myself of the dream of bringing a border collie into our lives. We just weren't "enough owners," as Don would say, for these brilliant and intense working dogs. I had to concede his point, having learned from all the top breeders that underutilized border collies are miserable, neurotic, and destructive. If you don't buy them to actually work sheep, as they have been selectively bred to do for centuries, then you must do full-time dog sports or rescue work of some kind with them, or suffer the quite wretched consequences. Every border collie owner and/or trialling competitor told me this, time and again. Sternly.

Instead, in June of 2012, we invited Talisker's Frankly Speaking into our lives, another Shetland sheepdog, a female, to keep Talisker's Seadog MacTavish, our six-year-old male Sheltie, company. The two dogs are from the same Middle Sackville kennel, but are not blood-related. They have as close a friendship as you could ever hope for. And we four are a close and contented pack.

I didn't do much other freelance writing in 2012, though I was back in the writing game, and "producing," as the expression goes. I also managed to complete my Master of Arts Research degree, specializing in memoir studies, that year. To my astonishment, I even won Gold at the Atlantic Journalism Awards for an article on Newfoundland's own Shaun Majumder, the well-loved television comedian and film actor. That summer we mostly stayed in Halifax.

By 2013, I had a book accepted for publication and I was a full-time freelance journalist again. I rode at Adrienne's barn in Dundee, Cape Breton, several times over the summer, and then in the winter of 2014, asked Adrienne if there was a barn near Halifax with a coach she'd recommend.

"Sure!" said Adrienne. "I know just the barn and just the coach for you. One More Time Stable, in Brooklyn, near Windsor. Sherry Clark is terrific. You'll learn a lot from her."

She was, and I did. I never did learn, however, why Sherry called her barn One More Time Stable, but it sure made me laugh to myself. *One more canter around the ring* – wasn't that what got me into trouble? Welcome to the irony in your life, I thought. *One more shot at riding, too.* If I was serious about that, I had to try and ride regularly. It was irregular riding that had brought such trouble into my life. Just because I'd started back at Adrienne's and made some good progress in strengthening my seat didn't mean I could take off a whole long Maritime winter and not expect yet another difficult resumption of the sport. Use your head, I told myself. Here's another top-notch certified Western coach who's willing to help you get strong again.

With Sherry, then, I started to learn more about Western Showmanship (showing at halter, which involves putting a horse through various paces and patterns with the rider on the ground). I also took several regular lessons from her, working on a smooth and engaged Western jog, and a similarly put-together and attractive walk. No cantering, not with Sherry's schooling horse, Simon, then, or on Adrienne's horses earlier. That was the eject gait. Both coaches want me more confident before I graduate back to the canter. Me, I am getting impatient, but it's also nice to have fun progressions to anticipate.

Sherry, like Adrienne, a few years older than I am, was accommodating and knowledgeable. Also like Adrienne, she is a long-time horse owner and competitor. She chided me for moving too quickly around Simon – "*Whoa!*

Slow down! Are you always this speedy?" – then solved the mystery herself, before I could explain. "Probably all those schooling barns you were in and out of, right? Lessons had to be on time and the whole schedule could be thrown off by one slowpoke."

I nodded, but it was more a case of yes, and no. She was right about the zippy pace of some of the schooling barns I've known, but I am wired up at times, especially when I am nervous, as I was then, with yet another new horse, coach, and barn. I was glad for the reminder to slow down while I was grooming. For a horse, whirring hands are buzzing bees circling around them. The motion does not endear the human to them.

I slowed right down as I groomed calm, capable quarter horse Simon. I'm always a sucker for chestnuts and when I first saw his gentle face, with a star, strip, snip blaze so similar to Coqeyn's, I knew I was yet again in the right barn. Under saddle, he did not disappoint. At twenty-six years old, fit and sound, he was a real old pro.

It was a wicked cold winter that year and I didn't ride as much as I wanted to at Sherry's place. I found that I just didn't learn very well at minus ten degrees Celsius – not doing new-to-me ground work, at any rate. Nor did my back do well with the frigid cold. My spine felt wooden some days. My numb lower back didn't ache so much as it seized up. One foot after another was not the unthinking, fluid motion most people make, but instead, was carefully calculated and timid in range. I often halfway wondered if something "in there" might not snap, before ease of motion returned. I wasn't motivated by anger any more, but I often felt discouraged. Riding with a numb back must be similar to skiing with straight legs, over moguls. No matter, I could still strengthen my legs and arms.

That was back in February. Now it's July 2014. All continues well with my writing work. I'm still doing profiles of various sorts for city magazines – which I started doing years ago, primarily as a way to get to know Halifax, after Don and I moved there from Cape Breton in 2006 – but mostly I want to write about animals: dogs, horses, farm animals – the animals we share our lives with, work with, and enjoy for their special attributes, either close-up or from afar.

I spent months researching the article I wrote on barns in Atlantic Canada ("Marjorie," laughed Don, when I slipped into month three of research, "you have enough for two *books* on barns! It's just one article. Enough already, wind up!"), and nearly as long on the article on oxen. I could have happily gone to every one of dozens of ox pulls around mainland Nova Scotia and Cape Breton. The summer of bells, that's how I think of the early summer of 2014, the oxen barns full of tinkling bells, which the oxen wear around their necks. The sound is like fairy spears of crystal, tangled and touching in the wind. I loved the drama of the pulls, and I admired all the young people I met who were involved with oxen, both in the ox-pull worlds and in 4-H, a youth development organization, often focused on farm animals and the farming life. The youngsters were so genuine and caring. The juxtaposition of the small, light boys and girls and the bulky or rangy oxen, all heavy, somehow smote my heart. Mutual trust and liking was as common as the dirt under their boots and hooves. Young humans and animals looked after each other well, as did the adult teamsters and their oxen.

Oxen. Those benign animals sucker-punched me in how my heart opened to them. Neutered bulls, I thought at first, what's the big deal? Then, as I wrote about in the article, I experienced oxen in their own barns – and be-damned if they didn't have "presence," as photographer Terry James noted. At first I was more interested in their presence in historical art forms of the region. Be-ribboned and belled, standing shoulder to shoulder in peaceful solidarity, the mostly rusty-coloured oxen with white faces were portrayed in oil, watercolour or acrylic paintings, and wooden carvings of every size. I found them all charming.

Then I spent hours and hours around actual oxen. Their coats are soft, buffed to vibrant shades of ruddy or golden brown or shining black and white, by slow, repetitive, grooming hands. Their bodies smell like bread that has just begun to toast. Oxen are calm; they don't startle and flee as horses can, when they hear loud noises. They even chew slowly and stand quietly in whatever stall they find themselves. Their teamsters are men, primarily – reserved, hard-working men who nonetheless don't hesitate to express deep affection for their animal co-workers and friends. They know the stories far better than any freelance journalist of how the oxen have saved human lives for as long as the two species have worked together on any endeavour. They know all the details, have lived many of them, or have had parents or grandparents who did. Oxen and humans – it struck me as one of the most respectful partnerships between humans and animals I've ever seen.

It's so easy to fall in love, isn't it? I wrote about border collies, and wanted one. I wrote about oxen, and wanted a team of oxen, too. But it's not so easy to stay in love. I write about horses – and I want their company, most of all. Once and always. True, too, for a certain man I know, who I married sixteen years ago.

Mid-July already – and I only rode once in June. Summer in Atlantic Canada is an ice cube on hot pavement. Next thing you know you spot red leaves on the trees. *Slow down*, summer of 2014, please. *Year of the Horse*. It's still a drumbeat in my blood. With only one full month left in the summer, and so much catch-up writing work for me, I am still determined to make this one of my best horse years ever. Even if I don't know how.

8

SUMMER 2014

D'ESCOUSSE, ISLE MADAME, CAPE BRETON

The fourth week in July and Isle Madame's gardens are still colourful and sweet smelling. They're at their peak, though, or just beyond it. Don and I are having lunch out on our back deck. The dogs are alternating between chasing one another around the large, fenced yard and coming back to mooch where we sit, our plates set on the low table before us. *If you don't need the second half of your sandwich, we can help,* is the clear message in their caramel-brown eyes. I'll give them each a raw baby carrot in a minute. A squirrel runs pell-mell down the power line out in the yard, and the dogs are off howling in proprietary indignation. In general, the Shelties are quiet here at our country home. There's more for them to do, and a bigger yard to run in. They get so bored – and vocal – in the city. But in either venue, intruders must be vanquished.

"You're having a dream first-year experience with your new book," says Don, over the roar of Sheltie fury. "You understand that, don't you?"

Yes, I guess I do. Mostly I am just doing everything – and I mean *everything,* at least one task or activity every day, for months now – that I can to promote the book and encourage sales – and yes, I am grateful the process is going along well. A friend of mine from Vancouver days, who I once worked with, and then for, told me that I "take directives very well." I was offended at the time, thinking it was a queenly comment to a slow-witted servant, but I've come to see it was a compliment, as I am sure now it was intended, and not a condescending one. I *do* take directives well – particularly when I see the sense of them, and how they serve either me or the collective.

It suits my list-loving brain to check my way along through my days. I also like to do what I say I am going to do, and receive the nods that usually come from that. Now that some of the biggest items on that list have been checked off – the book launch, readings, book signings, some radio and television appearances, organizing cross-country book reviews – I am starting to feel less anxious and driven. But there are still many more of these promotional activities to do again or for the first time in coming months. Here on Isle Madame, Cape Breton, too, where they're not too keen on bragging or "big feeling" ...

I actually find the self-promotion torturous some days. No matter what people might think, this isn't a question of vanity and self-aggrandizement. Don and I are writers, and writing and communications are how we make our living. Moreover, writers aim to create books that are of value to people. Only three months after the book's publication, I have been overwhelmed by the positive response to *Coastal Lives*. I examined universal themes within a personal life story, and have been graced by readers' phone calls, letters, and conversations about feeling included, or understood, or even given a voice of their own, when I wrote about subjects common to many lives.

I had a lot of catching up to do with my freelance writing and general working life after my accident. I went a long time without a paycheque. My biggest job right now, as a first-time author, is to sell that book. "Enjoy yourself!" Don encourages me each week. "Relax a bit – you'll never have a first year with a first book again!" He's right, of course. And if I remember to breathe regularly – as you must, when riding – all goes well.

No one but Don sees how wired I am before book-related events or appearances, and how it can take me days to feel rested and calm again. It's exactly the same when I teach: I give everything I have, perform my way through day-long memoir writing seminars, offering up as much information as I can, in what I hope is humorous and accessible form. I want everyone I read to or teach to get everything they could possibly want from the experience. As this is only possible to a degree, the Type A-ish part of me suffers inside. That said, I can experience satisfaction when I believe I've done the best I can. And then I allow myself to feel the fatigue. By day's end I collapse onto a couch at home. Tea, rum, a fire if possible, and a homemade meal, and sharing all of these with my guy, and our two Shelties beside us, usually restores me.

We're in a good, if slightly off-kilter period right now, Don and me. Early in May, Don lost his friend of over forty years, the writer Farley Mowat, who died just days before his ninety-third birthday. I was lucky enough to know Farley and Claire for almost twenty years and felt gutted myself when he died. *No more Farley stories.* My heart pounded that hollow reality over and over. No more meals and high-spirited times together, the four of us up in Cape Breton, where the Mowats have a summer home in River Bourgeois and we're a half-hour away on Isle Madame. No more MacTavish and Franki romping around the property with Chester, the Mowats' mixed-breed sweetheart of a rescue dog. He's gone now, too. Too much loss this past year.

We didn't go to Farley's funeral in Port Hope on May 23. Claire said no, don't come to the Ontario funeral, but do, please, come to our gathering in Cape Breton later in

July. Yes, we said, we will be there, and so we will this Friday, along with the rest of the Mowat Family, Farley's and Claire's cherished neighbours, and other lifelong friends such as Elizabeth May, federal leader of the Green Party. Farley and Claire have known Elizabeth since she was a teenager, and was even then a committed environmental warrior. Elizabeth, who is studying to be an Anglican priest, will read a service for us, and some of Farley's family members will speak, too.

The venue is Farley's and Claire's "backyard," a small, mowed section of grass behind their house on a hill, with ocean-facing acres on the right and many treed acres all around. There we'll gather to say fare thee well to the man who fought for wolves and whales and all the world's creatures – but felt little compassion for the future of his fellow man. Man, argued Farley, never saw an animal he didn't want to butcher or make extinct, or a world he didn't want to pollute or choke and money-make the life out of. After all the savagery Farley had experienced as a very young man in the Second World War, and all the changes he'd seen in the twentieth and twenty-first centuries of his lifespan, most Canadians felt he was entitled to those raw feelings. We did.

On a softer note, we visited with Claire several weeks back, when she was en route to Cape Breton, and we are looking forward to visiting with her again after the funeral, next week sometime, when all the family has gone home to Ontario and she's on her own at the hillside home. Gentle, thoughtful Claire, such a fine writer, too, misses her husband of nearly fifty years terribly. We weren't actually sure if she could or would come back to Cape Breton on her own, or in this first year without Farley, at least, and we were happy that she had decided on the Cape Breton memorial for him. We and so many others need to say an extended hello to her – and a heartfelt goodbye to Farley, among the people who loved him so long and fiercely. But again, we are glad we can visit with her after the memorial and into the autumn,

112 – Marjorie Simmins

before she returns to Port Hope. She looks so odd, so profoundly different without Farley nearby. She also looks new-dawn beautiful, too, in that vulnerable way of those who love deeply and are then bereft.

It's been such a demanding summer. Now, finally, we're here in D'Escousse, still working, but able to feel summer in a way that you cannot in the city. And Adrienne's barn is only a half-hour away.

I've already booked a lesson for Thursday, the day before we gather to honour Farley. I am glad I'll be riding this week, but I am frustrated. What have I really accomplished related to my long-term riding hopes? So little. Year of the Horse began with such high hopes, and I've done practically everything but ride. *It's taken so long to reclaim my life after the accident.*

It's all too nebulous. This is my fault. I need to make some iron-clad riding goals – and the sooner I talk to Adrienne about these, the better. I have to do something *real*, measurable, before the summer is over. It's fine to say I don't have time, but I'll just have to make it, if not at one end of the day then the other. "Don," I say, thinking aloud, "we can really stay here in Cape Breton for the next two weeks, and then the last two weeks of August, right?"

He beams. If ever a man's heart was happiest in Cape Breton, it's the man I married, who has spent most of his life here. Toronto-born, Vancouver-raised, and heart-in-Cape-Breton Silver Donald Cameron, complete with a Cape Breton nickname, which noted his prematurely silver hair and separated him from the numerous other Donald Camerons in Celtic-rich Atlantic Canada.

"Sure," says the silver-haired scribe, as I enjoy calling him, "we've been through this. The project I'm working on requires me to be here, and you can do your work on-line." He laughs. "And I know what the *real* question is. It's 'How much can I ride in this time?' Ride as much as you can!" He grimaces, obviously remembering some of the desperate days in 2011. "I can hardly believe I just said, 'Ride as much as you can.'" He folds me into his arms. "Just be careful."

* * *

Thursday already and I was on the road by 7:25 a.m., to be on time for my eight o'clock riding lesson. The mosquitoes, deer and black flies can be bad at Adrienne's in the summer, even by late morning, some days. We coat the horses in fly spray and hope for the best. The flies can be vicious and the horses, unsurprisingly, react badly when they're bitten. Not much fun for the humans, either. We use insect repellent, too. I had an excellent lesson on Gofor, who is one of the smoothest gaited horses I've ever ridden. I'm stiff after the ride, but nothing is hurting today and the parts of me that are complaining – legs and stomach muscles – are supposed to complain. Means I've made a good effort. I'm actually liking the physical discomfort. It's a virtuous ache.

Gofor is untacked, groomed, and out in the small field behind the barn. Adrienne and I left him with a flake of hay and then walked to her house for the chat I'd requested. The mug of tea she puts down in front of me, along with a plate of oat cakes for us both, is a welcome sight. I am parched. We sip and chew for a few minutes and make small talk about horses and family. This is such a horse-lovers' home: comfortable, bright, and welcoming, accented with horse art and photographs. And when we came in the house, stepping onto the beautiful hardwood floors, Adrienne said my favourite post-lesson words: "Don't worry about your boots – just go on in." Nothing nicer when you're tired and just want to clump towards a chair.

"OK, so what's on your mind?"

Goals, that's what's on my mind, goals. I don't want

to bob in place, like a mooring buoy on the water. I want milestones that we can plan for, execute, and with luck, celebrate. I've heard Adrienne and some of the young riders she teaches talk about the "rider levels" they are studying for. So I went online and did some snooping. These levels or courses are a part of the Learn to Ride program, run by Equine Canada. So it's a national program with national standards. It recognizes all riders, recreational to competitive, for advancing their knowledge about horses and skill as riders. At each level, the riders do riding and written exams, and if successful, receive certificates of achievement. The program's aims are to provide new riders with a safe and knowledgeable introduction to the discipline of their choice, produce able horsemen/women, and to assist in the development of future instructors and coaches.

Do I want to teach one of these days? No, without my own horses or barn, I can't really imagine that. But I would love to brush up on all my skills, general safety skills very much included. I used to take my cherished niece, Jocelyn, now twenty-nine, for pony rides in Vancouver when she was small. Now she has a daughter of her own, Leila, age five, and when I am in Vancouver visiting, I take my great-niece for pony rides, too. I want everyone safe when we go for these around-Southlands walks. I am so grateful I still have contacts down on "The Flats." My friend Nancy Brook's "pony barn," as I've always called it, remains almost unchanged in over forty years. Wildwood Paddocks is sited on the very corner I said my summertime goodbye to Coqeyn, before I sold him to a young junior who loved him well, I believe, for the time she owned him.

I only saw Coqeyn once after I sold him in 1975. He was with his second owner after me, another motivated young junior, about whom I remember nothing, except she was kind and chatty, and had blonde hair. Standing in his stall next to him – *so strange to think about now, as it was Ryan's barn, though Ryan was many years ahead of me in the future* – I couldn't breathe or speak properly. The owner asked me questions about my time with Coqeyn. The sounds that came out of my mouth made no sense to me and, increasingly, to her. She talked to fill the uncomfortable spaces, and we both nodded a lot. She was old beyond her years, though, and her eyes told me I didn't have to do anything, except what I was doing, stroking Coqeyn's sleek neck. It was obvious he was well cared for and loved again – and really, what else did I have the right to ask about, I remember thinking to myself. We'd sold him for cash money, which Mum was glad to have. He belonged to my heart, but not my life – ever again. I thanked the young lady for the visit, and fled to my car.

When you sell your horse and love is involved – you feel as though you've sold a member of your family. It's not just heartbreaking, it's sickening.

Ironically, Kaber's owner, Shannon Low, a farrier, used to shoe Coqeyn over on Bowen Island, just north of Vancouver. Shannon said he looked well, into great old age. Sometimes I could breathe when she told me these stories; sometimes I was back in his stall that last visit in the late 1970s, once again breathless with layered emotion, and wishing Coqeyn and I were back at our very first barn, just starting our time together. I could ride my bicycle to see him, late on a mild summer night ...

Thank you for your loyalty and brilliance, Coqeyn. Thank you for filling our lives with adventure and beauty.

I explain the briefest bits of all this to Adrienne, focusing on other, current details.

"I really want to improve my seat," I say. "I've lost all my core strength and I hate that. I can 'fake it' up there because I've ridden for so long. But I know I am weak and inconsistent, and you sure know it, too. Maybe I can't get back to being as good as I was years ago – but I really want to improve, claim the sport again, as best I can. Is that possible?"

I look down to my tea mug – because, dammit, my eyes are brimming. No way to explain to my new friend that these aren't pity-tears, they are wanting-tears. I want this badly.

For the first time in half an hour, the room is silent. I haven't known Adrienne that long, but I do understand, I think, her essential life-stance of enthusiasm tempered by realism. She's not going to make me any impossible promises, but she's all about hard work and determination in her own life, and pushes her students to have the same ethic. *I can work hard, Adrienne,* I say silently. *Really hard. I won't let you down.*

"Sure, we can do your rider levels if you want," she says. She's got that taffy-pull stretch to her syllables, obviously thinking like mad about the details of our conversation, but wanting to respond to my request now, too. "We can do them this summer or maybe by the autumn."

"Them?" I say.

"Yeah, we can certainly do Level One this summer and maybe even Level Two by the end of September or early October."

Be careful what you ask for – so the adage goes. *Two* rider levels, is it? Well, you're the one who asked. And oh, well, I've gone this far –

"I'd also like to compete again," I say. "Just a schooling show –"

"Hmmm," she says. "There's always Sherry Clark's – I've told you about that, right? The Heritage Championships show Sherry puts on each year in Windsor? It's great. Too soon for you this year, but we could aim for that next August."

I gulp. "A real show?" As in a formal, Nova Scotia Equestrian Federation "sanctioned" show with people who compete all the time, and really know what they're doing? I knew my other coach, Sherry, was a fine horsewoman, but I'd forgotten about this big event she organizes each year.

"Sure, why not? We'll put you in the Senior Novice walk/trot, Western. Yeah, that would work."

Seniors' class? Oh, right, seniors as opposed to juniors, which is anyone eighteen years and under. Not seniors as in getting my social security cheque already, which I am not. As for novice at Western riding, that would be me. I can feel my eyelids fluttering as I think. There's a lot to take in. Adrienne is portentously quiet, then: "No, you won't just go in the show, you'll win your class."

I am going to what? Whoa d'ere, Nelly! Triple-be-careful-what-you-ask-for! Especially when your coach is not only an ambitious rider in her own right, but ambitious for her students, apparently, too.

Happily, it seems to be a short-lived burst of enthusiasm. Or more to the point, Adrienne is a first things first kind of person. She has never pushed me faster than I am comfortable with, but she doesn't baby me, either. In two words: perfect instructor.

"Let's book you for two lessons next week – and get started on Level One, Western Rider. What do you think?"

"Yes."

Can't wait.

* * *

A hoot of teenage laughter and the observation that is obvious to all: "You need to go to the gym!" My young friend Kendra, who leases Juanashine or M, one of Adrienne's horses, can't resist teasing me as I stagger down the aisleway towards Gofor, wondering how in hell I am going to raise this bloody cement saddle over my head and up onto his back. He's taller than Winnie, that's for sure, about ten miles taller, it seems today. Then, when I am about five feet away from him, he does something I've never seen before: out go his front legs, up comes his rear end, and Gofor the horse stretches just the way a dog would, his back so low to the ground I could throw a leg over and be mounted. It's as though the centre of his back, which I usually would look up to see, has a big X on it – as in, X marks the spot. I plop that big old thirty-five-pound saddle right on top of the saddle pad I placed there a few minutes ago. Bingo! Didn't need to go to the gym to do that!

I am triumphant and boggle-eyed, but Kendra and Adrienne are unsurprised. "Gofor does this all the time," says Adrienne. "He loves to stretch."

"But does he start to stretch when he sees someone coming with a saddle?" I ask. Reason number forty-four to love this big grey gelding: he's obviously mad-keen about me.

"No, not really," she answers, dashing that hope. "He just stretches when he wants to, but yes, often when he's on the cross-ties."

A gift is a gift; don't check the mouth. With the most grateful of hands I finish tacking up.

Tack – equipment or accessories for riding. Every single piece of tack I am handling, I will need to know the proper name of, for my test later this summer. Thank you, teasing Kendra, for lending me your *Western Rider Level I* booklet, which I am studying now. *Horn* – knew that part of the saddle already. *Pommel,* too; that's the upward curving bit of the saddle, right in front of you. *Saddle fork* or *swell* – didn't know those. The *saddle fork,* then, is the front of the *saddle tree,* a frame around which the saddle is built. Holding the two parallel bars together, it provides a base for mounting the horn – which yes, is the knob-like leather piece you grab onto when you mount, or you can tie the reins to, or you hang onto for dear life if you feel yourself becoming unseated.

The horn, in my view, is the best feature of the Western saddle – next to the cushy *seat*, which provides far superior comfort to many English saddles. Western saddles, after all, were designed for the cowboy to spend long hours in, working with cattle on the ranges, or just covering long country miles to do other work or errands in surrounding communities and towns. Then there's the *gullet*; it holds the bars of the saddle together. Its angle determines how the saddle is going to fit the horse. The *cantle* is still the *cantle* – the back of any saddle, but almost everything below this is different from the English saddle: *concho; back jockey; seat jockey; skirt; latigo and latigo keeper; D ring; rear D ring; fender; cinch; stirrup hobble; stirrup* (same name!); *billet of back cinch; billet keeper; back cinch; cinch hobble.*

Can't you just see the plains of Texas and Mexico, the prairie lands of Alberta, and the desert-lands of British Columbia's Cariboo and Interior when you repeat some of these tack names? Can't you just envision the countless bobbing heads of moving cattle stretched over these flat lands – and the tanned, wind-scorched faces of the *gauchos* and *gauchas,* shadowed darker yet under their Stetsons? Yesteryear, the cattle drives moved out, all across North, Central, and South America, and cattle ranching was sustainable. Today, of course, the industry is not sustainable. Our North American hunger for beef seems limitless, and too many acres of wetlands and jungles are sacrificed for grazing lands and feedlots.

But I don't just think about cattle ranching as I tack up Gofor. Unsurprisingly, I think about horsewomen. One of the most fascinating horse stories I ever read was *The Hearts of Horses* by Molly Gloss. In this 2007 novel, Gloss recounts the life of Martha Lessen, a nineteen-year-old "horse-breaker" or "horse-gentler," living in the American West at the time of the First World War. Martha travels such great distances to offer the horse training services more often done by the young men of the era, then off fighting overseas, that she travels with several saddle horses, to "spell" them off, over the endless grassy plains. The injuries Martha suffers while schooling young horses made me blanch when I read the book, several years before my accident. Her overall life was no picnic, either. But she always came back to train another horse, always managed to live on her own terms. I absolutely believe this work of fiction could have described a real, early horsewoman's life. Our imaginations are so limited at times, when it comes to women pioneers and settlers in North America.

I'd actually like to reread the book now, for inspiration. It may have been a novel, but the premise was entirely believable. There are many gifted horsewomen between the covers of books, and in actual life, around the world. They ride in rodeos or in international dressage shows or gruelling, cross-country "point to point" competitions (horse racing over stone walls, ditches, and hedges) in the U.K. They barrel-race, or they're "reiners," a competition where the riders guide the horses through a precise pattern of circles, spins, and stops. Or they race Thoroughbreds or drive Standardbreds in sulkies. They train horses, train riders, compete against themselves and the world, and are dedicated lifelong learners. I don't think we hear enough about these stalwart women. I am fortunate enough to be training with one right now. I mean, for heaven's sakes, Adrienne is the president of the Nova Scotia Equestrian Federation, and she and her daughter Helen, who's ridden and competed since she was tiny, have bred and trained every horse in their stable. How did I get so lucky to meet these people?

"Marjorie, you about ready?" Adrienne's voice is amused, not impatient. It's true, I have been wool-gathering.

"Yes," I say, grinning. "Ready as I'se gonna get."

We have an intense lesson – much that is new to me, much that may as well be – discussing, among other concepts, one- and two-handed rein positions. These include the bridge, the two-hand two-rein (English position), the three-rein, and one-handed (neck-reining). Every position feels strange except the one I am used to, the two-hand, two-rein, and even that's a bit odd, as even with the reins crossed over the horse's neck, I am still nervous about somehow dropping one side of the split reins. Altogether, the reins are far longer than I am used to. I've noticed that Adrienne and her students seem to use the bridge rein most often. The reins are indeed bridged in this position, one strip of leather over the other, with the hands set at either corner. In my mind, I think of this as the "box" position. I try all the positions, feeling ham-fisted and clumsy and guiltily ask, "Is it OK if I use the two-handed rein?" "Go ahead," says Adrienne. "That's fine – for now."

Good, now I can focus on brushing up on other information, such as the rein effects, of which there are four: Direct, Open, Neck (indirect), and Rein of Opposition. As with every movement by the rider on the horse, rein effects are first executed grossly and ineffectively, and many rides later, appear discreet and are effective, used in tandem with other natural aids such as the seat and legs. I'm at the "gross" execution level today. I am at least cognizant of the terms "inside" and "outside" reins, but it's been many years since I thought about rein effects in depth.

But even rusty me knows that reins are not for hauling a horse to the left or the right, though you'd often wonder, from what you see at times, or even – *blush* – what I find myself doing at times. In fact, I read somewhere that the kids who grow up riding Western and neck-reining their horses don't have to "un-learn" the unfortunate business of being taught to "steer" the horse directly by its head – or more accurately, by the mouth. This steering makes it impossible to bring back the centre of gravity under the rider, where it must be, for any lightness and balance.

One-handed riding was also originally true for dressage, with the riders thundering into battle with one hand on the reins and the other grasping a weapon, meeting their opponent mid-field, and thereupon *pirouetting* and *piaffe-ing* them to death. Kidding! (Blame the lapse on British comedian Eddie Izzard, and his killer funny skit on dressage.) If you spend any time around dressage riders – and again, there is Western dressage now, too – you see them and their horses for the phenomenal athletes they are. *Dressage*: the art of riding and training a horse to develop obedience, flexibility, and balance. Or just plain training, which is what the word translates as, from the French. It's one tough discipline, with so few rising to the highest levels.

Back to reins.

Two-handed or one-handed, the new or returning rider is taught that the outside or indirect rein always controls and directs the horse – never the inside rein. The inside rein is supposed to "soften" (ease up) until gradually, you are not relying on it at all.

Back to rein effects.

Happily, I only have to learn the Direct and Open Rein aids for my Level One. The Direct Rein, unsurprisingly, is applied parallel with the horse's neck. When one Direct Rein is applied, it tips the nose toward the shoulders; when both Direct Reins are applied, it tips the horse's nose toward the chest. Direct reins are used in stopping, backing, flexion (changing or "rounding" the physical body shape), correction (asking for and getting a different physical response), and transitions (change of gait, either faster or slower). The Open or "leading" Rein bends the horse toward the rein and leads it into a large circle. The rein hand moves out and to the side, which applies pressure. The "off" or outside rein must give, as it shouldn't counter-effect the Open Rein.

Clear as mud, right? It's easier when you're aboard the horse – sometimes. Some days the horse feels serpent-twisty and every "rein effect" you try on is the wrong one, or incorrectly applied. When they twist like that, it's not their fault, it's yours. And, of course, that can be so frustrating, because you know you're in the wrong, but you can't seem to fix it. Gofor was kind to me most days, but even as good-natured as he is, he could get fed up with confusing directives. Today, he's a star – so I must be doing all right, too.

Walk, jog, halt. Large circles, smaller circles. We work on the left rein, then reverse to the right, for more of the same. My muscles are warmed up nicely now, and for once, I seem to be keeping my chin and eyes up, and even my hands are nice and steady. We do some rising trot. This is also called a "posting trot." The rider makes an up-and-down movement each stride, rising out of the saddle for one beat and lowering (sitting) for the second beat. Both Western and English riders post, for warm-up purposes, and to spare the horse's back from the unremitting impact of a "sitting trot," where the rider does not rise. Horses aren't the only ones who warm up during this exercise. I soon peel off my jean shirt to the T-shirt below.

"Guess how long we've been out here," says Adrienne. I shake my head, call back, "No idea." Maybe a half-hour? "An hour," she replies. "Over an hour, actually."

Really? Is that possible?

"How are you feeling? Are you tired?"

"Not at all. I feel great."

"OK, time to canter."

At last!

Western horses are trained to pick up the canter or *lope*, which is slower, with the same aids as an English-trained horse, but they also have an aid that is solely theirs: the *kiss*. English riders can be mad "cluckers," that funny sound you can make by clicking your tongue against your teeth at the side of your mouth. It's supposed to be an encouraging sound, used when a horse is being lazy or needs reassurance, say, as you are approaching a jump. The problem is, English riders often overuse this sound – it's almost a third leg! – and horses can become indifferent to it. But if you reserve a sound for one reason only – to canter, that lovely three-beat, rocking gait that riders live for – chances are the horse will remain wonderfully responsive to it.

"OK, let's move forward with some energy, and prepare to canter," says Adrienne. "Soften that inside rein and connect with the right. Left leg at the girth, right leg just behind the girth. Now, *kiss!*"

Feeling self-conscious, I obey. It's like throwing the horse an air-kiss. *Here you go, Gofor, a kiss just for you.* Gofor strikes off perfectly and we are cantering! No, we are loping, and it is beyond rocking-chair comfortable. I could do this foreverevererever. *La-de-dah-de-di-daw-day!*

"Marjorie, come on over here!" Adrienne's got the biggest grin on her face I've seen yet. I slow to a jog and then a walk and Adrienne is walking on over to me, where I've now stopped on the rail. Adrienne is such a lovely tall drink of water, *slim as a reed*, as my mother would say. Up come her arms for a hug, and down I lean, to hug back. *Don't cry, don't be any idiot, keep it together.*

"You did it."

"Gofor's the best."

"Yeah, he's a good guy." She pats his shoulder, then heads towards the gate. "Come on, that's it for today."

I teared up – but the tears didn't spill. I'm almost back to me.

* * *

I drove back to D'Escousse stinking of horse, hands dried-sweat-sticky on the wheel.

And now I cried. I cried so much I had to pull over to the side of the road, because the world became a blurry place and I might have driven off its edges. I didn't sob, but the tears were a steady stream from both eyes. Left-hand swipe, right-hand swipe – over and over. I couldn't find a Kleenex and I didn't care. Then I started using my sleeve under my nose, like a little kid with no tissue. And still the tears came on. I turned off the air conditioning, opened both truck windows, wanting to feel the warm air, breathe it in, from toes to nostrils. That air, that horse, that coach, this day – *don't forget a single moment –*

You didn't get me, Life, you didn't kick the shit out of me and win. I did not go down with my face in the dirt. Fuckyoufuckyoufuckyou. I am back to me!

Mostly, I could have just passed out from happiness. I felt like Boadicea after a bloody and successful battle. How would I know what that feels like? Because history's horse-sisters were whispering in my ear. They said, *Not so bad – good effort today.* Not just history's horse-sisters, either. *Well, of course you rode well today,* said Karin – *couldn't you hear me cheer you on? You'll never be a one-woman cheerleading team, not with all your old West Coast horse friends and the new ones you're making on the East Coast, and not with the stash of horse-time memories you have, and all the shiny new ones you're creating. Don't you know that yet?*

I did then.

Don took one look at me when I came in the back door and said, "You're different when you're riding." To put it mildly, he has had mixed feelings about my return to the horse world. But his voice was full of admiration that day.

"Different?" I asked, grinning – and oh-so-obviously fishing for compliments. I was also interested in what he'd say, exactly.

"Yeah," he said obligingly. "Different. Stronger, happier, more sure of yourself. It's attractive, nice to see."

I thanked him, and thought, *It's even nicer to feel.*

It was time to float down to the ground and think about what came next. Don and I were returning to the city tomorrow morning and there was much to do before we left: laundry, pack, clean the refrigerator, tidy the house, and pack up our offices and files. We try to leave the house the exact way we'd want to see it when we come to it after the long drive from Halifax, which takes three and a half hours – if we make no stops along the way, and with two dogs in the car and a Frenchy's used clothing store en route, we always do. I frankly didn't want to go anywhere, but the article on oxen wasn't going to write itself. Thinking about that, I smiled. At least I'd be back in some animal barns again, if not horse barns. If I just settled into that work, the two weeks would fly by.

9
LEVEL ONE WESTERN RIDER

The days did fly by. Now it was mid-August. It was time to really strategize about getting that Level One done.

"We've got less than two weeks to do it," Adrienne said, when I returned to the barn for a lesson on August 19, my late mother's birthday. "Four lessons this week, three next, then the exam on the twenty-ninth. Are you up for it?"

I didn't know if I had been hungrier for a goal such as this – in years. Maybe that long-delayed master's degree. This was oddly similar. Despite high hopes, it took quite a while to get here.

One thing for sure, I would be cantering a lot these next two weeks, along with lots of sitting and rising trot. For my Level One exam, I would need to show competency in "Stable Management" (parts of the horse; horse identification; care of the horse; horse handling; tack; how to saddle and bridle), and competency in "Riding" (how to mount and dismount; body and leg position; one- and two-handed position; rein effects – Direct and Open Rein; aids – the categories of and the aids for walk, jog, and lope, and for stop and back up). We'd also do some mounted exercises, and I'd need to describe the horse's gaits – which leg moved when and how – at the walk, jog, and lope. All this and more has to be done in an "acceptable manner." Then I'd write an exam, mostly related to the safe care and use of the horse, which would take about an hour. *Bring it on.*

"Oh, yeah," I said. "I'm up for it."

* * *

"Withers, back, loin, point of hip, croup, buttock, hip, thigh, flank, stifle, gaskin, hock –" when I am not muttering horse body parts, I am listing off general safety rules or basic horse handling points. "Always lead a horse with a halter and a shank from the left side; never approach a horse from directly in front or behind, because both are blind-spots to the horse, and they may become frightened."

I laugh, because I know all this, admittedly some of it sketchily by now, but I certainly haven't listed any of these points off in a long time. And I have indeed gotten into some bad habits over the years, like ducking under the horse's head when they're on the cross-ties. It's a good way to get bashed by the horse's head, or to alarm the horse and have them throw a fit. Not good. So finally, I seem to have broken myself of that long-standing bad habit. I know there are others, so I'll just keep working on those. I spent a long time hacking by myself – no riding instructors checking up on me, and toward the end of my leasing time, no experienced riding friends to natter at me, either. It's what riders do, primarily to keep themselves and others safe. That said, we can also be a bossy lot.

"Ears, forelock, forehead, face, bridge of nose, muzzle, nostril, chin groove, jowl, and throat latch –"

"Getting better," says Don. We are having breakfast at the small kitchen table in our attractive, gingerbread-trimmed house in D'Escousse. "Now, tell me, what's the normal temperature range for an adult horse at rest?"

"Thirty-seven point five to thirty-eight point five degrees Celsius," I fire back. "Same as us." I add a bonus answer: "And the respiration rate is between eight to sixteen breaths per minute."

"Not bad," he allows. "Now, what about –"

"I'm out of time – gotta go." I push the small container of Greek yogurt to one side – couldn't possibly eat anything more – and start collecting up my gear and purse. Then I stop. "Do you have your camera nearby?" I ask. Don glances into the living room and sees it on the coffee table. I follow his glance. "Could you take a quick photo – for luck?" I ask.

The photo is as amusing as I'd hoped it would be. I'm outside in the treed backyard, where the striped summer light, along with my baseball cap, shadows my face. I pretend to be a boxer, raising my hands up to my chin with a *come-'n'-get-me* expression in my eyes. I'm grinning like a sailor on leave, but only someone who knows me well would see how nervous I am, too.

"Go git 'em!" shouts Don as I run out the gate with a river of barking Shelties following me. "I'll see you back here in the afternoon."

The air is warm, the sky full blue. It's a carefree summer day in the country. But the barn is a serious place today. Adrienne is temporarily not my friend, only my coach, on test day. She explains how the morning will unfold, with the stable management component and riding test first, and the written test second. I will not know the results right away. Probably late in the day. Adrienne watches as I groom and tack up, and notes how I move around Gofor generally, using "best horse handling and safety practices." Gofor, who has several times in recent days bowed low to help me hoist the saddle, does not do this today. I manage, but it's not a graceful hoist. No matter, the saddle is on, with the latigo pulled through the cinch and done up. Gofor takes the bridle's bit in a purposeful way and seems eager for the ride to begin. I swear, he knows it's test day, too.

I mount using the mounting block, ride the best I can, that honest, smooth-gaited gelding making me look far better than I really am. Adrienne puts us through our "paces," and we execute them as we must do. I answer queries about Direct and Open Reins, describe the footfalls for the gaits Gofor and I do, and then execute these. Four-beat: walk. Two-beat: trot. Three-beat: canter. My position at the walk and jog feel good to me; my position at the lope feels passable. That numb back of mine doesn't help me there; with it, there is very little "give" at my waist. Don't worry about that, I tell myself. *Chin up! Pay attention.*

Then suddenly we are done. The test is over. Gofor has apparently untacked himself, and now grazes out in the small field behind the barn. Tack and brushes also put themselves away. Then just as suddenly I am in the house, sitting at the big oak dining room table, pencil in hand, exam in front of me.

"You can start now," Adrienne. "You have an hour." She slips away to her office.

The house is library quiet.

Have I always written tests this way – head down, only inches above the page, left arm curled around the page, stomach and chest pulled in tight to the edge of the table? Yes, I am sure I have. It is as though I physically wear the exam, as much as write it. I am making good progress down the list of questions, then get to the "horse handling, general safety rules" section. I am asked to list ten or so of these. I start off well – then falter. It's not that I didn't study this part of the booklet, or, indeed, that I don't know all sorts of safety rules and bloody well, too. It's that I am confusing two lists in my mind: the points they want me to list, and all the rules I have in my head and memory. I write down two or three points that I am certain were not listed in the booklet. After all, there are endless numbers of safety-related points one could write. I know this will bring my mark down, but it's better than leaving a blank space, I think. I keep on writing. Copiously.

"I'll mark your written exam, tally up the two tests, and email you later on this afternoon," says Adrienne, collecting up the papers. She is still my coach on test day, not my friend again just yet. I stand from the table, dithering a bit as I collect up my gear, sunglasses, and truck keys. "I am sure you did fine," she says neutrally – and then smiles, my friend for one reassuring flash. I smile back. "Great. Thanks for everything. Talk to you soon."

Back at the house I check my email obsessively for the next two hours – nothing yet. Finally realizing the futility of this behaviour, I change out of my sweaty clothes and shower, then put on a light summer dress. I even reapply my makeup – which I'd never ordinarily do twice in a day – in an effort to give busy Adrienne just that much more time to do some more of her barn work and mark my tests. Gee, I might even permit her time to have some lunch.

Lunch. What a good idea.

"Don?" I call up the stairway to his office, as I have countless times, in numerous dwellings over the years, "would you like some lunch?" Once again we take our sandwiches out to the deck, and are followed by a brigade of eight eager paws, a-topped with sable and white coats. Once again, I have baby carrots on each side-plate, some of which apparently starving Shelties will be given when we've finished eating. I make it halfway through my lunch. "I'll be right back," I say – and we both know I am heading into my main-floor office to check my email again.

In a moment I am back: "Did it – I did it." My arms and legs are rag doll boneless, but my smile is firm.

Don is on his feet, arms outstretched. "Congratulations! Well done, my love." He gives me a bear hug. I settle in happily to that, then pull back and look up at him. I cannot help myself, it's a "big feeling" kind of day: "There are three totals I could get – Standard, Meets Standard, or Exceeds Standard." Worried though I was about the improvisation I did in the "general safety rules" section, I didn't bring my mark down there enough to affect the overall score. "I got Exceeds Standard," I say. "Don, I did it!"

The Shelties bark, Don and I hug again. A sudden gust of wind tosses the tree branches in the backyard, clearing our faces of the shadows that were there only moments ago.

10
Autumn 2014

September 2014 was as busy as almost all the Septembers of my life have been – just the way I love it. When I wasn't learning myself, keeping on with all sorts of book promotion events, including reading as a "new author" at the Word on the Street celebration on the Halifax waterfront, my first appearance at this nationwide festival, I was teaching memoir writing courses and writing articles for magazines. I adore the autumn season, no matter where I am living. However, the autumn foliage is breathtaking in the Maritimes and to me, each year is "the best ever." Halifax's generous wooded environs and parks showed a range of colours an easy two rainbows' worth, certainly in the lower, warmer shades, while the skies dawned and darkened in the higher hues of blue, indigo, and violet, and the Atlantic Ocean surrounding the city peninsula swirled together the missing, richer greens of the summer gone by. And so September passed, another best ever. I did not ride at Adrienne's barn, though. Level Two Western Rider was slipping away from probability for 2014 …

In October, Don and I did the freelancers' usual "business with pleasure" jaunt, driving back to Cape Breton for the first time since August and staying for two exceptionally fun weeks. The focus of the trip for me was to be the keynote speaker at The Second Annual Women's Health Expo, held in St. Peter's, at the Bras d'Or Lakes Inn. It was an honour and a privilege to present there, and I couldn't wait to talk about the healing magic of old-fashioned snail-mail letters and cards, as well as journals, and memoir writing. All these types of writing had helped me through the regular and irregular demands of my life.

In truth, I don't know how I would have managed, in the Karin years and the troubled late teenage and young adult years beyond, without the stabilizing, revelatory effects of journals and letters to family. I love to share knowledge about the beneficial effects of writing because I know for a certainty that someone – maybe several someones in audiences of more than one hundred – will buy themselves a journal after hearing me talk about them. They may even post a letter to their sister or brother or parents – or better yet, their grandparents, who don't have to be taught the value of a paper letter. If they buy a journal, then someone just found themselves a new best friend, even if they struggle with their cursive writing, or have to print the words. If they start a meaningful correspondence with a family member or friend, they immediately lessen the feelings of loneliness and isolation we all feel at times, by reaching out and expressing interest in and caring to others. My brother Geoffrey says our family is "Edwardian" in our devotion to letters, but I know for a fact we are not the only ones left, that there are even some younger and much younger ones among us, too. I will always encourage others to pick up pen and paper.

The only thing better than September in Halifax is October in Cape Breton. The autumn colours almost always peak at Thanksgiving. Then there's the music. For over nine days mid-month, Cape Breton Island is home to the Celtic Colours International Festival, a celebration of Celtic music and culture. Started in 1997, the festival is bolder and broader in international scope every year, presenting dozens of concerts all over the island, along with community events and a nightly "Festival Club," held at the Gaelic College in St. Ann's, near Englishtown, on the Cabot Trail.

Musicians from around the world join with Cape Breton's finest musicians, dancers, singers, and storytellers for the annual celebration. Scottish airs, played hauntingly on fiddles, bring the hair standing up on your arms, prickle tears in your eyes. A half-hour later, it's *Give 'er!* and those same fiddles are set near on fire, by the likes of internationally known Cape Breton stars Ashley MacIsaac and Natalie MacMaster, both step-dancing all the while. Tin flutes add high notes, birdsong at dawn, while the round, tight-skinned bodhrans, or Celtic drums, add the heartbeat low notes.

All this occurs mainly in venues so small you bump shoulders with the fellows on either side of you. There are bigger venues, certainly, such as the Civic Centre in Port Hawkesbury or Strathspey Place in Mabou, and these, too, attract sell-out crowds. In either small or large venues, you can spot the "Capers" in any crowd, their feet driving the beat to the floor, their hands the first to clap, their voices first to roar to the rafters when a favourite "tune" is done scorchingly note-perfect.

My favourite places to hear music, though, are the small community or Lions Clubs' halls, which dot every village and town in Cape Breton. In these, you can watch close-up the pounding feet of the step-dancers or the dexterity of Celtic guitarists, the strings blurring under their hummingbird hands. As for the thundering, cyclonic riffs performed by the piano or keyboard accompanists – "Oh, well yes, it's a mystery," confess those who know them best.

Don and I were lucky to take in several concerts over the Thanksgiving week and, on the holiday Sunday, roasted a local organic chicken for supper, which we shared with friends. I managed a few lessons on Gofor at Adrienne's, as well. I even got to meet Kendra's sweet new quarter horse mare, Carlie, which she boarded not at Adrienne's barn in Dundee, but at a barn nearer to her own home in Louisdale. To my delight, Kendra even asked, "Wanna ride her?" and so I did for a few minutes, in the ring at the barn. Compact, beautiful, and *comfy*, Carlie the sorrel mare is a happiness-maker. I had forgotten that particular gleam you often see in a new horse owner's eyes – a gleam I see in brilliant measure in Acadian Kendra's warm brown ones. Horse and person are perfectly matched, judging from the affectionate and easy interactions I observed that day. Joy whirled all around them, like errant autumn leaves on the breeze.

Of course, I remembered Coqeyn then, and the press of excitement in my stomach each time I had thought of him, in the first weeks and months we owned him. *A real horse, of our very own.* I don't know if I ever took that in on a cellular level. Most days I felt much more that I belonged to him than the other way around. I still do. I don't care how much money does or doesn't change hands – how can a human being ever "own" an animal and its spirit? Co-adventurers and -creatures, more like. I hope Kendra co-adventures and shares the world with kind-hearted Carlie, all their lives long.

We went back to Halifax in mid-October, then returned to Cape Breton for one last trip of the year in November. Then, on November 5, I had my "1st unsupervised ride." That's how I wrote it down in my calendar day-book – with a big asterisk inked above. *Remember this*, that asterisk signifies.

And yet, to be truthful, I don't. I think all it means is that Adrienne allowed herself to slip away from the ring for a few minutes, sometime during the course of our lesson, that she trusted me enough to *carry on as if you're normal*, as the joke runs in Cape Breton, and to choose my gaits and pacing aboard Gofor however I wanted, without her direction. Heaven knows she could trust reliable Gofor, but *if* he spooked/*if* he shied/*if* he bucked/stumbled/disobeyed in minor or major form – well, then, she could apparently trust me, too, to react appropriately, to be *just fine*.

It was as though I were just another one of her students who had fallen once or twice, painfully but uneventfully, or perhaps one of the lucky few just starting out, yet to fall off. To some degree, you have to think this way – *I will not fall* – or you wouldn't ride at all. No different than life overall, really. You can live it with no expectation of harm, or with every fear that harm lurks, waiting to catch you in an unguarded moment.

I guess with one experience and another, I'm somewhere in the middle of that equation. I know for sure I sat a little taller in the saddle that day, when Adrienne ducked into the barn or house. It was time for more independence.

11
COUNTRY CHRISTMAS PARTY AND HOUSEWARMING

Riding families can share uniquely close ties, especially if they've spent a lifetime not only riding and caring for horses together, but breeding and training their own horses, and showing together. If the family is lucky enough to have a farrier in their midst as well, as the Smith family does, with Adrienne's husband Scott, then they are fortunate. Every four to six weeks, regardless whether the horse has worn down his shoes, the shoes still need to be removed, and the feet trimmed. Prices vary widely, especially from city to country. In Nova Scotia, new shoes cost around $140 to $160 a set, one Annapolis Valley farrier told me. This is for a regular set of shoes, nothing fancy such as ones with "corks," which act as cleats, and cost more yet. Even simply changing the front shoes, which wear down more quickly than the hind ones, costs around $90 to $100. Good farriers are also booked up for weeks ahead and are not always available, when horses do as they often do and "throw" or lose a shoe.

The Smiths' adult daughter, Helen, is now a barn-owner herself. And today, December 20, 2014, Helen and her partner Neil Morley are hosting a housewarming and Christmas party at their new home in Ardoise, near Windsor, which is about a forty-five-minute drive outside of Halifax.

Don and I were delighted to be asked to join in the fun. Don has never met Helen, or Neil. I've never met Neil and have only talked with Helen a couple of times over the past two years. She, like her mother, is a horse owner, lifelong competitive rider, and a certified Western coach, trained in all Western disciplines. She is also a dynamite reiner. The property she and Neil bought is 132 broad acres, with about fifteen acres of fields. Today is a Hallmark Christmas card, the long driveway leading enticingly to a stand of spruce trees and beyond this, an older, substantial barn with a gambrel roof and greyed wood siding, the two front doors painted Wedgewood blue. The doors are decorated with two evergreen wreaths, complete with scarlet bows. Such an inviting, bold colour ...

As for the property's name, Helen and Neil decided on Roseway Stables, because of the wild rose bushes that are plentiful around the house and barn.

When Helen asked us if we'd like to come to the party, she also told me that she'd have one of the schooling horses tacked up to offer rides, probably Shania, their new horse. Winnie's here, too, of course, she reminded me, so you can visit with her. *Of course, I remember now,* I'd said – *Winnie is actually your horse.* Now that Helen had a barn of her own, they'd trucked Winnie down from Adrienne's some weeks ago. It would be a treat to see her. Food, grog, happy friends and family, pre-Christmas merriment in a gorgeous country setting – and maybe a short ride – it all sounded great to me.

I have dressed to ride and am keen as mustard to do so, having not ridden since the last time at Adrienne's in November. Around Helen in her great new riding ring are a group of young girls, students and family, all of whom have had a turn on the horse now. I am hanging back a bit, toasting my hands over the fire pit near the ring, as I don't want to spoil their girlish fun.

"Hey, Marjorie," calls Helen, "do you want to ride next?" She beckons with her hand for me to come in the ring. That's good enough for me. I shoot a smile over towards Adrienne, standing in the rear doorway of the barn, but she's talking animatedly with someone and does not see the smile; I feel strangely shy to ride with my coach watching – as though I have to ride extra well, to represent her fine coaching, not so much to her daughter, obviously, who learned from Adrienne herself, as a tiny child, but to all the other people assembled. Along with Neil's family, who live in Halifax, Adrienne and Scott are here from Cape Breton to share this happy day with their daughter and Neil. Adding to the crowd are old friends and new neighbours, many of whom are horse-owners.

"I'd love to ride!" I shout back to Helen. I am dressed in riding breeches and several layers up top, finishing in a down jacket. It's a raw day.

"I'll get you a hard hat," says Helen.

"Don't bother," I say, beaming. "I brought my own." She waves to indicate she's heard, and I jog towards our Ford parked in the wide area beside the barn. Hat retrieved, I jog back toward Helen and all the vivacious, beanpole girls.

Helen is holding a tall Paint mare by the bridle, in this wonderful riding ring that she and Neil have worked so hard on in recent months. Even in a month that has seen tropical-strength rains, the ring is a thing of beauty. It should be a lake. Instead, the footing is mostly firm and well-drained, thanks to the couple's clever choice of septic sands, through which the rain descends easily. After barns, lifelong riders notice rings right away, instantly gauging the ride they will give. Soggy, firm, hard, each condition affects the impact on the horse's feet, legs, and back – the whole body. This in turn affects the person's ride in the saddle, making it smooth or uneven. I have already spontaneously complimented Helen and Neil three times on the ring's obvious good footing, which can only be laboriously achieved.

The ring's fencing is new and stout, too. Everything is done well, which doesn't surprise me. Helen was raised by smart, hard-working country people who know the value of a job done right. City-reared Neil, an accountant and vice-president of a development company, is just as smart and hard-working, and in love with his partner, their new property near Windsor – and his vivid green, new John Deere tractor. It's astonishing what the couple have done to improve the property in only a few short months.

Helen pats the mare's neck. "This is Shania."

Well, hullo, Shania, I think – *who are you?*

Whenever you ride a new horse, especially after a life-changing fall from one, you are always on edge, wondering about their personality and quirks. Individuals – every person and every animal is an individual. It's just that horses' personalities are mostly harder to figure out, at least before you've spent many hours together. Maybe people are the same, after all. But horses don't have the words to help you understand them and their needs and desires. They don't have human beings' mobile, informative faces, either. Horses' expressions are subtler and their actions can be anything but subtle, even explosive at times. Watch the ears: they tell the rider so much. Take clues from the eyes, too, though don't face them head-on, because a horse's vision is peripheral. They won't respond as most dogs do, instantly friendly and submissive. Mostly they'll be watching you as discreetly as you are watching them openly, looking for clues to your ways and wiles, and deciding, like you, if there's trouble or peace ahead.

Unlike you, for most people anyway, they are also giving you a good smell. Today I made sure I wore no perfume or hair products. I do smell of woodsmoke from standing beside the fire pit, and I smell like me – whatever unique, human-y scent that might be. As for smelling horses, I confess to being one of those riders who loves the scents of horses, especially a well-groomed, sun-warmed horse, but even an everyday horse makes me smile with olfactory pleasure. The smell of adventure.

Helen pats the mare's neck again. "Shania's great, you'll love her," she says. Big smile: "She's Neil's horse."

Right, someone told me that Shania was Neil's horse first, but she is also used for lessons, or just for fun, like today. The "husband horse," as horse folk call these gentle equine loves, intended for novice riders, as the men in horse-riding couples often are.

"Yes, I know," I reply to Helen, smiling just as big. "Your mum told me you really lucked out finding her." Shania is "nicely put together," as the expression goes. The Paint is an American breed of horse that combines both the conformational characteristics of a Western stock horse with a pinto spotting pattern of white and dark coat colours. Unusually for most horses, Shania has one blue eye and one brown eye. Her overall expression is also unusually mild. She is quiet and attentive.

I swing aboard using the mounting block. Shania is 15.2 hands high, which is a nice medium size for a horse, but a bit tall for a petite woman to mount from the ground, unless she's good and fit.

I settle in the saddle, adjust the stirrups and reins. I sit straight, take a deep breath, full up from my diaphragm. So, what is this horse all about?

Her spine is pure kindness. I can feel it running both down the neck from her poll to her withers, and the opposite direction, from the base of her tail over her croup, loins, and back. The current is a silent hum. A hum of good humour and gentleness. I am startled and surprised to feel it – so much so that I don't say a word. Over forty years of riding and I don't recall an intuition like this before. This mare would hurt herself before she'd ever hurt a human.

She likes people. And she wants to do a good, predictable job for them. She is as benign a horse presence as I've ever known. If spirits have colours, then hers is daffodil yellow. This mare is not simple, but she simply wants a peaceful co-existence with her human caretakers and her fellow stable-mates. I bet she's even nice to the barn cats. If my long-ago lease-friend Cliquot the Thoroughbred was nine-tenths sunny and giving, then Shania is entirely this way.

"What do you think?" says Helen, as I pick up a jog, which the mare wants to make bigger. Does she somehow know I've ridden English all my life? *Come on, rider, let's do a nice big working trot.* I post the one full circuit of the ring, then resume the jog I started out with. The second I use my seat to slow her, Shania comes down to a walk. I must have pulled back on the reins, too – a mixed message to which she responded perfectly. I lighten my seat and hands, squeeze with my legs, and she recommences the jog.

"She's lovely," I say, when I am once again abeam of Helen. "A real sweetheart." I have never been surer in my life that I could trust a horse such as this every day, in every way.

As if to tease me, the mare stops, and then starts a softly rumbling bugle, because she has caught sight of her stablemates in a close-by field. Her body is alert and she is minutely resistant to my hand and leg aids to move along. Winnie and Shania are best friends, Helen told me earlier. Winnie's in the barn right now, but Shania is keenly interested in the comings and goings of all the horses at Roseway. I can't see who it is in the nearby field, but Shania can, and she is acting like the small child left out of the party. Horses can be fiercely devoted to one another and even the most emotionally remote ones usually have a good friend among a lifetime of stablemates – just as dogs do. But horses, who are herd animals, can act up when they feel separated from their kind. That can mean any number of things that are unsettling or unseating to a rider.

Shania isn't the only sensitive one.

"Are you all right?" asks Helen, who has seen and heard Shania become distracted. She knows a little bit about my accident, knows there are vestiges of unease for me when I ride now. "Just turn her head away – she'll be fine," she says. I knew that, knew that she just needed to be re-engaged with her rider, me, but hadn't responded quickly.

Am I all right? The question still hangs in the air, even though Shania and I have now turned, breaking the mare's line of vision to the field. Helen is still waiting, poised to begin another task. "I'm fine, Helen," I belatedly respond. "In fact, I am doing really well now." *Thanks to your mother,* is the clear subtext. We exchange a smile and Helen ducks into her barn, knowing, as her mother did back in November, that I am fine on my own.

I once again ask Shania for a bolder trot and she responds without hesitation. The hum in her spine never ceased, even when she obviously wanted to be somewhere else. This is a consistent, giving mare. I would love to get to know her better.

"Congratulations on your new horse," I say to Neil some time later. His eyes gleam as Kendra's did, when we talked about her new mare Carlie, back in the summer.

"Isn't she great?" he says, smile as broad as the winter sky above, and the acreage around us. Neil is obviously thrilled. It's nice to see a fellow that daffy about his horse. As they say in Cape Breton, "You couldn't beat the smile off his face with a stick."

Mine, either. What a prime winter day in the country, with friends, furry and otherwise.

12

YOGA AND RIDING

On February 19, 2015, two days after my fifty-sixth birthday, Year of the Horse would flip over to Year of the Sheep. But for now, it was mainstream European New Year's Day, 2015, and horses still ruled the Chinese zodiac. I, in turn, gave horses every spare hour away from work that I could. I was still focused, still committed to improving my seat and moving ahead with my milestone goals. Our slightly unrealistic plan to achieve my Western Rider Level Two accreditation last fall had indeed not come to pass – we were both far too busy with work commitments – but neither Adrienne nor I was disappointed. Achieving that Level One in the brief time we both had to work together was miracle enough.

For me, the satisfaction from that gain was both lingering and freshly inspiring. I wanted to push on, as effectively as I could. In the interests of improving my flexibility and core strength, and also because yoga does wonders for my emotional health, I signed up for a second year of wintertime Gentle Yoga at my local community centre. The yoga we are learning is from the Kripalu tradition, a word which translates as compassion, and indicates a core philosophy of the practice. The classes do indeed begin gently, with a focus on being present in your body, and sustaining a flowing breath and warming up. Kripalu also allows you to choose the level of physical intensity that is right for your body, recognizing that all practitioners have different bodies.

I had taken classes with this particular instructor, Lynn Bowditch, before; she knows about my accident in 2011, and provides the perfect selection of poses to help me and others with ongoing physical "issues" get strong and balanced again. I enjoy and admire Lynn. She is my age or perhaps older, I am not sure, and fit, flexible, and beautiful. Practising yoga with Lynn won't give me her thick chestnut hair and violet-blue eyes, but if I stick with the classes, I can work towards gaining as strong an overall frame and keeping a fine, health-enhancing posture.

I always see immediate benefits from yoga classes – physically, mentally, emotionally, and spiritually. It felt great to get back to once-a-week classes with most of the usual crew from the year before, many of whom were either coming back from surgeries or had chronic physical conditions of one sort or another. One classmate in particular, a trim and supple retired doctor in her eighties, inspired us all. Her erect bearing strongly reminded me of the older horsewoman I spoke to as a fourteen-year-old, all those years ago, at Southlands. Then and now, two strong senior women. *Just keep riding*, and to further facilitate that, take yoga, too. It's a good combination for me and other riders, I am sure.

I was also still interested in setting and achieving riding goals. What could I accomplish in the next nearly two months – before I lost the extra impetus and sparkle of the horse-titled year? And, based in Halifax for the winter, where was I going to ride? Should I go back to One More Time Stable in Brooklyn? Or should I start up at Roseway Stables, Helen's new barn, which she kindly offered that I could do? Finally, it was firmly winter now, temperatures low and unforgiving. Surely the late-to-start snow would commence sooner than later and interfere with any riding schedule I tried to put in place? I certainly hadn't done very well last winter, with only a handful of rides at Sherry's and she had the added perk of an indoor arena. Last winter was bitter, and I frankly found it just as cold inside as outside the arena walls, but it was possible to ride on snowy days, which it probably wouldn't be at Neil's and Helen's. Perhaps my goal was simple, just to get tougher and ride on the really cold days, no matter where I did this.

I knew Helen did not want to influence my decision about where to ride. Helen, Adrienne, and Sherry are long-time friends and colleagues. The day of the Christmas party, Helen simply said she was taking on new students, and I would be welcome if I wanted to start some lessons with her. A part of me thought, *A third coach in as many years – they're all great, but am I up for this?* And the other, more insistent thought was merely two linked names: *Winnie & Shania; Shania & Winnie.* If I rode at Helen's I could ride the good-luck palomino mare, and the safe-as-houses Paint mare.

I couldn't know for sure, but it seemed likely that Helen's teaching style would be similar to her mother's. From the little I'd seen, their riding styles were definitely similar. So the transition from training with Adrienne to training with Helen shouldn't be that hard. Just a question of getting to know someone better, ride by ride, lesson by lesson …

"Oh, that's great news!" said Helen, when I called her the day after thinking all this through. "We can start tomorrow, Saturday, January 3. How does 12:30 work for you?"

13

TRUST
JANUARY 3, 2105, 12:20 P.M.

For my first lesson at Roseway Stables, I am back on Winnie – oh, happy day – and back on the lunge line, as we did that first post-accident lesson at Caberfeidh Stables in the summer of 2012. Unlike that warm day, today is minus ten degrees Celsius. I am wearing a turtleneck, a down vest and down jacket, thick breeches, and the wooliest of wool socks under my boots. The sky is a dark-for-winter blue and the yellow sun ignites rainbows on the dusting of snow. The bright sky-high world hurts my eyes, but sunglasses mostly don't work for riding. You have to be keenly aware of the natural world around you and your mount – birds or small animals darting above or below, tractors or other vehicles starting up or suddenly heaving into view, anything a horse could react or overreact to – and you must be observant about the footing, even when you're on a lunge line and someone else is making the decisions about what gait to pick up, and when. If your shades are too dark, and you don't see what the horse sees or doesn't see, you won't be prepared when your horse either trips or spooks.

Thanks to the septic sands and no recent rains, the

footing in the ring is firm. The ground is hard with frost, though, so it's walk-trot only today, and for some time ahead, I'd guess. It's just too hard on the horses' legs and feet to canter over this unforgiving, ridged ground. The horses are wearing ingenious winter shoes, put on by Helen's father, Scott – corks on the perimeters, and rubber snowball pads over the sole and "frog" (a triangle of hard tissue in the centre of the foot), to prevent snow from filling the area. Footing in winter and any other season, really, is a horse person's obsession. Without healthy feet and legs, you have no horse.

"Today's lesson is all about trust," says Helen, from where she stands by Winnie's head. "Trust of the horse, and trust of the process of riding." She attaches the lunge line to the inside side ring of the halter, not the ring under the jaw, as this provides greater lateral leverage and control. The halter, previously, had been placed over the bridle. Thanks to the mounting block, I am already in the saddle. Helen has half-hitched my reins to the saddle's horn – *Always do a lunge lesson with a halter and bridle,* she'd said earlier. *That way, if something goes wrong at my end, you can untie the reins and use them if you need them* – though to start, I will be riding without the reins.

"Remember," she says, patting that secure half-hitch, "at this barn, it's safety first, then fun – right?" I nod and smile. Sounds fine by me.

When I was grooming Winnie, we went through some of the barn's rules – regular, common-sense barn rules, none of which surprised me – and then, when we got in the ring, we covered another safety rule that did surprise me – and I'd never heard a coach or instructor say before.

"You need to know this," said Helen firmly, 'that if I am injured while we are riding together, and am on the ground, unresponsive, get yourself and your horse out of the ring, and call 911. You can't help me. But paramedics can. And the sooner the better." I didn't tell her that the very idea of my coach being on the ground, unconscious and gravely hurt, made my heart lurch.

My coach, of course, like her mother, is fast becoming another special friend of mine, so small wonder thoughts of riding accidents are unsettling to me. I understand why Helen told me this safety rule, and I agree with the logic. It's basic first-aid procedure, really. So whether the horse hurt her unexpectedly when she was standing on the ground, or if she was giving a lesson while riding a horse of her own and her horse unseated her and she became unconscious, the person who is able-bodied can't waste time trying to in-effectively assess the situation. Collect up the horse(s) – one at a time, if needs be – and get out of the ring and phone for help. It would be wrenching to walk away from a friend, though, lying motionless on the ground, with her eyes closed.

A flash in my mind of the young stable-worker at the barn where my accident occurred, her distressed face look-ing down at me. Then another image of her running away from me "to get Buddy, so he doesn't trample you." Being trampled was the last thing on my mind. Mostly I was con-fused that I couldn't stand up. There was no pain at that point, just the strange icy ripples of nerve damage to my leg and spine beginning, then the warmer waves of shock set-tling in from head to toes ...

Helen's relaxed voice disperses the dark memory. "Now, let's just get comfortable at the walk first, then we're going to do something a little different."

We start on a circle to the left. Helen has the folded lunge line in her right hand, and a lunge whip (an aid to help direct the horse). With her left hand, she feeds out the lunge line until Winnie and I have a big circle to work in.

"Put your hands on your legs and sit up nice and tall." We circle around several times and work on getting "weight" into the heel and general leg placement and pos-ture. Even at a walk, I am warming up pleasantly.

"Keep walking – and close your eyes," come the next requests.

"Close my eyes?" I can't imagine why I would do this.

"Yes, I want you to really feel that four-beat gait and feel connected to Winnie at the walk." She doesn't say it, but I know she's thinking, *Winnie will take good care of you, don't worry.*

Right, I'll try not to, but I may as well be riding blindfolded, not something I associate with safety. I close my eyes. The world vanishes. There is only essence of horse below me, winter air on my face, and the discreet sounds of country lands, as though the trees and fields are breathing all around me, in time with my own breaths. I am more aware of the saddle than I am when my eyes are open. It's deep, comfy, and holds me safely, and erect. I know there's a universe above me and that it's vast. Today and this very moment, that sky's benign, even protective. My legs bracket warm horse body and my hands don't feel as peculiar as they did, resting flat on my thighs, not folded around the reins. They're just there, minding their own business, the fingers spread a bit, but not clutching at my breeches. Piano hands, and me playing the song of a woman on a fairytale horse, its immense and muscular wings pushing us through navy-black skies and galaxies glowing with stars …

Only one problem: I can't really "see" my body as I ride here and now, in real time. I could be turned backwards, for all I can properly sense.

"Am I folded over at all?" That's just a guess, and it doesn't really feel that way, but with riding – let alone with eyes closed – you're hardly ever sitting tall or straight enough, consistently enough.

"No, you look fine," comes the literally disembodied voice nearby. "How do you feel?"

"Bizarre, and great," I answer. "Hard to describe. The whole world is horse." I want to laugh, but then feel my first pang of nervousness at that idea. I have a fairly physical laugh at times. Whatever movement accommodates the heartiest guffaw. A contained titterer, I am not. At the moment I am balanced – and wish to stay that way. Don't even think that word, *dizzy.*

"Time for a posting trot."

My eyes blink open: "With my eyes shut?"

"Yes, eyes shut. And then picking up the correct diagonal."

I am good at diagonals, can mostly do them without looking down to see if I am rising on the "correct" leg. But the lazy man's way of looking for the diagonal by checking the movement of the horse's shoulders is another one of my bad habits. I have a feeling I am about to start working on that bad habit, along with the others I've been addressing.

To rise or "post" upwards at the trot, you need to be able to feel your "diagonals," which refers to the diagonal configuration of the two-beat trotting gait. When the horse's left front leg moves forward, so does the right hind leg. Many students were raised with the saying, "Rise and fall with the leg on the wall," and that's referring to the front outside leg. And so, if you were trotting around the arena to the right, you'd rise as the left front leg moved forward.

But the reason you do so has to do with the hind legs. When you are going in a circle or around an arena fence, the inside leg bears more weight. This is because of how the horse's body is arced. So by lifting your weight out of the saddle as that hind leg bears weight, you're relieving the horse of extra pressure.

My brain sometimes takes "the route less travelled by," as the Robert Frost poem says. When I glance down to check a diagonal, I look for the inside front leg to be in the "down" or weight-bearing position and rise when I see that; I just couldn't make the other explanation work for me.

New riders are also taught to alternate the posting diagonal, if they are, say, trotting for long periods of time in straight lines. This allows for the horse's haunches to be worked equally. Karin and I were conscientious about this when we rode up the trails for hours at a time. We also found we had a preferred diagonal we rose on, the left, and tried to vary this.

"Ready to trot?" asks Helen.

"Sure," I say. "Let's go."

Winnie being Winnie, trained to her attractive diva eyeballs by the very woman who holds the lunge line and lunge whip, she responds immediately to Helen's voice command to trot. We're underway!

And if I thought that walking on a horse with my eyes closed was revelatory, then trotting with my eyes closed is doubly so. I sit to the trot for several strides – *one-two, one-two* – then rise.

"You got the diagonal," says Helen. "Can you feel that you got it?"

"Yes," I say, "I can." But this short statement doesn't begin to cover how wonderful this all feels. I am posting, aware which horse leg is placed where, most of the time, and yet I am also back up in that starry night sky again. Baby, forget the horse, I am riding the *wind*. Forget the stars, too, because I am a supernova all on my very ow – *uh, oh, where am I?*

"Sitting trot again. You OK?"

I blithely lie. "Yeah, fine – just lost where I was for a sec. Can I cheat and open my eyes for a minute?"

Helens laughs. "Sure, and that's not cheating."

I open my eyes only long enough to reassure myself I am on a horse, in a ring, on a lunge line, most securely in the saddle. Beyond that, I take in no other environmental details, not wanting to spoil the out-of-body experience I just had.

"Ready."

And so we work a bit longer. I am four for four on picking up the correct diagonal and feel great about that. Later, we do some other work off the lunge line and after one full hour altogether, we stop. I am warm as a seat by the fire, but Helen must be frozen. You'd never know it from her happy chatter. Like her mother, Helen loves to teach.

"So, what did you think of riding with your eyes closed?"

"Bizarre, great," I repeat. I loved every moment, actually, even the wobbly bits. I mean, really – a day when the whole world was horse and I was a several-second supernova? Best of all, my whole self felt trusting – of the horse, the coach and the natural, breathing world. Even when the universe blacked right out, save for starlight.

CRYING
JANUARY 2015

There are times when the sky thins and magic breaks through. The world has been gold on paper-white fields for all of January. Above the riders who come to Roseway Stables, horizon to horizon of Confederate blue. Around us, groves of evergreen, long lines of fencing and barn cats running and tumbling in soft whorls of snow. Yesterday. Then three days before that, too. Then four days prior to those days. Starting it all off, that first lesson at Roseway when I rode with my eyes closed and hands at my sides. Altogether I rode four *give 'er* days (to revert to Cape Breton-ese) during hell-cold January. That's already one more ride than all of last winter. We're soon to be busting into February and I'll be riding regularly then, too, I hope.

Outside. No inside arena. In the ring, open to the sky. Bitter cold.

The cold was not a problem. Not one bit. I would have preferred warmer temperatures, and I silently cheered when the minus numbers were in the single digits, but I was learning and enjoying myself so much that the cold was incidental. There hasn't been much snow, either – there's a bit of luck. Sometimes I rode Shania, other times Winnie. Sometimes Helen taught from the ground, other times she rode whatever horse I wasn't on, and gave the lesson from "on board." Yet other times I shared a lesson with a junior rider, Avery McLean, who'd only been riding a few months, but was doing well, despite being an alarmingly loose noodle in the saddle. Out of the saddle, as we talked in the barn while we groomed and tacked up, she was so polite and sweet – just like her mother, Karen – she just made my eyes tear up.

That's the problem. I can't stop crying.

I listen to the radio in our truck on the way out to the barn – and I cry at the sappy songs that I seek out on the dial, and listen to. *Love, sweet love and comfort, baby* – sings one artist after another.

I listen to the radio on the way home from the barn, hours later, and don't even hear what song is playing – and I cry, because my body feels trashed and my spirit is humming with purpose. *I am progressing.*

I cry when I get to the driveway of Roseway Stables, because I love long driveways that end with barns, and I know at the end of this one, there's a barn with kind people and horses in it. Even the barn cats are cheerful and welcoming to the visitors in their home, jumping up on the table in the tack room and pushing their striped heads under your hands, as you sort through your gear bag, looking for gloves. *I am so lucky to spend time here!*

Other times I cry because Helen and Neil got engaged over Christmastime and their happiness and excitement is great to see. I love it that Neil got Helen a beautiful diamond ring – the diamond set low and snugly, specially designed to be as "barn-proof" as possible. That's one cool and thoughtful fiancé. My fiancé did the same back in 1998. I can wear either my wedding band or my year-fifteen anniversary ring to the barn and not worry about them. Often, I ride with both of the rings pushed close together on my ring finger. *Once and always, my silver-haired scribe and spouse.*

Seventeen years married now, and nineteen years together – and yes, that makes me cry happy tears, too.

Mostly I cry because I couldn't, when I was down and nearly out in 2011. I couldn't do anything but exist, in a monotone, circumscribed way. If I had succumbed to tears, I think self-pity would have done me in. Even if the tears acknowledged the monstrous levels of pain I was dealing with – I think it somehow would have retarded my healing. I felt so feral and even nasty, lying in one place day after day like an animal stabbed through with a spear, pinned to the ground, heartbeat slow and unchallenged by exertion – *going, going, gone* – the world around me indistinct, even possibly not existing at all – except in memory. Was everything from now on going to be a memory of what was real before? I asked myself. Walking, running, holding my husband in my arms – even tiny triumphs like turning over in bed on my own?

The recuperative years also have been mostly tearless. I was too busy concentrating on getting back to some sort of normal, which mostly means oblivious, insouciant existence. I don't want to think about my physical self, or at least not the parts of me that still complain or wave self-absorbed little flags in front of me, saying, *Look, look, we're not all better yet. Aren't we special and deserving of your attention?* No, you're not. Family, friends, horses, writing, teaching, our charming, gorgeous dogs, the natural world – these deserve attention, not leftover physical nonsense from a riding accident.

The fact that the lowest band of my back is still numb after all this time is something I've in greatest measure accepted. It doesn't hurt, or prevent me from doing what I want to do. I know I look awkward and stiff at times, and I know I am not the "pretty rider" I'd like to be, a phrase we used when I was learning to ride as a girl, meaning that attractive combination of suppleness, quietness, and strength, but these are not hanging offenses. I do all right.

That makes my eyes blur some days, too. Took so long to get back to adequate.

Call this the month of tears then. Four long years later and similar to the day I cried in the truck after a great ride at Adrienne's, I don't actually cry long, only allow a few hot tears to spill down my cheeks. Swipe, swipe, go the back of my hands on my face each time this happens, most often in the truck. I turn up the radio, grateful for sappiness and solitude. The tears are a backlog from the wretched times long gone now.

It doesn't seem like it, but I am certain there is a finite amount of these waterworks. It's got something to do with the fact that I don't have to be brittle and marginally coping anymore. I can be soft in expression on the outside, and soft-hearted and receptive within. I don't have to fight every second to feel anywhere near normal. I even ran down a flight of stairs last week – then nearly tripped the last few stairs because I was so startled I'd done that. People ask me – not so often now, of course, usually only those with physical troubles of their own – *How is your back? Are you feeling well these days?* – and I respond, truthfully, "Better every day." Something changes in my musculature and tissues every day – for the better. I think of it as tiny, adjusting tweaks, made by an horologist, on the complicated clock that is my body.

"Soft-tissue damage, complex and long-lasting," said the ER doctor the day I arrived in an ambulance at the Halifax Infirmary.

But I'll be damned if I'll let that be a life-dictate. *I am moving ahead now.*

I hope the weather holds for February.

14
A WAKENING

The first of February was at least minus seventeen with the wind chill. We did not walk the dogs. I don't think we left the house at all that day.

I drove the few blocks to yoga class the next day, feeling resentful and silly. Walking to yoga is an effective warm-up for the class, especially when I take the longer, neighbourhood route that has a steep hill and then a steeper staircase leading up to the community centre's playing field and parking lot. Two more sets of stairs inside the building and I arrive at our practice room pleasantly out of puff and ready to peel off my numerous layers of outer wear and start working. Instead, on that morning, I felt the laziest person ever driving down my road one block and then up Herring Cove Road for another two blocks – all to avoid the razor wind that made me involuntarily gasp and moan when it hit me full in the face and body. It was "not fit," as I have learned to say about numerous weather conditions since living in the Maritimes.

At least I gave myself points for going to yoga at all. Our class was a small one that day. As I had requested, we did lots of stretching and strengthening poses. I even did a fair job on the Child's Pose, which used to be my favourite yoga pose, the body all tucked over, under, and tidy the way a wood-bug rounds into himself when you touch him. I allowed myself to spread my knees apart for this pose, instead of having them tightly together, which often strains my back and tautly healed calves more than I can stand. But I got my head right down to the floor, and let gravity pull down my shoulders and back as much as I could manage. The effort felt good yet strenuous – and I hid the limp that occurred in the aftermath from our teacher, knowing she would be unnecessarily concerned. It was just my right calf being grumpy. From times past, I knew it was nothing that an Epsom salt bath wouldn't take care of. No pain, no gain, and all that.

The following day I rose from a good night's sleep feeling peculiar.

"What do you mean, 'peculiar'?" asked Don.

"I don't know how else to explain it," I said. I also felt low-grade anxious, as though I had studied for an exam but didn't feel confident about all the material I'd be tested on. My mind roved in ever-widening circles, looking for the right word, the right concept, to describe how I felt. I did what I always did when something happened related to the accident – for I'd figured that much out, at least – and I told myself, "You're not in pain – and so, you are fine. Get on with it." I did just that, putting in an hour or so at my computer writing, thinking now and again about what to make for lunch or cook for supper. At a pause in the writing, when I'd decided on scallops for supper, I got up from my chair to take them out of the freezer. I rose, stepped toward the kitchen, and stopped as though a wall had shot up in front of me, or I was one step shy of an edge I wasn't sure I would come back from, if I did walk over it. "Peculiar" had become disturbingly weird. What the hell was going on?

Sea changes can be weird; my psyche had that one spot-on. The sea of my body had gone through storm after storm, and then a prolonged lull. Then when healing "suddenly" occurred, my brain, heart, and spirit couldn't understand what they were experiencing.

"Don?" I stood in the doorway of his office. "C'n I talk to you for a moment?"

My tentative stance and tone of wonder turned his head sharply away from his computer screen. "Sure, what's up?"

"My back. It's hard to explain, but far as I can tell, well, my back isn't numb anymore." I don't know if Don knew how much of my back had still lacked feeling – I rarely talked about it – but he knew now, and knew this was an important moment. He shot to his feet and gathered me into a hug. "Wonderful! That's just bloody wonderful."

I hugged him back, silent.

"It *is* good news – isn't it?" he asked.

It was hard to articulate that yes, of course, this significant healing was a blessing, and I was vibrating with gratitude. My mind, though, was spinning with the newness of the experience. There was before – numb – and after – my back is mine again, doesn't belong to numb-land. I unquestionably felt more me again; it was just a me I hadn't been for a long time. That other me was a stranger who had had a portion of her back go on some kind of strange sabbatical, very much without my permission. But stranger or not, I'd lived with that woman for some years. I wasn't going to miss her, but I did wonder where she'd walked off to. *Walkabout*, as the Australian Aborigines say, about those among them who leave the company of all others and need to walk the vast desert lands, solitary, open to learning, experience, and mysticism. *Walk long and far away from me,* I told the most enduring of my injuries, that thick, numb back. *No need to return.*

Complicated injuries also have complicated resolutions, or can. That was the word I'd use again to describe how the physical change in my back feels – *complicated*. For all that the healing is a positive development, it was not an instantly positive sensation.

It would take some getting used to.

* * *

And it did. I soon discovered that having feeling – all sorts of feeling – in a part of my body that had been unfeeling for so long was disconcerting. My back became a place of ticks and clicks; I didn't want to know why, and I tried not to restrict my movements, to prevent the sounds, which only worked sometimes, anyway. While riding demands a quiet, controlled body, it also demands full use of it. You cannot hold back. There were days I came home from my lessons so stiff it took hours – or an Epsom salt bath and a full night's sleep – to limber up. I even started lurching down staircases again ... and feeling uncertain about my future with horses. I said nothing, kept on.

15

PLANS AND MILESTONES

The day after my back un-numbed, Helen and I had an exciting exchange of Facebook messages. I was Facebook "friends" with both Helen and her new business, Roseway Stables, and with Adrienne and Caberfeidh Stables. We all tended to communicate this way more often than by email, text, or cellphone, as it was fast and efficient, and also fun to post photographs of and comments about ride days. In addition to her coaching businesses, Helen is also a professional photographer and works for the provincial government. This meant I most often had lessons on the weekends, though Helen sometimes had time for lessons mid-week. I rarely said no when lesson times opened up, fitting my own more flexible freelance work around Helen's availability. So as we chatted online about lesson days and times, we also discussed plans for the year ahead.

To my delight, Helen first proposed a Ladies Trail-Riding Weekend, which she'd host at Roseway in June. The 132-acre property will have three kilometres of groomed trails when Helen and Neil have the time to do the work. We could also ride in the grassy fields, the one facing the road being a good twenty acres all on its own. Was I interested in a solid weekend of riding with a gang of women riders, which would include a barbeque, wine-drinking, and a sleepover at the house? "Not that I know where we'd fit everybody!" laughed Helen.

I tried not to squeal with delight, thinking there were few things in the world I'd enjoy more than a weekend that featured all those activities; if needs be, I'd sleep in the hay-loft. In all my years of riding, I have never done anything such as an organized riding weekend with other riders. The closest I came to that was just prior to my accident, when my brother Geoffrey, whom I hadn't seen in ages, had booked us a two-day mountain trail-riding adventure in Alberta, where he lives. I had been training to do that strenuous bit of riding when I got hurt. Geoffrey had already paid for the trip and sorry as he was that I was then injured and unable to go, he didn't want to cancel it and lose his considerable output of money. Fortunately, he was able to take his oldest son, David, on the trip. Both Geoffrey and David are serious athletes and while they hadn't done much riding before, with good horses and a careful trail boss, the trip was not a problem for them. They had a grand time.

As for me, if there had been a moment when I was going to lose it entirely and have the soggiest of wail-a-thons, it was when that June weekend came and passed – and Geoffrey and David went adventuring and I stayed home in Nova Scotia, in bed, still unable to walk.

So, asked Helen all these years later, was I up for the Ladies Trail-Riding Weekend? Hell yes, I replied.

There was more.

"I'd like to put on a schooling show at Roseway on July 4th," wrote Helen. "It would be the stable's first show, and would have both Western and English classes. How does that sound?" By now I was hyperventilating, unable to respond sensibly. One way or another, I managed to indicate that yes again, I was interested in going in the show. And on the plot thickened: "I may push back our show a week, as there's a big clinic that is scheduled in Windsor for July 4 through 7. I'd be open to you taking Winnie in the clinic if you want to pay your fee, which is $500 for four days, but well worth it!"

Me, going in a specialized horse-riding clinic? But that was only for the rich kids, when I was growing up. Horse experts from every discipline, most usually dressage at Southlands in those days, would come to the riding club and offer one- and two-day clinics to those who were literally well-heeled in their smart leather boots and had the bank accounts to prove it. The clinics were also for *serious* riders, the names you breathed like movie star names, the men and in greater numbers women who lived for nothing else but riding and competing and were very, very good at their sport and passion. Even though the fee was indeed worth four days of instruction, I still wasn't sure if I could justify the money from our household budget. Maybe if I started saving now, but was I even good enough to do this, or was I being silly?

And who was teaching the clinic? Not that I'd know the name, anyway. I don't even know who the stars are in the English riding world any more. Well, maybe a couple. Canadian open-jumper star Eric Lamaze and his gelding Hickstead, I remember that astonishing airborne duo, and I can't forget Hickstead's horrifying death in 2011 – the year I was hurt, too – right on television, for all the world to see. A ruptured aorta, of all improbable things, which occurred on the jump-course, just before a fence. The last thing the horse did was fall carefully, leaving Lamaze uninjured. So great was the bond between horse and rider that Lamaze was convinced that Hickstead had done this kind act deliberately. I choose to think he's right.

Of course, I also remember Canadian superstar open-jumper, Ian Millar, and his magnificent chestnut gelding Big Ben, who died of colic in 1999. I know Millar, sixty-eight now, is still hard at the sport, but I couldn't name his mounts. As for the Western worlds, I don't know anyone –

"Tommy McDowell," said Helen. "The clinic is with Tommy McDowell from Oklahoma. It doesn't matter how experienced you are. Just show up, ride, watch, listen, and learn." Adrienne had taken a clinic with him many years before, and loved it, said Helen. She might even take the clinic herself, on her Paint gelding, Lex.

Overall, Helen mused, if I wanted to take the clinic, which was going to be held at the Windsor Fairgrounds, "you would learn a lot, and it would be *great* for you to ride off site [from Roseway] in a show facility without actually having to show." Finally, the facility is the same one where Sherry Clark's Heritage Championships would be held later in the summer, on August 8 and 9 – the show that Adrienne wanted me to aim for, when we first started talking about goals late last summer. Helen didn't have to tell me twice that it would a fabulous psychological advantage for me to train and ride at a facility I'd come back to only weeks later, as a competitor ...

In summation, then: the ladies riding weekend, the Tommy McDowell clinic, Helen's schooling show, and Sherry Clark's Heritage Championships – what did I think?

Cream on the cream on the cream of my cream puff, is what I thought. Then a light bulb went on. Just the week prior, I had received notice from the Nova Scotia Equestrian Federation that there were $250-bursaries available for life-long riders interested in continuing rider education of every sort, from regular lessons to targeted training, to clinics. The bursary could pay for half the fee, which made the whole idea a lot more reasonable for me to consider.

Sure enough, when I double-checked the guidelines for applying for the senior riders' bursary, my goal of going to the clinic was a perfect fit. Adrienne, ever willing to help, agreed to write me a letter of recommendation and did so in short order. I was not surprised that the letter was generous about my in-progress comeback to riding – Adrienne is such a positive person – but I was surprised how those kind words hit my heart. I'd had my head down running for so many months that I tended to forget anyone else was noticing those strides were getting longer.

Two weeks after Helen and I had first talked about the clinic, I hand-delivered the envelope to the Nova Scotia Equestrian Federation, hoping for the best.

As I suspected, January's tears dried up and I almost missed the heightened, vulnerable edge I brought to most riding days of that month. Almost. The month of February at Roseway was demanding and exhilarating for all of us, humans and creatures alike. We needed to be made of stern stuff. The temperatures plummeted and settled around minus ten for most of the time. The snow spread out and piled up, as though every other season was permanently covered over. Neil got good at plowing the driveway and ring, and then he got brilliant at it. When the snows became record-setting, other neighbours pitched in with the plowing, too. One way or another, Vancouver-raised me managed the highway drive to Ardoise in our nimble little Ford Explorer Sport-Trac truck, all the while thanking the snowplow drivers for the consistently superb job they did of clearing the roads. The Maritimes are amazing that way, as I can only guess the other snow-generous provinces in the country may be. Vancouver, I'd also guess, might have a couple of snowplows for the whole Lower Mainland, let alone the city proper. Which is adequate, most years ...

Once at Roseway, I'd enter the driveway as though into a roofless snow-tunnel, the snowbanks rising high on either side, the purest of aqua-whites. Arriving at the barn, I'd admire anew Neil's work to clear the parking area, and to have the ring plowed and ready to ride in. The footing was surprisingly good, the snow compacted but not icy. Riders had to be careful, keep the trots slow and steady, but really, the ring was quite ride-able. The whole property was gaspingly gorgeous, winter charcoals and pastels the predominant colours, contrasted against the sunlit snow.

Personal milestones fell as steadily as the snowflakes. On Valentine's Day I led Winnie into the ring – and looked in vain for the mounting block I customarily used to mount my steed. It was buried under a hump of snow – I think. It was certainly missing in action. Helen couldn't help laughing at my crestfallen face. *How the hell was I going to do this?* First off, we lowered the stirrup on the left or "near" side, so I wouldn't have to lift my leg so high. Then my not-to-be-daunted coach helped me find the highest bit of snow-covered turf in the ring for me to stand on, and we laughed even harder when yes, by God, I did mount from the ground – with tall, strong Helen quick to push my backside upwards, and into the saddle. It was the first time I'd mounted from the ground in years beyond recollection. It felt good, although I was embarrassed at my weakness and clumsiness.

I balanced those hot feelings with the cool fact that I'd been at least hoisting on my own saddle for some weeks. I wouldn't want to walk a country mile with one of those sprawling babies in my arms, but I could tack up on my own now, and that felt great. One day, I'd even hoisted two saddles in a row, one on Winnie and the other on taller yet Shania. When Avery, the young rider I was having a lesson with that day, asked me to help her saddle Shania, she didn't actually take in the fact that I was as short or around the same height as she was. Avery only knew I was the closest available adult, and accordingly asked for aid. "Of course, dear," I'd smiled – thinking *oh dear*, indeed – and then just did it, because I had to.

Don't ask yourself how you feel, my mother used to say, at times of greatest challenge and distress in her life – *just do it.* It was a somewhat brutal dictate, which I have nonetheless found useful in my life.

Challenges aside, Helen and I had lots of laughs in February, and one side-splitting occurrence. I was once again mounting from the ground, tall Shania this time, and we'd once again lowered the stirrup – a lot, this time. If some is good, more is better, right? We were in accord that I should be able to just step right in and swing up, easy as a bird to the sky. What we forgot was, the lower the stirrup came down, the higher my right leg had to travel to get up to and over the saddle. I was swinging and pulling for all I was worth, and poor Helen was pushing for all she was worth, and I still wasn't anywhere near the saddle. At that point I was damn-near panicky with incomprehension. *What the fu–*

"You've run out of leg!" laughed Helen. "Try again, and I'll push harder." I did, and she did, and miracle of miracles, the short-legged warrior ascended her warhorse with an untidy thump.

"Well, that was fun," I dead-panned. *I will go somewhere now and croak, of mortification.* I wiggled my left foot, unencumbered by a stirrup, and then looked down to the stirrup, many inches below – and we cracked up all over again. *Ran out of leg ...* yet more new experiences in my comeback to horses ...

Then came the day after Valentine's, and no one was laughing.

ME, HORSE, AND THERE'S THE GROUND

Yellow mare, silver sun, toes in my boots numb, fingers on the reins number. We're going along at the kind of Western jog that you're melded to the saddle, the gait so smooth you could jog on through this endless winter right into summer – and not stop once for a meal. Winnie's relaxed, I'm relaxed and the only distraction for either of us is a world so exquisitely coloured, it's a Japanese silk fan, spread full in white, blue, and gold. "Eyes up," calls out Helen, as my wandering gaze flickers left, right, down, anywhere but where it should be focused, which is up and straight ahead. I know better. I smile, lift my chin – then everything changes. Suddenly, Winnie's head swivels to something we are passing, an object poking out from under the snow, just outside the ring. Bam, bam, bam: she stops, shies, and does a mini-buck crow-hop.

Me, horse, and there's the ground, is all I can think. Am I frightened? No, just instantly gut-sick. Big sick. Gonna vomit, I am sure of it, right here and now. Please, Winnie, no real bucks – and no bolts, God, no bolts. Haven't I had enough of those for a lifetime, several lifetimes? *Can't/can't/ can't fall to the ground/ground/ground – please, dear God, keep me in this saddle. I can't go through that agony again. This cat's only got so many lives to barter with –*

"Silly mare," says Helen calmly. "Turn her away, get her working again."

Turn her away? I don't understand. They used to tell us to make the horse confront its fears, pull its head right back again, to look at whatever it was they've shied from. If they did this shy-bucky number in front of a jump, we'd just cluck and whip them right over it. *Me, horse, and there's the ground* – oh, for God's sake, shut up, I tell my frantic mind. My body is rigid, heart smashing. Winnie is still fussing.

Helen, again: "Circle her, get her working – now."

What's left of my thinking brain obeys the command. Winnie and I make a small circle away from the rail, then trot to the end of the ring, and make a larger circle there. The "hot spot" mid-ring is well out of vision for now.

"There, good, see? She's working for you again. Aren't you glad this happened?" Helen sounds so happy.

Breathe, you need to breathe in order to answer your coach. "Well, I am glad it's over," I manage. "Thought I was gonna vomit."

"No, seriously," says Helen. "You need to know that Winnie won't hurt you. She's schooled to come back from anything – bucks, shies, whatever – you just have to make her listen to you, ask her to work. All our horses are safe like this. Bomb-proof. See how good she is now?

It's true. I sense no remaining nervousness or distraction in the mare. She's "in frame" and comfortable again, going about her business. Did I imagine what just happened?

"She wouldn't have done that to you when you first started back," says Helen, happier yet. "You're stronger now. She was just trying it on for size."

This rings so true that in answer, I just nod my head, not trusting my voice to assent. Horses are peculiar this way. More often than not, they will be kind to those who need kindness most: young children; beginners or disabled riders; returning, ineffective riders. Once they feel a rider get stronger, asking them to work more, all bets are off. Or less dramatically, they can be occasionally resistant and intent on their own plans.

Horses, like people, have individual personalities, quirks, and yes, moods. As I discovered with the lease crew, some give as regularly as they breathe, while others take you as their rider on sufferance. Even Kaber shied with me now and again, just to keep me honest and paying attention. But because he liked me, it seemed to me, after he shied, he would then wait quietly for me to rebalance, either in the saddle or bareback. Polite, that was Kaber – a lover, not a fighter.

And Coqeyn, hot-blooded as he could be, was for the far greater part of the time perhaps the gentlest and steadiest horse I've known. Coqeyn said a lot with those large, mahogany brown eyes of his. What he said most often was, *Hello, fellow creature, what are we doing today? I'm up for anything.* He was sweet-tempered and forgiving, too. He just got the devil in him some days.

Circumstances factor in as well, weather particularly. Crisp winter days make for crisp behaviour. Winnie did the smallest of shies and bucks, most likely because it felt good to be out of her stall and to dance around a bit, in addition to her earlier romp around the ring. Helen often lunges the horses pre-ride, or chases them around the ring with a lunge whip, to get their yah-yahs out. Karin and I did this with Coqeyn. This was just a leftover bit of highjinks. Very minor.

No hysterics or vomiting necessary, says my critical self. No, but it was dismaying to instantly remember that gagging pain again, says my fairer self. So ocean-vast, and gale-strong. *Sickening.*

* * *

In Shoppers Drug Mart, in my local shopping mall, just the week before. I have paid for my purchases and turn from the cashier's station to leave the store. At the door, by the stack of red plastic shopping baskets, an older woman has dropped her car or house keys. Clunk. She stands hunched over, looking down at the splayed keys. The distance from her hands to the floor is ...

... a round-trip to the Milky Way.

In the nanosecond that is pain-sharpened memory, I remember dropping something on the floor of the kitchen, not long after I was "back on my feet." I may have been that, but I wasn't functioning well in all other ways. I stared down at the linoleum. I remember the heated desire for the object, not what it was, and I remember being nonplussed how I might regain it. I was alone in the house that day.

The woman stares at her keys, on the drugstore floor.

I stared at the object of my desire, on the kitchen floor.

I stared for half a minute, or thereabouts and then came up with a plan. Holding onto the kitchen counter, I could drop down on one knee, then two, and reduce the continents between my eager fingers and the longed-for object. I could retrieve it, if I tried hard enough. The tricky part would be rising again. I grabbed once again onto the kitchen counter. The effort felt Samson-strong. Nothing in fact happened, other than I braced myself for the rise. One knee came up – fingers clawing on the counter now – then up came the other. I was upright. My back, as always, felt like someone had whacked it with a two-by-four, then wrapped it in lead.

The woman in the drugstore is neither upright nor kneeling. The keys are still on the floor. Three galactically slow seconds have passed, or thereabouts.

In one more second I run, then easily slip to one knee to pick up the woman's keys. I am flustered, far more than she is.

"Here you go," I pant, heart accelerated by the kitchen memory. Standing again, I hold out her keys. "Some days are hard, aren't they?" Smiling, she takes the keys, then thanks me. She is calm, I am sick at my core. A person should be able to pick up something they drop. Without ridiculous effort, without having to strategize how to do it.

"Thanks again," she says, not yet moving. There are days you can't rush. Many days in a row, sometimes, or even all the days to come. I can't guess what this woman is dealing with. One thing for sure, she wasn't getting those keys into her hands again any time soon. I smile, and turn my face away, so she doesn't see my eyes, filled with sadness from other days.

I hated being physically ineffectual, hated thinking about simple movements, and having no clue how to do them. Moving through the world was a chess game, requiring all the intellect and cunning I had. With whatever small bits of energy I had "left over," I was shocked that being physically challenged could result in mental exhaustion. I had to scheme about every movement, right down to pulling on underwear with one hand, the other hand braced on a bureau, so I wouldn't fall over.

I still can't get out of a bathtub by hoisting myself up

on my hands. I turn over on my hands and knees, and rise up backwards. Some days, I walk down stairs backwards, too, gripping the rail, always. The backwards descent is somehow easier on my taut calves, something to do with how we use our muscles, a friend told me, though the details didn't stick. It is also strangely comforting to walk backwards down a staircase. As though I am just pretending to be dysfunctional, do this only to remind myself how lucky I am to be walking at all.

I am extraordinarily lucky. And know this deep in my sticky ligaments and sore tendons, every day. Lucky for what did not occur, and that I am still "better every day."

* * *

On February 19, the Chinese New Year began. When you're raised in Vancouver, most non-Asians like to celebrate the new year with the Asian community. Even here in Halifax, there is now enough of an Asian community that residents of other ethnicities are aware of the celebration, and many take part in it, by going out for dim sum brunches or evening feasts. Don and I do every year.

As had been promised a year ago in my internet explorations, Year of the Horse had indeed been "thrilling" for me. Now, it was Year of the Sheep/Goat. And this year, too, said yet more internet sources, would be "generally positive" for all, and certainly for people born in the Year of the Pig, or Boar, as I had been. Better yet, the guiding influence of a "benign star, The Three Pillars," promised people of my sign enough "inner strength" to overcome obstacles, and to win over adversaries – and, here's the best bit, "ensuring that final goals will be achieved." I liked the sound of that.

Listen, you need to know, I don't make every significant life plan according to Chinese astrology or any other sort of astrology. But isn't it encouraging and supportive to make some of these plans, connected to positive life experiences from then and now? That's what I figured.

You should also know: *I have to keep going.* One year wasn't nearly long enough to do all I wanted to do. With goals already spilling out well beyond February into August, I had obviously passed Year of the Horse and was well launched in years of the horse.

Gimme two years to tell you all that happens. *Witch's honour,* as we said as kids – the best is yet to come. How do I know? As you recall, I did train in witchy business. And sometimes you just have to believe in the power of your own story.

16
IN SEARCH OF A LOST WAHOO

It happened again, after yesterday's excellent lesson at Rose-way Stables, a lesson that I didn't think was all that strenuous, but my body evidently did. This experience is so common for me, and yet, every time it happens, I think, "I feel strange." Then, without conscious thought, my hands go to the base of my back and I feel a lump on the right side, or a lump on the left, or a continuous plump band of congestion below my waist, above my tailbone. Below the apparent fluid, and deep in the muscle and tissue, a corkscrew of discomfort and sometimes, pain. There it is again, I think wonderingly, or, on stupider days, "What *is* this?"

And you thought after four years you were all better, says the taunting voice in my head. Better than waiting forever to be totally healed, and not attempting anything, I retort.

In fact, I live my life as though I were "all better." Who cares how I get in and out of a bathtub? I manage to get both myself and the tub clean, don't I? I know damn well I am not completely healed – and so what? I still compare my challenges to the strangers I see around me, or to people I know in my personal spheres, and then they seem so petty that I try hard to keep my mouth shut and just carry on.

I know superstars in my life. People managing miserable diseases. People whose physical lives are monstrously complicated, for whom pain and dysfunction are dawning suns of each day, and yet they themselves are sunny, minds and hearts engaged with ideas, and with the best that life offers. Men and women and children who do the impossible each day, who do not carp and complain, and do smile and invite the love of those around them. I am not in chronic pain. Nor are my general activities curtailed by my often unhappy back and leg. I didn't have back surgery recently, or a stroke or a heart attack, and I don't have cancer or Parkinson's disease. I'm not dealing with clinical depression or grieving the recent loss of someone crucial to my happiness and well-being. I simply feel old and fatigued when my back puffs up, or the pain-ghost in my right leg or foot gets decidedly unspirit-like and real.

You feel old and tired because you are old and tired, says the unkind part of me to regular me.

No, I answer, that's not it. Here's the truth of the matter, the part I am struggling with: I thought things would be so much better when my back un-numbed itself in February. I even thought – for one heady and silly moment – that I'd feel the way I did on the early morning of May 2, 2011, *before* 10:15, when I was still driving to the barn, anticipating a great ride, my back upright and silent, without a dissenting voice of its own. I never had back troubles before the accident.

Well, here it is mid-March, a month after the back woke up, and you feel like crap, don't you?

And this time, I can't push away the negativity. I am not a superstar. I am not a sun glowing in a morning sky. I am just cranky me. Try as I might to fend it off, the most current form of the personal "bad list" begins its chant: *fat* – up over ten pounds again from last summer; *old* – yes, fifty-six is old when you are not a lifelong athlete and have spent more years flabby than fit; *foolish* – oh, this one stings, but I do feel foolish at the barn some days, everyone around me younger and more limber, with generous decades ahead of them to progress from fine young riders to excellent ones.

Young or old, you were never excellent.

Thank you, I needed that reminder as well.

Well, you weren't. Even Karin wished you were more competitive, could win ribbons on Coqeyn the way she did, and didn't have those "issues" of yours, especially on a jump course.

Spatial issues. We didn't have a name for it then. I have spatial issues. Remember that "path less travelled" I mentioned earlier, in reference to how I recognize a diagonal when I am trotting on a horse? I've gotten light years better dealing with how things move and are put together, piece by piece, along with numbers, maps, and many other connective things, and all on my own, thank you very much. Even Don says I am monumentally better with spatial matters and all manner of logistics, year by year since he's known me. Because I work at it.

A moment's reprieve, then the old memory-tape resumes: *The oxer first, now left over the triple combination, a hard turn right over the brush jump. Hurry up, this is against the clock. Change that lead, over the barrels, now down the centre line to the vertical. Repeat the whole course. No, no, no, wrong way, again! How can you do it wrong again? I don't believe it! Pay attention, you aren't listening!* said this instructor or that one, sometimes in exasperation, sometimes angrily. The more frustration or pity I heard in their voices, the worse I did. Sometimes, tired of picking on me, they'd pick on Coqeyn. *Take the brush jump – it's only two feet – do you think your pony can do it?* I'd be so caught up inside my suddenly dust-bunny brain and fearful heart, I'd almost freeze, not seeing anything in front or even around me. Or, livid with anger on behalf of Coqeyn, guts jumbled and hands shaking, I'd execute the jump badly – again. *Coqeyn, I am so sorry.*

I didn't know then that I need more time than other

people to "see" a course in my brain and to keep it there. If it took someone without spatial troubles once or twice to "get" the course's pattern, following only verbal instructions, then it would take me four or five times, mutter-carving the words along my thought routes and if the instructor yelled at or belittled me, longer yet, or not at all. I really had to watch and process, then experience and digest, to get it right. As well, we couldn't afford regular lessons, so our progress was ye old three steps ahead, two back.

At a show, the confident girls on their expensive ponies who'd shown since they were toddlers would crowd around the bulletin board that had the course pattern tacked to it, stare a minute, then turn away with fire in their eyes and bellies, waiting for their number to be called. All I saw was an incomprehensible page full of lines, numbers, and shapes. All I felt was anxiety, enough to throw up. I'd memorize the first three jumps, and pray to remember the rest. There was no coach or instructor to pat my leg and say, *I know you can do this. Go get 'em.* Only Karin sitting in the stands, hoping for the best.

"Now on course, number forty-six, Marjorie Simmins on Nizzeyn's Coqeyn."

And finally, the voice memory I hate most: *"Thank you, competitor number xxx, you are excused."* That dismissal only happened once. But I may as well have been dismissed from the whole world, not just a show ring. The embarrassment made my skin hot, full of sharp tingles.

A rider is excused from a jumping show ring for several reasons, but most commonly because she or he has collected too many faults (knock-downs or time faults) or gone "off-course." I had not only gone off-course that long-ago day, I didn't know where I was on the planet. *Coqeyn, Coqeyn, where am I?* And he, good and proud pony that he was, trotted the two of us gaily out of the ring, not a moment of shame slowing his tidy feet. *It's just a jump-class,* his pert pace asserted. *The fact that we're here together, trying our best*

– that's the important bit.

He was right, of course.

To my relief and surprise, Karin never mocked or chided fourteen-year-old me that time I was "excused" from the ring, or other times, when I did not place. She sighed a bit, and wished aloud she was eighteen years old again, not nineteen, which she'd turned on her last birthday. As a junior (under nineteen), she'd competed on our pony against other juniors riding ponies. Now a senior, she could not compete on our pony against other seniors, all of whom had "outgrown" their childhood ponies and now rode horses. The horse classes and pony classes were separate.

When my mother bought Coqeyn for us, we didn't even know he was a pony. We knew nothing about how to measure a horse or pony. We only knew "our horse" was heart-skip beautiful. Not that we would have been able to judge, but he did indeed have excellent "conformation," meaning his physical shape was optimally well put together. He was also one of those attractive ponies who looked like a small horse anyway – a quarter horse, most people commented. He had none of the often short-necked, short-strided cuteness of some ponies. Karin and I were both small, though Karin was taller than me. At five feet, five inches and 115 pounds or so, she did not look too big on Coqeyn, by any means. If we hadn't started showing, this whole subject of "being too old for a pony" would never have come up. But everyone around us at Southlands showed, and we were encouraged by our instructors to do so. In the end, we were just like everyone else and wanted to show off our lovely boy …

Karin had only had one year riding Coqeyn as a junior. That's when the troubles with her drug usage really started up again, as she dealt unsuccessfully with that heavy disappointment. She was a strong, serious competitor.

And you aren't.

That's not true! We'd only been riding for a year when

we started to go in schooling shows, and we only went in one formal, Equine Canada sanctioned show that I remember, and it was the 1973 Southlands Summer Show, held at Southlands Riding Club. I'm as keen a competitor as anyone else who's interested in what they're doing – and a lot keener than I used to be, because a learning disability and fear used to block my efforts.

That learning disability doesn't hold you back now, nor fear neither?

No to both, not the way they used to. I know more about my learning style now, how best to take in information, and I don't mind one bit saying, *Could you repeat that? I didn't understand.* Or, *Could I repeat doing that? I didn't do it right.* Nowadays I care a lot more about competition and achievement than I did as a teenager or even in my twenties and yet, sometimes, I care a lot less. Any day on the green side of the sod is a good one, and all that. For that matter, any day I can walk to the bathroom on my own – and sit down on the toilet and get up again – is a great one.

Suddenly I am smiling, thinking of a quotation Don likes to cite now and again: "Old age and treachery will beat youth and enthusiasm every time." So said the playwright David Mamet, Don tells me. I am not treacherous – only if you equate treachery with the mature person's more common ability to focus on a goal and work doggedly toward it.

That negative inner voice isn't quite through with me, though. *You won't say it, so I will: you have never won a red ribbon in a formal show. A first-place ribbon, that is. You're just stubborn enough to want to – at fifty-six improbable years of age. But even that driving desire may not be enough to get you back in the ring. You're going to blame that puffy back of yours, and all your ancient and unsuccessful experiences in a show ring, maybe even your poor long-dead sister, and somehow weasel out of this year's plan for competing in a provincially sanctioned show, aren't you? Oh, and by the way, I mean both shows. Remember, Helen's "schooling show" is a Scotia Series show, too, which means that it, like Sherry's bigger show, the Heritage Championships, is sanctioned by the Nova Scotia Equestrian Federation, or is a "formal show," as you keep erroneously thinking of it. All riders competing at these shows earn points in their classes, to work toward provincial standings. Of course, you won't have to worry about any of this, if you wiggle out of the commitments, will you?*

The silence stretches out. I've tried out a lot of retorts in my mind, but they sound, as my psyche intimated, pathetic and childish. And fearful.

As we said when I was a teenager, lips curled with disdain: *slack.*

The only response I can come up with is: *Bugger off.* I detest bullies, no matter where they live, in the public or private worlds we all move in, even the bully under my own skin. Against all odds and some would say common sense, I've come back to a sport and passion that has sustained and nourished me as much as my writing has, all my life. I've found two distinguished and kind coaches and I work hard with both of them. I have set attainable or at least enticing goals for myself as a rider, and am supported in these aims by *three* coaches, actually, counting my part-time coach, Sherry Clark. All this is not *slack.*

I do not know what will happen next. I never did have a crystal ball, only an unchanging love of horses that I couldn't sacrifice to a dysfunctional back and leg, or a sometimes timid heart. And no, I don't blame Karin one bit – I fiercely do not blame her for anything. *She did the best she damn well could, with the cards she was dealt in this life.* In the best, brightest way – are the nightmares and hauntings gone, finally? – she'll be in the bleachers if I compete this summer, and wahooing at highest cowgirl volume, no matter what happens. So will Zoë and Geoffrey, my older siblings, and Jessica and Fiona, our younger siblings, all robustly well and living across this country, be there in spirit to cheer me on. The same for my old friends I used to ride with, too.

As will my best friend, my beloved Don, be there in real time. Don, who shot to his feet and wahooed like a bronco-bustin' cowboy at the Calgary Stampede, the evening I won Gold at the Atlantic Journalism Awards in 2012. I adored him for that. I'd give anything to be able to do a genuine wahoo of my own, for any reason, any time this year or any year. I just can't. Those hollers from my youth got stuck way down in my gut, never to rise again, after I turned thirty or so. Much, much joy and contentment in the years that followed, but not that screaming, irreverent life vitality we had as teenagers and in our twenties. I can do a damn good shout for someone else, at a performance or a wedding reception, maybe, but I even think about making a cowgirl wahoo only for me, the way we used to, roaring and totally disregarding of anyone around us – and my throat closes over and I feel desolate.

Such a strange thing, that my mother, who was both conventional and deeply unconventional, but really couldn't stomach fusses in public, simply loved it when I and my girlfriends howled in unison, offering the loudest proof that: *We were alive! We were there to play by our own rules and play hard! We were hot sauce and champagne, daggers and sugar, curved lips and clenched fists, hungry, harum-scarum and on the run to life* – and we never apologized for any of it. Maybe it wasn't so strange that Mum loved our intensity and hunger. She'd carried that flag and run with it, too, marrying a man who proposed to her after three days, having four strong-willed, complicated children with him, all of whom she deeply loved, and filling her post-divorce life with everything she'd always loved: family, travel, study, reading, work, dogs, cats, and gratitude. *You never do your cowgirl hollers, anymore,* she'd say to me now and again. *I miss them.*

I do, too.

Of course, Karin, our friends, and I first started making those sounds at horse shows, when people we knew and liked did well in their "flat" or equitation classes (the rider's position and riding ability while mounted) or jumping over fences. We were loudest of all at the jump-offs, when everyone's hearts were pounding as the fences in the shortened course were raised higher and higher, and the competition had come down to two riders. Someone had to win – and someone had to lose. We didn't enjoy that last bit much, but fair was fair; someone's horse would jump that final round high and clear in the fastest time, making the win unequivocal.

Years later, my friends and I shouted to purple night skies, city lights intersecting with star-shine on our raised faces, our merry booted feet dancing on the roof of a friend's commercial fishing vessel moored down on "A Float," at the government wharf at False Creek across from downtown Vancouver. Sometimes all it took to warble was a Friday night after a long week of high school, or a Saturday afternoon, when we took the train to Squamish, north of Vancouver, and hiked to the summit of craggy mountaintops. Wolf-women in our chorus, armed not with slicing teeth or claws, but sketch pads and pencils. Howls over, we settled down on smooth stone outcrops or the dried grass lulls between, and contemplated the immense cap of surrounding skies and the silver-lipped Pacific Ocean. Silent then, save for the scratching of our charcoals. The heron-blue rain-coast world darkened to lavender and then it was time to slide our way down the steep, once-walked path we'd broken through on our ascent. We stumbled and tumbled and slid, sometimes shooting off sideways into dense bush, then pulled ourselves back onto the path, and started our haphazard journey downward all over again. The descents should have been harrowing – or at least harmful.

And yet I never remember a single bruise or cut, only a lot of giddy laughter, and a sodden, muddy backside to my jeans. *Sorry, Mum, teenage business.* At least I did my own laundry and some cooking at that point, didn't add endlessly to her burdens.

G'wan, holler again, you can do it. Regular me.

I don't know how. I forget. Worried me.

You don't forget the sound, and you don't forget how it feels – do you? Maybe, maybe not. I'm not sure.

I take that back. Yes. I remember how it feels. Truthful me.

Right, then, we'll work on all the rest. You need another strengthening memory, another memory-jewel.

* * *

Riding with someone else can be wonderful – or miserable. It depends on so much. Do the two horses get along? Is your rider-partner observant, does she/he practise good trail sense/good trail and ring manners? Does she talk too much – insist on silence?

Most of all, do you feel safe riding with them?

"Are you ready?"

Not Karin this time, and yet I am looking over to another pair of vivid blue eyes I love, these ones lit with excitement. I check the chin-strap on my helmet, shorten my reins a tad, adjust my feet in my stirrups, then nod to my childhood friend, Ann Gunderson, whom I've known since I was thirteen. We are in our thirties now.

"Ready."

Two cannonballs roar forward, in sync. Ann rides Kitty, her powerful grey quarter horse; I ride Boo the Brave, an Appaloosa hunter, rounded and strong. We stand in our stirrups, backs crouched low over our horses' necks, grinning jockeys, shoulder to shoulder, an arm's length or so apart on the wide forest path. Both horses have their ears flattened, their necks stretched out. The drumming of their hooves on the firm ground is a sound I could listen to each day – the past is behind us, this is the sound of the future, a giant's knuckles rapping on an oak door: let me in now, let me in now. That's the gallop-sound, a four-beat, scorching gait, with the horses averaging about twenty-five to thirty miles per hour (forty to forty-five km/h). Horses in the wild gallop for the joy of it, or when fleeing from predators. Horses in captivity, so few of them with fields to run in or owners who take the time to chase them around a ring, hardly ever get to gallop. They need it, they love it – and they are very, very good at making the world a blur.

Boo is one fast, competitive boy. And yet the younger Kitty is pulling ahead. She is also a quarter horse, the breed named such because they run the fastest quarter mile of any horse on earth. Now I am watching her haunches as she puts two horse-lengths between us. I don't mind – we're going quite fast enough, thank you – though Boo does. I can practically hear him grinding his long teeth, trying to catch up to that bad-ass grey mare. He's probably not too keen that I have a big chunk of his mane in my hands, either. Just a bit of extra gripping insurance, in the event that a recreational walker should unexpectedly step out from the brush, or an unattended dog should jump out. You'd have to be looking for trouble to walk in front of either of these horses, their hell-bent hooves sparking on the occasional embedded stone, but gotta be prepared all the same.

It's a long, pounding gallop, but finally, we're coming up to the bright yellow, heavy metal swing-gate at the end of the path; I don't know why park officials gated it here, but they have. End of gallop time. Good thing, as my heart is burning with exertion and even gasping hard, I just can't seem to get enough air into my lungs. And my legs are Jello. A determined Boo catches up to Kitty and then, eyes glowering, passes her. I would never tell him that, in fact, Kitty has slowed down to a canter, which is why still-galloping Boo passed her.

"Maggie! Slow down!"

Jesus, Ann is right. We're nearly at the gate. We'll gallop right into it if I don't haul him back. Oh, Jesus again, what's he doing?

Former open-jumper Boo is preparing to nail this real-life "fence," as if it were a single, towering jump in a Puissance jump-off. He may have had his ass kicked by his horse buddy at the gallop, but he'd show her a thing or two about jumping, so he would. His neck is still stretched out; I'd have to be Hercules to haul back using the two reins. We won't jump that gate, we'll crash it.

"Sit down! Pull your right rein – now!"

I sat, I pulled. Boo slowed, then stopped. We stayed on the right side of the fence.

"Maggie!" *says Ann, shaking her head, as she and Kitty jog toward Boo and me.*

"It wasn't my idea" *– pant, pant –* "I assure you." *I want to laugh, but can't. Takes too much air and I need every scrap I can get right now.* "Little bugger," *I manage, my sides heaving as hard as Boo's. My face is sweaty and hot, my legs feel shaky and useless.*

A cascade of laughter comes from my left. I look over to Ann, whose face is also flushed, the blue eyes one shade more sky than usual. "Weeellll," *she says, the word drawn out and suitcase-full of meaning.* "That gallop was –" *she's laughing harder now and I join in, can't help myself, because I think I know what's coming –*

She grabs a breath, starts again. "That was ... better than sex!"

Now there are two spirals of laughter rising to the treetops, mixed in with some earthy snorts and howls. "It was!" *I laugh back.* "Ceeeelestial!" *Weak in the knees, our stomach muscles warm and loose from laughing and tear-tracks drying on our cheeks, we start back down the trail, one of only two "breezeways" which are safe to gallop on in Pacific Spirit Regional Park. It is called, fittingly, "Imperial" ...*

The humans may be spent, but even as we slowly make our way back to Southlands, Boo the Brash is tangibly pleased with himself: Showed that Kitty-mare, so I did, he tells us with every head shake and spraying snort. Didn't take the fence, but didn't have to. Everyone knows I coulda done it, and more besides. Don't mess with Puissance-kid. Only stopped because she, yon rider-woman atop, asked me to. I am a gentleman, after all, as well as a jumper.

Kitty, on a loose rein, her neck stretched out low and deep, was also a gentlewoman: she never once reminded Boo who was the faster horse – at least over the quarter mile.

Every part of this long ride was fun, but it's good to be nearing our home barns. We are tired and thirsty. We'll go to our favourite watering hole, the clubhouse at McCleery's Golf Course, for a coffee, after we've untacked, groomed, and put the horses away. Our barns are a ways apart, so it will take some time to meet up again. That's fine. Days such as this are rare and shouldn't be hurried. It's nearly as much fun to rehash and dissect all that went on as it was to experience it the first time round. We'll be laughing about this day again and again, for years to come. Better than sex, indeed …

On or off a horse, I am blessed to have a friend like Ann. We are both blessed to have horses we trust, as we blaze or amble down the trails. Together, we can handle anything that comes at us during these trail rides of ours. Anything.

Little bugger.

Would Boo have actually taken that four-foot metal gate that mild spring day back in the 1980s? No, I am sure he wouldn't have. He was one of the safest, smartest horses I've ever ridden. It would have been supreme folly to jump an immovable metal gate that high. Boo was a canny old pro. I think he just had to make a point to Jaguar-footed Kitty, by passing her, and then he almost incidentally refocused on the barrier, and went for it. After all, he was indeed a fine jumper, though his owners, Letsa and Tash, knew his jumping days were behind him, and I was soon enough to be told by them not to jump him anymore, even small fences. Ann and I went on to have many safe and exhilarating rides together. We were always laughing by the end of the day.

Safe and exhilarating rides. Laughter. Striving, now, in my own time, in my own way. Thankful for these opportunities, but most of all, proving to myself I can make a tough plan and follow it through, no matter what the outcome. Trying counts, in and of itself. I'll give it my all.

Helping me, inspiring me ... memories of Fleet-Footed Kitty-Mare and her Ann, and Boo of the Bountiful Heart.

17
SLOWER THAN MOLASSES SPRING

I rode twice in March. The second time was the day I'd had a great lesson, and felt so awful physically and emotionally the next day. Our seventeenth anniversary also came and went that day and after my ride, Helen, Don, and I went to the Spitfire Pub in Windsor and had a tasty meal and a relaxed, chatty evening. We missed Neil, who was away on business. I guess my back was already starting to bother me and we did have the near-to-an-hour's drive home yet to go, so we didn't stay late. But it was a warm-hearted anniversary all the same, full of laughter and storytelling. It was nice to see Helen enjoying Don's amusing stories as much as I do. Cape Breton-raised Helen is a lively storyteller herself. I felt proud of my Don that night, seventy-seven years young and handsome, his wavy silver hair shining and hazel eyes as bright with intelligence and wit. I remember thinking, *Helen, this is what two decades with the right fellow looks like; I wish you and your fiancé Neil all the luck and love I've had with Don.*

March: The snow kept falling and the temperatures stayed cold. Adding to the fun was the regular appearance of freezing rain – a phenomenon that, growing up in Van-

190 – Marjorie Simmins

couver, I knew nothing about. The view out of our house windows would disappear under the blurry swathes of ice. Our cars got covered in a thick layer of it, too, taking Herculean efforts to de-ice and enter. That was after, of course, digging the vehicles out of the snow in the first place.

The world in general was a hero sandwich of layered cold bits. The landscape was pristine to look at, deadly to walk on. We wore pull-on corks on our boots, as the horses did, and prayed to every god and goddess not to fall anyway, and break a bone or otherwise harm ourselves. To all appearances I was an ancient one, mincing along over the ice, Don within arm's reach, and both of us with a hesitant dog on leash. We did not go far, some days only a block, other days less than that. Sometimes the ice was too cold for the dogs' feet, or the salt burned their pads as badly. We didn't use booties for them because they patently hate them, feeling clumsy and unsafe. One day we made it to the mailbox, a single block away – and it was buried under a snowbank. The letter to family I had in my pocket stayed there, until I made it out to the post office, days later. That neighbourhood mailbox stayed buried for weeks.

Eventually, there was so much snow that there was nowhere to put it. We would open our front door to a wall of white – and have to dig a path out for our dogs to urinate outside. Our tiny front yard rose in a vertical hill of snow, a good fifteen or twenty feet. The highest snow points were the edges of the yard; on the left, we chucked over the snow from our driveway up above; on the right, everyone chucked the snow from the central staircase that we and numerous other neighbours share. Everyone was exhausted; everyone felt desperate and at times shack-wacky and depressed.

Every night, we'd light a fire in our energy-efficient fireplace, which has a glass door and a new "insert" fitted into the old masonry, handily taking care of the heat loss of a traditional fireplace. As a part of the conversion, a small fan was also added. When the fan's on, it can heat the whole house, not just the den.

But you still need wood to make the initial fire. Retrieving wood from the wood shed attached to one side of our house became a daily, life-in-your-hands chore. Onto our boots went the slip-on corks again, to deal with the ten-foot walk on ice from the front porch to the door of the woodshed. Then the shed door wouldn't open, because it was deeply iced in place. Finally, Don had to saw a hatch through the shed door, which could not be opened for a further six weeks. Ducking in and out of the hatch with a basket-load of wood was tricky. It was trickier yet covering that same icy ten feet back to the house with your heavy burden.

There were good moments, though. All around the city, neighbours checked with neighbours that all was well. Our own street was remarkably convivial and even fun some days, with all hands out shovelling, bitching, and laughing. I didn't laugh when I fell badly on the staircase one day; instead, I bellowed and swore enough to make a sailor blush. If the air was blue, the pain was red and pervasive, spreading across the base of my back. Inside the house again, I discovered I'd also scraped my forearm on the staircase rail, that it was bruised and bleeding. I was so focused on my back, I hadn't even noticed I'd bashed my arm. It ached for days, as did my body.

The thirty-one days that comprised March were like a dozen winters in one month. I felt claustrophobic and antsy. Roseway Stables and the world of horses became nothing more than emails and Facebook messages between Helen and me. *Are you guys OK??!!* I'd type. *OMG,* Helen would type back, *at 7:00 a.m. the snow was three inches over my knees and I am tall!* Helen's and Neil's first winter together at their new property was demanding, and could have been demoralizing and dangerous, if not for the steady and generous help from neighbours. Mornings started at five o'clock or earlier, and one way or another, horses got fed and watered, the stables cleaned and swept, and human residents went to and returned from work in the city, and blessedly, no mishaps occurred. I, too, went about my business, guest-teaching a writing class for two days at a junior high in the suburbs, checking out some city venues where I might teach memoir writing classes, working on my own freelance article writing.

Messages from Caberfeidh Stables, Adrienne's and Scott's place in Cape Breton, were sobering. Adrienne always found a tiny ray of humour or gratitude when she posted on Facebook, but the photos of the thick ice and mounds of snow around their property made me gasp. It's not that far from their house to the barn. Nonetheless, I often felt spikes of worry thinking about their comings and goings. Adrienne had broken her wrist during another recent winter, slipping on ice on her way either to or from barn. The distance from Helen's house to her barn is further. No one at either barn complained, but you knew daily life was a challenge.

In truth, I have no clue how all the horse people I knew, along with all the others in the province, did what had to be done, caring for themselves, their families, and their barns full of horses, and for some, caring for resident feral and barn cats. I don't even know how city people looked after themselves, especially those with physical disabilities. Even for the able-bodied, winter was an exhausting, full-time job.

With no time off.

On March 10, I received an email from an old horse friend, Edie Sutter, from Vancouver. She included a joke – which prompted the biggest smile I'd had all that chilly month.

"Beware. I ride horses. This means I own a pitchfork. I have the strength to lift bales of hay and the guts to ride a half-tonne animal. You will not be a problem."

One month earlier, Edie had had a birthday, she told

me. *Her seventieth.* There's that number again.

"Yes, I am still riding," she wrote in response to my instant query. "Albeit on a small cob/quarter horse that is really my landlady's grandkids' pony. Daisy's so small I am embarrassed to use a mounting block, but I do. 'Wouldn't want to shift the saddle,' is my excuse, and I am sticking with it! I have good fun. She's my own mini-warmblood." She included a few photographs with the email.

She looked trim and happy and sat that wee cob a treat.

"Then there's a big warmblood mare, Lucille," continued Edie. She spliced in that keen sense of humour I remembered so fondly: "I can ride her, too, but it's just too much work to get all that bulk *moving.*" Oh, did my ineffective calves know about *that*, some days. "And last, there's always the mini-horse, Maybelle, to drive a cart around the neighbourhood, and stop traffic because of the cuteness factor. Here's a photo from Christmas Day last year. You can just see the halo she is sporting. Christmas Angel. So yes again, still horsey after all these years." There was another activity I'd always wanted to learn: how to drive a cart with a horse or pony; maybe I'd add that to the wishlist for coming years.

I obviously needed to raise that number up from seventy to ... eighty? Then I suddenly remembered Queen Elizabeth II – who, the newspaper told me recently, was turning eighty-nine on April 21 – and still went for weekly hacks on a variety of her favourite horses.

Right. Here was the new chant: *Just keep riding, as long as you possibly can.*

"One last thing I thought you'd want to know," wrote Edie. "I still see your old lease horse Boo's owners, Tash and Letsa Bantassios. I see Letsa a couple of times a month. She's a good friend. Her retirement home for horses has had anywhere from fourteen to twenty-one senior equines over the years. She still has quite the rep on the Flats as an excellent caregiver of horses, so everyone sends her their seniors or injured. And she has her own collection of riding horses, mostly given to her! A big warmblood gelding, a talented hunter, to name a couple."

Of course, sisters Tash and Letsa still ride, still care for horses as brilliantly as they always have. No surprise there, but it sure made my spirit sing! They're around my age, probably younger – seems everyone is – and among my most favourite and genuine Southlands people ever, over all those years of riding there. Well, ex-Southlands people, as many who stayed with the sport are now. It's just too expensive to ride at Southlands. Always was, and now it's off the charts. It's also cramped by new and ugly "Mac-mansions," most of the grassy fields of my youth gone or greatly reduced now. So many people I knew moved to the green suburbs of Langley, Abbotsford, even nearby Richmond, on the modest delta acreage still available there. Langley, that's where Edie lives in a small cottage on a horse farm, working as an occasional caretaker, and that's where Letsa's barn is, too, the one she took the spectacular Boo to in his retirement, many years ago now. Blessed is the horse who comes to Letsa's barn, whether sound or otherwise. Those who are "otherwise" are in fact doubly blessed. Old, lame horses rarely fare well in this world unless someone cares enough to make a difference, throughout a lifetime. Hats off to you, Tash and Letsa Bantassios.

The Bantassios sisters and Edie inspire you, don't they? says the voice of resolve I've been hoping to hear from, for some weeks now.

Yes, of course they do. If I can be half as active and animated as Edie at seventy, and half as admirable and caring as Letsa and Tash, who have looked after so many horses of their own and others, many old and lame, all these years – I'd be well pleased with myself.

But really, what's so admirable about looking after old horses? asks this same voice, determined to make me work for my spiritual progress. *You can just euthanize them when they are no longer sound or healthy.*

Now that makes me angry. Don't you get it – as Tash and Letsa so resoundingly do? Horses have infinite merit beyond their immediate use to you; as living, breathing co-adventurers in this world, they don't actually have to give you something tangible to keep their lives. Maybe you truly can't afford to keep a horse that will never be ridden again, can't find a non-riding home for them, and so you call the vet, arrange to say goodbye. I understand that. I also agree that some older horses are in too much pain to humanely keep alive. But many others are just like older animals of any sort, or older people. They love life, but can't gallop into it any more. They still deserve walks with friends, time for leisurely stops to enjoy the sun above, the world around. Their sentient, scented company is gift enough, and more.

I wish there was more time to just be with Winnie and the other horses in my life, and not just ride them. As someone who doesn't own a horse, however, the time I spend with Adrienne's and Helen's horses is more circumscribed than I'd like, and more narrowly goal-oriented. I rarely ride Winnie just for fun, no lesson. I've never ridden her bareback, either, or taken her for a meandering halter walk, her and I and a big old sky above. Then again, and unlike some of the horses of my youth, she doesn't need to go for halter walks to graze. She has many acres of fields in which to do that. The horses of Southlands have even fewer acres to graze in now.

I remember when Tash used to walk her old mustang gelding Rick, who couldn't be ridden any more, but could enjoy a stroll around the block, with leisurely stops along the way to graze. What I really remember is the joy she took in that time with him. Rain or shine, and most days, there went the two of them down 55th Avenue towards Carrington Avenue, blonde-haired Tash beaming, scuffing her wellingtons against the pebbled, muddy margin of the road, and Rick, her matching, small buckskin, with his black and blond mane and feathered legs, walking at her shoulder. The lead line that connected them was more of a gossamer strand held in the lightest of fairy hands. There was no "leading," really, only two friends out for an amble. You could see the slow-motion contentment from a full block away. They were both exactly where they wanted to be, in the best company either could imagine.

"... still horsey, after all these years," seventy-year-old Edie had written, her happiness as evident as the image I have in memory of Tash and Rick sharing an hour's walk together, every day they could.

And I'm bellyaching at age fifty-six? Sit up, woman, and *walk on*. Let all the horse people you did know, and still do know, encourage those steps.

Even those long gone.

18
SOUTHLANDS CHARACTERS –
BARNS, HORSES, AND HUMANS

Many of the horse barns of my youth, all in the low-lying area of Vancouver known as Southlands, or more casually "The Flats," no longer exist, or are barely recognizable in their reconfigurations. But in the early 1970s, apart from the one much-despised rental stable, Green Acres, which treated the horses badly, truly comparable to something out of a melodramatic Victorian novel, there were two obvious categories of barns in 99-acre, rurally-zoned Southlands, which improbably, is bordered by the Fraser River, two golf courses, and 49th Avenue, one of the busiest arteries of the city, leading west to the University of British Columbia. First, there were large or mid-sized schooling and boarding barns, each with their own resident trainer, and second, the small or mid-sized family barns, which might also take in a boarder or three to help with the costs, and were usually managed by a family matriarch. In terms of poshness, the barns ranged from lavish (high ceilings, wide cement aisleways, automatic water in each stall, big riding rings and well-made jumps, lunge rings, even on-site tack stores) to dismal (not really barns at all, just squat, cheaply built buildings with a row of narrow stalls, with no covered area for grooming or tacking up, and no riding rings), with lots of barns in the middle range.

We loved the stable names, many of which were fanciful: Camelot, Willows, Tamarack, Chesley, Casita, Wildwood Paddocks, Greyross, Shannon, The Flying B. Other barns were simply known by the families' names: the Mills' place, the Calders', the McCarthys', the Maynards', the Gretzingers'. Even the more modest barns usually had large, rain-forest verdant fields for turnout for the horses. It was long before Vancouver real estate became astronomically expensive, and fields could just be fields, green and welcoming to eyes and feet, satisfying horses' bellies.

A third category of barns was the rich-family enclave. There have always been staggeringly rich families at Southlands, among them the Belkins, of Belkorp Industries Inc., and the Taylors, as in mining, lumber, and oil magnate Austin Cotterall Taylor, who was also a racehorse enthusiast. His son, Austin Edward George, or simply Austin Taylor Jr., also loved horses. Early in the 1970s, he built a large barn to stable his and his children's horses, along with the Belkins' horses. Nicknamed "Austintatious," he is fondly remembered in Vancouver and Toronto for being a colourful character and, later in his life, for being a brilliant investment banker.

I never met him, but I do remember seeing 300-pound, six-foot-four Austin Taylor Jr. astride his own saddle horse, an equally immense draft-Appaloosa-cross, that stood at least 18 hands high. The mare had an impressive barrel, and oddly thin, dainty legs and hooves. He rode well, as did the whole family. I remember one slim, petite daughter in particular, Michelle, who was one of the gutsiest riders I've ever seen storm a jump-course. She and her dark, dappled-grey Connemara spent more time above ground than on it. *Fearless*, for all anyone could see. I was in awe of her drive, which seemed artless and was in fact a blend of natural athleticism and hard work. She was a fierce competitor, as were so many of the children and young people in Southlands in those days.

In stark contrast to the wealthy family barns were the ones that looked as though a strong West Coast sou'easterly would whisk them skyward into the Coast Mountains, as poor Dorothy and Toto were borne aloft to Oz. One of these properties, Foxtrot Stables, was owned by a woman of German origin, Mrs. Groening, a.k.a. "Granny," who never saw an older horse she didn't feel honour-bound to care for. Long before we understood that there truly is no "average age" for a horse to die, the phrasing more correctly being "average age range" that an owner can bring themselves to euthanize their horse, Karin and I would pass this property on Blenheim, which had large and monumentally muddy front fields and several rickety shelters, and stare goggle-eyed at the herd of ancients collected therein.

And I do guess they were collected, from people who could not bear to have their horses put down, but also felt they couldn't afford to keep a horse who couldn't be ridden, due to the complications of old age or permanent or recurring unsoundness. I don't know for sure, but I think Mrs. Groening, like my marshmallow-hearted old friends Tash and Letsa, believed horses had great value beyond what they gave as mounts, or as literal vehicles for competition. And Mrs. Groening, Letsa, and Tash would not be the only ones to believe that horses have incalculable worth as fellow creatures in the world, that by their peaceful presences on their properties, the horses give back merely by breathing. While the frail ones make the landscape more odd than beautiful, they always, always, make it more compelling.

Karin and I were not the only ones who stopped to watch and wonder. The sheer scope of the horses' histories – some were forty years old and older, we were told by those in the know – was enough to get our imaginations working. As for their appearance, the horses could have been on display in a Ripley's Believe It or Not museum.

It is one thing to see a singular old horse in a field; unremarkable, that is, even sweet and nostalgic, in the way of an autumn bonfire burning low, winter winds soon to come. It is quite another to see a herd of them, each one seemingly vying for the title of Oldest Horse Ever. Even their hooves were bizarre – they had grown so grotesquely long that the customary farrier-rounded edge had sharpened, the point curling up like an elf's shoe. There were so many horses and ponies. It must have been too expensive for Granny to provide hoof care for all of them, all the time. That is the kindest, most probable spin I can put on this memory. Perhaps, in current-day lingo, she would be called an animal hoarder ...

I was never tempted to be a veterinarian, but if I had been, the interest may have been piqued in those earliest days at Southlands, before I'd even started riding, when we'd cycle by Granny's and regard this strangest-of-the-strange assembly. I knew they were real, that their elderly hearts still thudded, however irregularly, and yet they presented more as inanimate textbooks of the older equine, walking photographs of horses at great ages, sure to take their last breath as you watched.

Presumably well-fed, their ribs and backbones were still alarmingly visible, as were their hip bones. Their backs seemed longer than usual, forming peculiar sideways "s"es, with the middle bit sagging low. These are called swaybacks, we learned later, a condition that happens as soft-tissue attachments slacken and muscle tone is lost. Withers, too, the outcrop of bone at the base of a horse's neck, rose starkly, without the surrounding fat and muscle of the young horse. And nary a patch of gloss to their coats. Instead, these were mostly soft and clumpy, or sparse and harsh. Manes and tails were not much brighter. Eyes, too, were sunken in their sockets, dull.

As for movement, the animals did not walk as much as lose balance one way, and then the other. The movement was not even reliably forward or lateral, but more an occasional, stationary weight-shift. Sometimes their heads sank low to eat hay, but mostly they did not move at all. Staring was their primary activity.

It was a beautiful place to stare, and live out last days. The fresh air from the North Shore Mountains mingled with estuary salt from the close-by confluence of the Pacific Ocean and Fraser River waters. Other scents on the air included wild roses, sweet pea, flowering blackberry bushes, cottonwood trees, and the bright yellow "broom" that grew along the river paths. The sun shone or the skies dripped. Cars and bicycles passed and radios in surrounding barns played cheerful pop music. I can't remember if there was an actual barn on Granny's property, or only the three-sided shelters, sometimes called "loafing sheds," where the horses can get out of the rain, or take shade on a hot day. If there was a main barn, then at some point the horses would be gathered up and returned to their stalls, I suppose, but for most of the daytime hours they simply took their stoic place in the world. Their dignity was palpable, even from a distance.

The Southlands of the late 1960s and '70s was ruled primarily by the Thoroughbred hunter, some quarter horses, Paints, Appaloosas and Anglo-Arabs, and swarms of stunningly talented show ponies, mostly of United Kingdom breed-origin (Welsh, Connemara, Exmoor, Shetland, etc.). Coqeyn, of Welsh and Arabian origin, was at the far end of the BRP (British Riding Pony) trend. This category began in Britain in the 1920s, when horse shows first offered pony classes. British show-pony breeders crossed native breeds with Arabians or small Thoroughbreds, resulting in exquisite ponies that often resembled small horses. Coqeyn, with his strong and compact build, looked less miniature Thoroughbred and more miniature quarter horse. Warmbloods had yet to claim the stage, as they have so thoroughly in many horse communities, though interest in these breeds – Hanoverians, Trekehaners, Westphalians, to name but three of many – was growing.

"Warmbloods" were created when the "cold-blooded" or heavy, even-tempered war horses of Europe were crossbred with the smaller, fleeter "hot-blooded" horses of Arabia. "Cart horses," an old horse friend of mine from Vancouver used to snort, "warmbloods are really nothing more than European cart horses." She was not a fan, but countless horse people around the world are, and the warmbloods themselves have had the last laugh, by becoming so ubiquitous. Tall, big-boned, and often brilliant at complex disciplines such as dressage, warmbloods command sizable dollars nowadays – and you'll pay extra for any cart.

In the Southlands of my childhood, hunter-jumper was the discipline of the day, with fewer people riding dressage ("horse ballet," as non-riders sometimes call it) and a very few riding Western. The horse and pony names were delicious. Among the horses: Soroya, Woodwait (Woody), Dudley Do-Right, Little Jon, Chinook, Thistledown, Quasiak, Popeye, Mimic, Ratzo, and Splash. Among the ponies were amiable Stardust and dainty Dimity, and three for which I remember their full registered names: Cricket's Little Tomboy, Cricket's Early Dawn, Cricket's Mountain Rebel. These were three stunning, light-dapple or charcoal-grey Connemaras, called "Cricket ponies," as they were all sired by a local stud of that name. Fine-boned but muscular, they all jumped far above their "weight-class." All were well under 14 hands, as I remember them. Powerhouses, as were their fearless, diminutive riders.

Another flashy grey pony – I was riding my own pony then, and more aware of them than the horses – was the half-Arab/Welsh gelding Turls Hill Reno, nicknamed Popcorn. The same breeding as our pony, Coqeyn, though a tad smaller, but just as gifted in all the disciplines. Popcorn was tidy and cute as a raccoon washing his supper, both on the flat and over fences. He and his owner, Susan Coghlan, were consistently "in the ribbons," riding both English and Western. In 2006, the last year I had word of him from Susan, Popcorn was retired to the country, healthy and happy at age *forty-two*. Not all horses and ponies look skinny and pathetic when they live to a great age. Health-luck and genes go a long way, as it does for all of us. I bet this pony looked as attractive as ever.

Speaking of – Pepper Pot was a tiny Shetland pony with a large appetite for mischief; I don't know how many times I saw his wee riders on the ground, and Pepper Pot flying down the track at Southlands Riding Club, soon to be flying down the road to his home, several blocks away. At least the riders didn't have far to fall. Shaggy, dun-coloured Pepper Pot was an escapee from one of English cartoonist Norman Thelwell's books, where all the riders' legs stick out horizontally and their backsides are perpetually airborne.

I don't forget Pistol Pete, either, only 12 or so hands high, a chestnut and white pinto, and one of those head-turning "horse ponies." His equally tiny owner asked me to "give him a good gallop, so he stops bucking." Instead, the small pinto neatly bucked me off at a hand-gallop, and did victory laps around the ring, electrically pleased to be a solo operator again. (I remember missing a tall metal garbage can by only a few feet. Whatever was it doing placed in the ring?)

A less bruised memory is connected to Snuffy, a dear red roan schooling pony who was built low and wide, and tended to waddle a bit at the trot. If Humpty-Dumpty were a pony, that would have been Snuffy. But he wouldn't have fallen off any wall, especially not with a rider on. He was the steadiest, safest of schooling ponies. The first time I ever rode with Western tack was on Snuffy. I couldn't believe how comfortable the saddle was, or his ultra-slow, steady jog, which came on with the smallest of "clucks" and didn't stop till the sun went down, as far as I could tell.

Karin and I weren't the only sister team to share a horse. Rita Sapanon and her younger sibling Lisa shared Beya, I believe it was spelled, a flashy, big-boned pony (barely), who bombed around a hunter course as though his hooves were on fire. Rita and Lisa, like Karin and me, looked physically similar, but they were much fairer overall. (Their surname indicates a Finnish, or Scandinavian background.) The two young women rode well and placed consistently. Both sisters were blonde, attractive, and fun, and obviously good friends. They were devoted to Beya. I can't help wondering if they kept on riding, either together or separately. I hope they're still close; I hope they're still riding.

In my early years at Southlands, there was also, improbably, another "Marjorie S." Her surname was Smith, and we even went to the same high school. This talented junior, a year or two younger than me as I recall, rode a genius of a chestnut hunter-jumper pony named Paddy's Surprise. Their consistency in the winner's circle was daunting. They were a crackerjack team.

Schooling horses and ponies – the scale of giving, animal to human, is so uneven. Such kind and generous animals. It is almost as though they know they have a mission in life, connected to the humans who ride them. The mission is to take excellent care of you, the good, bad, or indifferent rider, and build up your confidence so that you think you can do anything.

"You're going to jump another small course today, including the coop," said David Woodley, the new co-owner, along with his wife Carol, of the newly renamed Casita Stables. The stable had been called Chesley, and was owned by the Ledingham family – husband and wife, two daughters, and a son, attractive, sunny-natured people all – and it was Joan Ledingham who had invited Karin and me to the barn as boarders in the fall of 1972.

Now it was the late spring of 1973. And the coop, a trian-

gular wooden jump painted flat brown, was just over three feet high. To me, it may as well have been thirteen feet. I'd only ever jumped about two and a half feet, and that seemed plenty high enough. Also, unlike poles, which are set in cups and fastened to "standards," or tall wooden braces, the coop wouldn't "give" or fall down if you knocked against it. This was not a jump to make mistakes on.

I'd also had a difficult lesson on Coqeyn the week before – which further tamped down my confidence. Coqeyn had oodles of talent over fences, but he was still a young, green pony and did things in his own time and way. With an experienced rider aboard, he was Pegasus over a jump-course. With his green riders aboard, who often "dropped" him or lost contact via the bridle and seat before the jump (this is also sometimes called "abandoning" the horse), Coqeyn often "refused" the jump. Essentially, Coqeyn did not feel properly guided, may even have felt frightened. Thus he would either slide to a stop or, worse yet, "deke out" or run to one side of the jump. A rider should not give a release or rise out of the saddle until the horse's feet are leaving the ground, we were told by David and other instructors. And yet Coqeyn was agile enough to deke out after his forelegs left the ground, and had done this to me several times during my last lesson with David. I had stayed on with great difficulty – a limp spaghetti noodle all over his neck – and had fallen off when he'd done this other times.

The solution for Karin and me was to drive Coqeyn with full-on leg and unwavering will, waiting until the very last second before throwing our weight over his neck. This could lead to being "left behind" – horse going forward, rider going backward – which didn't necessarily also mean an unseating. Form aside, the greater objective was to get horse and rider over the fence.

With a lump of stone in my gut, I turned toward Coqeyn's stall to start grooming and tacking up for my lesson.

"No," said David firmly. "I want you to ride Musicman."

Musicman? His own retired open jumper, now used occasionally as a schooling horse?

"He's just what you need right now." As he spoke, he pointed to the ring, where a talented young student had just finished a flat lesson on Musicman. She was still aboard, chatting with another young friend on her own horse. As though feeling our gaze, she waved towards us, then hopped off the big bay gelding, who I remember as a Thoroughbred. She stood at his shoulder, reins in hand.

"Get your helmet, let's go," said David.

I'd always thought dark-haired, slim David was so well-suited to dark-coated, slim Musicman, and loved the times I'd seen him ride, especially over fences. They were a quiet, frugal team, not a stride or movement wasted. But they didn't ride together often. David had multiple sclerosis, had had it for some years. Fortunately, at the moment, he was in a remission, his wife Carol had told us. Nonetheless, David didn't ride much. He might have been too busy as a family man, co-running the barn, and instructing, or perhaps, after years of competing, he wasn't that keen any more. It's also possible he just wasn't up for it physically, remission or not. I don't know. I do know it was very generous to allow me, such a new rider, to ride his cherished old horse. And Musicman was fairly old at that point – at least twenty, perhaps even twenty-five.

Hands cupped low to take my bent knee, David gave me a brisk leg up, which nearly raised me too high to ascend the saddle without a thump. One giddy second airborne, and I was astride the saddle, left foot in the stirrup, right foot still wiggling to find its iron. My hands, thank goodness, instantly held the two braided reins firmly, at much the right length. Score a point for that, I told my jiggedy-jaggedy heart.

"Start your warm-up," David smiled. *"Right rein."*

I started our ride going to the right, then, loving the good-natured gelding's animated working trot. I felt that I was working well, too – heels down, hands steady, eyes up, ready for whatever came next.

"Pick up your canter, please," asked David. I did, whispering my left heel against the horse's side, and thrilled with

the instant strike-off from the walk. Trying not to grin, I was nonetheless captivated by Musicman's soft, cat-paws canter – bah-bah-dump, bah-bah-dump, bah-bah-dump.

Next, we did some figure-eights around the ring, changing canter leads (the leading leg) as we loped through the centre. They weren't "flying changes" – executed with no stride between – as that was too advanced a maneuver for me, but near enough, as Musicman knew exactly what was needed. I soon discovered that the less I did to direct the horse, the better we both did. All I really had to do was think what was needed, and Musicman did it. For myself, I tried not to flick my eyes left or right, at the lines of jumps we passed, or at the fat immovable coop, set over by itself on the right side of the ring.

"How're you doing?"

I nodded, attempted a smile, once again concentrating on maintaining an energetic canter. I could do that, at least, I hoped. As for the jumps ... "Fine," I squeaked, all my air used up.

"Start with the cross-pole, then onto the combination – okay?"

One, two, three jumps – the job was done.

"Nice!"

Nice didn't begin to cover it. Heaven, more like.

"Don't stop. Circle round, do it again."

More heaven.

"You're a bit tight on his face – no need. Longer rein. Let him do his job. He's very good at it."

I could feel my instructor's smile from twenty feet away; no one knew better how well this horse did his job, and he had the ribbons and trophies to prove it. I loosened my reins a touch, felt Musicman shake his face into the extra room. His stride had stayed cat-paw smooth.

"Ready for the coop?"

Now or never. Never was fine. "Yes."

One-two-one-two-one-two. I counted the strides, as we had been taught to do. Then I felt a surge of gasoline under the pedal as Musicman focused in on the coop. Finally, a jump worth his time, he might have thought. He bounded over it.

Musicman wasn't the only one who was excited. A sparrow-line of young women, including Karin, all sitting on the fence nearest the barn, set up a warbling array of whoops and hollers. "You did it! Yehaw! Looked great! Do it again!"

I looked over at David. He nodded. Around the ring we came once more, and up we Porsche-powered again. This time, I felt as supple as Musicman did. Instead of just bending my back over the jump, I gave through the waist, which in turn gave the horse every bit of locomotion and forward balance he deserved, and made for a more put-together landing. It wasn't a big challenge for an old professional horse – but it was a big accomplishment for an inexperienced rider of fourteen.

No, it was more than that. It was chocolate cake and a big, brass band, the gifts of a Musicman, all on an ordinary Wednesday afternoon.

* * *

The Southlands of long ago is an earth-sphere's quantity of memories for me. I was shy enough to be heartily in awe of the many instructors and, in the way of the young and impressionable, can remember nearly all their names, and peccadilloes. Most were effective communicators and kind human beings, both to their student charges and to the horses they trained. Others cared little for the less well-heeled of their students, who weren't on the "A Circuit" and wouldn't go on to show full-time and bring ribbons home to their "show barn," and mostly regarded horses as commodities to further their ambitions. Some took horses out behind the fancier of the barns to the "rapping row," and thought nothing of bashing a wooden pole against a young horse's legs as he jumped, to teach him to "tuck" his knees or lift his hind legs higher, which ultimately meant less chance of a downed pole in competition.

"The Dirties" of the horse world exist at all levels of riding, and in every discipline, in myriad form, around the world: drugs, abuse of all sorts, neglect, outright cruelty, lack of protocols for end of life care, unregulated and unsupervised slaughterhouses, etc. Each rider of conscience does the best they can to behave thoughtfully and well within their own spheres, and if they are able, beyond these.

I have had the great good fortune to board and lease at excellent, horse-first barns over my many years of riding. Even though Ryan had occasional difficult times, that big, sensitive gelding had people in his life who cared about him, and his day-to-day barn life was excellent. No one even talked about people being "depressed" in those days, let alone horses, though any experienced horse person knew the difference between a mentally healthy horse and the opposite of this. The hard-ridden rental horses at Green Acres fared worse, in all ways.

In fairness, I must say that even at that barn, there were a few kind and capable young women working with the horses. I remember two charmers in particular, who "jumped ship" to our barn, just across the road, bringing their own horses with them. From their experiences of galloping many different horses up the trails several times a day, small hurricanes couldn't unseat them. Grace was somewhat lacking, but steady lessons saw big gains there, too. There was a lot to admire about these two girls who knew horses at their worst and best, loved them equally, and for themselves, did all they could to improve and progress as riders. Unsurpisingly, they knew how to laugh at life's turns and twists, too.

When I came back to riding in my twenties, in the early 1980s, I knew I should start with some lessons again, before I even thought about leasing a horse. Some of the instructors I first knew were still teaching at Southlands, but many had moved or perhaps gone on to other endeavours.

With an adult's broader perspective, I realized how tough being an instructor could be – essentially, being responsible for another human being's safety and well-being, let alone their steady progress at a sport, or lack thereof – though I still had my favourites such as David Woodley from my early years, and still thought ridicule was not an effective teaching method.

Once again and lucky me, the new instructors I "took" from ("Who are you taking from?" we used to ask, when we first started riding in the '70s) were a bright and hardworking bunch, and expected their students to be the same. It was a good kind of pressure. By default, I returned to hunter-jumper instruction first. As for the barn, the name that comes to mind is Canterbury Stables, long gone now, from that southeast corner at 51st Avenue and Balaclava Street. I rode all sorts of different horses, my first big-boned warmbloods, among them, which I found exciting, if a bit daunting. I even found myself back at Southlands Riding Club as a visitor, for lessons, jumping the extensive hunt course there.

Yolanda Blommers was my instructor at the time. I learned a lot from her and enjoyed her drive and enthusiasm. As I remember it, Yolanda was a big fan of practising the "two-point" or "forward position," called such because the rider has only two points of contact with the horse: their two legs against the horse's sides. There are two basic seats for a hunter rider, full seat and half-seat. In the "full" or "three-point seat," you have contact with your seat in the saddle, on the horse's back, along with your two legs against their sides. It's the seat you use in rail or "flat," non-jumping work. In the half-seat, which you need to learn for jumping, you rise out of the saddle and find a balance that's a little more forward. This position allows you to get your balance up and over your lower leg and over the horse's centre of gravity in his shoulder and wither. This all sounds lofty, when in fact the only thing that is aloft is your butt, and the only thing you really want to hear is, "You can stop now," and not, as Yolanda often cheerfully intoned, "One more time around, everyone."

Two-point is practised at all the gaits, but most often at the trot and canter. It is murder on the stomach and thigh muscles – if you have them. If not, then double murder. Takes a toll on the ankles, too, as you jam down a lot of "weight" into your heel when you're in the standing position. Groans aside, I was grateful to Yolanda for strengthening my seat, and getting me capable enough again to jump good-sized jumps. From the get-go, she had far more faith in me than I had in myself, which eventually, and as she intended, did bolster my self-confidence.

As with any other small community, The Flats had its residents or regulars who were notable for their bold or eccentric personalities, and manifold skills.

Everyone knew Mrs. Mills. I knew her daughter Georgann, first, from elementary school; I was older by a year, but even still, we talked to one another now and again. In my high school years, I came to know the Mills' son, too, a brilliant, gentle, and soft-spoken man, who, tragically, would die young from disease. I believe Richie was a couple of years older than I was. The Mills family lived on Blenheim and 53rd Avenue; their property was right beside the Calders' barn, the very first barn at which we stabled Coqeyn. I remember being so excited to tell Georgann at school that I was about to enter into the Southlands horse world as a horse owner. She was and is a brilliant rider and continues to have an exciting life involving horses. Her success as a competitor, and now also as an instructor and trainer, is due to hard work, inborn natural talent – and the cyclonic force of nature that was her mother.

Just as with everyone else's mother in the '60s and '70s, Mrs. Mills did not have a first name. She did, of course, and it was Sue, but I don't think I even thought of her that way until I was well into my thirties (and even then I'd think

Sue Mills – and still feel I was being disrespectful). The fact that she was British-born and very correct about how things should be done – or so it seemed to young Canadian me – also made me think of her only as Mrs. Mills. She was the brisk and capable sort of individual you respected on sight.

And rightly so. The Mills' property had a modest home on its west side, a small ring, and close by, an L-shaped shed-row barn filled with horses and ponies for the family, with some for hire, as lesson horses. Mrs. Mills taught hundreds of children to ride. She excelled at every sort of riding herself and even "rode to the hunt" in the Fraser Valley, in the autumn. Legend had it she once took a bad fall one year. She apparently remounted her horse and finished the hunt – with a broken collarbone. Sources further reported that post-hunt and -hospital, she had no idea what the fuss was all about. It had been a lovely day at the hunt, hadn't it? Furthermore, the horse was fine, wasn't he?

Mrs. Mills also rode side-saddle. She had all the proper tack, and all the proper dress. Slack-jawed with admiration and incomprehension, I would watch her ride. How could she possibly stay on her horse with her two legs set on one side of the saddle, the right leg tucked neatly into a second, lower pommel, the left leg snugged under this, that foot set in a stirrup? She rode with a "cane," or whip of sorts in her right hand, the artificial aid replacing the aids for gait changes that a right leg would ordinarily give the horse.

She looked upright and elegant, a Victorian gentle-woman, cantering in from an earlier epoch. I never saw her jump in her side-saddle, but I have no doubt she could and did. Mrs. Mills did everything well, especially when it came to the equine life. As far as I can gauge, "I can't" was not in her vocabulary. Indomitable was.

I haven't told my beleaguered spouse yet – but yes, I do aim to ride side-saddle sometime in coming years. Perhaps not on a hunt, though, as courageous British women first came to do, centuries ago ...

A few – a very few – riders at Southlands in the 1960s, '70s, '80s, and '90s rode Western exclusively. With my current focus on Western riding, it is informative and fun for me to look back on those riders. And surprising.

I can only blame my ignorance on my youth, and the fact that Karin and I, and possibly a good portion of Southlands' younger English-riding populace, had no clue we had a Western superstar in our midst. Teenage me was only just observant enough to note that Western-clad David Esworthy seemed to judge a lot of shows. I also loved his own riding style, which was both crisp and soft. I couldn't quite figure out how that worked. One look at him jogging or loping his bay quarter horse (as memory suggests the colour was) around the track at Southlands, the two creatures forming a single, tall shadow, and I'd somehow want to pull back my shoulders just as I walked around the barn, doing chores. At the very least, looking at his straw hat, well-fitted jeans, and immaculate shirts with pearl snap-buttons, I'd feel the urge, before I rode myself, to redo my straggly ponytail, perhaps even tuck in my T-shirt.

What's that expression? Yes, a "natty dresser."

And, it turns out, a distinguished man. The late David Esworthy (1929-2015) had a fifty-year career "in horses." He has been called "one of the most influential individuals in Canadian equestrian history" by Jason Beck, Curator of the B.C. Sports Hall of Fame, of which he became an inductee in 2012. Esworthy was recognized for his successes as a rider, judge, horse-show organizer and chair, and industry advisor. He helped to organize equestrian events for the 1976 and 1984 Olympic Games, and of more durable effect, helped to write a constitution and bylaws for the rebirthed Canadian Equestrian Federation, now known as Equine Canada. Over a lifetime, he supported every aspect of the equestrian life, both as an individual, and as a board member or president of numerous equestrian organizations.

David Esworthy – I think of him with both names, always – was also the president of Southlands Riding Club from 1969 to 1972. That latter year was my first as a horse owner at Southlands. He rode with his family, wife Patricia, and son Phil, fine equestrians both, and mentored countless young riders, locally, nationally, and internationally. Beyond horses, he was a successful Vancouver businessman.

A splendid, "worthy" life. I sincerely hope he rode right up to his passing, at age eighty-six.

It was always a pleasure to see David Esworthy ride. There were other Western riders at Southlands who also made you happy to see in the saddle. As though they were born to it. Owned it, in the most natural and relaxed way.

Palmer Rutledge was born in 1903 and died in 2005, at a prodigious 102 years old. I knew him by sight when I started riding at Southlands as a horse owner at twelve years old; he and his family had a home and small barn on one of the prettier lanes in the area, Prestwick Avenue. I saw him riding regularly then, and throughout my twenties and thirties, when I was leasing horses at Southlands. I am sure I would have said, *Hello, lovely day/beautiful morning/great summer we're having, isn't it?* many times to him over the years, as he would have said, in one ever-courteous form or another, to me, and everyone else he passed. He was the essence of geniality. I like to think he even doffed his Western hat to me now and again, but I couldn't swear to that memory.

When I recall Mr. Rutledge – as with Mrs. Mills, I can think of him no other way – I think of smiles. The man was always smiling. He was always riding, too; I don't actually remember seeing him anywhere but on his horse. He owned several horses, I believe, but seemed to favour a rangy, "leopard" or spotted Appaloosa, on which he used a Western saddle and bridle.

I didn't see Western tack very much all those years riding at Southlands, and always found it interesting. The saddles seemed so big – beyond the saddle seat itself was the surrounding leather "skirt," which made the entire apparatus seem so rectangular and long – and the bridles were unusual to my eye, too. Some had only a one-earpiece headstall, a rakish look for sure, one ear moving rather nakedly, unencumbered by leather, instead of a regular headstall with a browband. Some bridles had no nosebands, either. There were also bosal bridles, a type of noseband, always made of braided rawhide, used on the classic hackamore of the *vaquero* (Spanish-speaking cowboy) tradition. A bosal has no bit, and the cowboy "neck-reins" – changes the direction of the horse – whispering the reins against the horse's neck, to the left or right. Neck-reining moves the horse laterally or in a circle. Other aids are used to execute "spins" (a turn on one spot on the haunches) or "roll-backs" (a rapid turn, followed immediately by a gallop in the other direction). Both these maneuvers are used in Western reining classes, along with the ever-fun "sliding stop" (executed from a full gallop).

Yet other Western bridles and saddles had "bling" detailing, either real sterling silver or shining silver metal of some other sort. Unaccountably, those shiny bits set my teenage heart aflutter. I must have had a magpie-draw to bling in every manifestation, even then. Diamonds, sequins, silver, gold, gems, and brilliants of every sort, they always catch my eye. Good thing, as Western show clothing and tack shimmers with bling.

But of all the things that sometimes made me stare unashamedly at Mr. Rutledge's small, retreating form on horseback, sometimes turning around in the saddle on my own horse to do so, were his chaps. The word "chaps" is a short-form of *chaperejos* or *chaparreras,* Mexican Spanish words for the garment, derived earlier from the Spanish *chaparro,* which includes among its meanings a low-growing thicket, difficult to ride through without damaging clothing. I still don't know the proper name for the chaps he wore, but they looked voluminous and old-fashioned. All the gear, tack, and clothing he wore looked authentic. Reviewing photographs of chaps now, I think he may have been wearing batwing chaps, which are cut wide with a flair at the bottom. Commonly made of smooth leather, they have only a few fasteners around the thigh, which permits great freedom of movement for the lower leg. The open design also allows for more air circulation, a boon in summer.

Memory is a tricky business: it would be fun to tell you he wore chaps that had long cattle hair on them – you know, like the cartoon cowboys you see – but there was nothing cartoonish about this dignified and pleasant man, and I am certain I am just imagining things. I can tell you with authority that as a cowboy and Western rider, Mr. Rutledge was The Real Thing. He was also a deeply respected and enjoyed member of the various communities within which he lived, worked, and rode.

I later learned that Mr. Rutledge was born in Goderich, Ontario, moved with his family of origin to Medicine Hat, Alberta, and then grew up in Nelson, British Columbia. (Some years ago, I was surprised to find out that my husband's late, cherished Aunt Ethel Wait, née Cameron, knew him from the Nelson days, where she brought up her own family. Unsurprisingly, she told me she had regard for him and his family. I love "small world" connections such as these.)

Mr. Rutledge was a "bike man," starting and running his own motorcycle dealership, supplying and servicing these for Kootenay bike enthusiasts. Then with his family of making, he moved to the Southlands area of Vancouver in 1944. He would have been forty-one then, and around seventy when I first saw him in the early 1970s. He was an early member of Southlands Riding Club, which was founded in 1943, and rode, apparently, nearly all his life, both on his own horses along the river trails near Southlands and working as a back-country guide around Penticton for thirty-five years – the latter until he was eighty-two. *Well, of course,* I can easily imagine him saying, *ride for as long as you can. Why wouldn't you?*

Mr. Rutledge, I aim to. I may even buy myself a bling-covered saddle one of these years, perhaps even Western chaps ...

Last, I want to tip my memory-hat to Janice Devitt, one of only two Western riders at the Ledingham's barn, Chesley Stables, who rode a big, muscled gelding called Sonny, a yellow-hued dun, complete with a brown-black mane and tail, and the brown "dorsal stripe" down his back. Janice, too, was the real thing. At that entirely "English barn," full of skinny Thoroughbred hunters and skinnier young women, strong, not-skinny Janice unapologetically rode Western and boy/girl, did she ride. In memory's eye, I see Sonny's curiously upright movements and only just-suppressed need to gallop at every opportunity. Tall, beaming Janice rode him straight-backed and proud, her joy in his vast life-energy a perfect match for her own. Her hands were soft on the reins, and her will was unrelenting. Sonny may have been allowed to gallop on straight stretches up the river trails, but in the ring, he accepted his schooling sweet as a kitten. That still didn't prevent him from launching into one gallop stride under Janice before he settled into his easy lope. I almost wonder if it wasn't a game they played – *one gallop stride, banana boy, now you listen.*

Of course, there were other accomplished Western riders at Southlands during the two extended riding periods I enjoyed there, but I moved in the "English" circles and just didn't notice or meet riders doing something different. Then, as now, there can be tension – and snobbery – between the two disciplines. *Oh, you're transitioning from English to Western?* said a young clerk in a tack store to me just last week. *I couldn't ride Western. I would find it so boring.* I just smiled, paid for the card I bought, and left the store. *Boring?* Watch an Ultimate Trail class sometime, I thought, as I drove away. Those classes take guts, smarts, and great teamwork between horse and rider. Or watch champion reiners, and the ultra-sensitive bond those horses have with their riders. (While there are similarities between reining and Western dressage, the latter does not use spins, sliding stops, or run down movements as part of the discipline's training or tests.) Watch those smokin'-hot (in every way) barrel-racing cowgirls, or consider the compelling grace of Western dressage riders. Then there's Showmanship (every step, movement, and stance counts, for horse and rider, and the patterns can be complicated), Horsemanship (equitation, or having a graceful riding seat) and Western Pleasure (a comfy pleasure to ride, and a perfect pleasure to watch). Sheesh – *boring*?

There were many more inspiring and sometimes outrageous "characters" I knew over the years at Southlands, both horse and human. Southlands' tales from the past could easily take over this story, and we'd all go for a lively ride. Current-day Southlands is just as fascinating, its residents more committed than ever to creating a vital future for this enchanting, in-the-city horse community. It remains one of my favourite places on earth. I even know old horse friends who plan to have their ashes scattered "up the bridle path," alongside the Fraser River. Many years from now, I do hope!

Right now, it's April 2015, and I have news to share.

19

GOOD NEWS AND GOOD LUCK

I won the bursary! The good news arrived via email on April 28 that I had won the Long-Term Equestrian Development Bursary, in the amount of $250. I shook my head in surprise and happiness. In my whole life, the only things I'd ever won were a "Texas mickey" of rye (three litres, or 101 ounces; I detest rye), and a gorgeously illustrated book, *The Atlantic Coast, A Natural History*, by Nova Scotia writer Harry Thurston, which was a win indeed. With these funds then, from the Nova Scotia Equestrian Federation, I registered for two of four days of "the Tommy Clinic," which is what we had started calling the Tommy McDowell Clinic, scheduled for July 4 through 7, at the Windsor Exhibition Grounds. Two full days would cost $250, and was quite long enough for me and my still-cranky back to be in a saddle.

Helen and I would attend on the weekend, July 4 and 5, she riding Lex, and me riding Winnie. We would truck the horses down from Helen's place in Ardoise, a fifteen-minute drive away, the evening before. I'd never helped to truck horses before; I learned later that the protocols for this are also part of the Level Two Western Rider exam. At this

point I was excited to learn about trucking, and I was dancing to go to my very first clinic. The fact that I had no idea
what to expect added to the spice.

Distracted though I was, I was still thinking ahead
to the other events of the summer. Unsurprisingly, Helen
had had to cancel the Ladies Trail Weekend. Organizing
a schooling show, teaching lessons, riding and training her
own horses, working full-time, and planning a wedding
for August, among other life-changing events – Helen was
busy to a degree I'd rarely ever seen. Something had had to
give. As there had been no time to groom and extend the
trails on Helen's and Neil's property, and the summer had
plenty of horse-related events packed into it already, it was
the trail riding party that was put off for another year. I was
disappointed for about two minutes. There was work and
fun galore for all, keeping steady with lessons and preparing
for the clinic, Helen's schooling show, and Sherry's big show.

If I was able to complete my Level Two Western Rider,
I thought it made best sense to study for it with Adrienne,
up in Cape Breton. She'd been my good-luck charm the
summer prior, and I liked the symmetry of studying with
her for the Level Two, which I thought might work for
August, after the Heritage Championships on the 8th and
9th. I emailed Adrienne to see if this would work for her.

Full-on work and fun runs in the Smith family. With
a barn to operate, lessons to give, shows for herself and her
students to compete in, and her cherished only child, Helen,
getting married on August 29 – Adrienne was a little less
sure we might complete Level Two that month. I confessed
to having a lot of work on the go myself, what with freelance writing and teaching filling the spring and summer
months. We also had my brother's youngest son, Michael,
age twenty, coming to live with us in May, likely for a few
months, and then there was the small matter of working in
and around my husband's schedule of writing and filmmak-
ing, which would bring a team of mules to their knees, and

sustained us all. This meant I was Chief Cook and Bottle Washer on the home-front. Fair enough.

Adding to life's complexities was the fact that we had our home in the city, which also has a ground-floor suite rented to tenants, up for sale. Our plan was to sell it this summer and make our seasonal home in Cape Breton our primary home. One house, no more tenants to look after. And no mortgage, either. Meanwhile, the housing market in Halifax was the slowest it had been in many years. Keen as I was to have the house sold, I was keener yet to keep steady with training generally, and for the rider levels. I found it hard not to fret – audibly.

"This is a journey," Adrienne wrote me in an email. "There will be detours. You just have to go along as best you can and when things change or get delayed, you go along with that, too. The most important thing is to keep on riding."

Typically, she focused on my good news and was philosophical and calm about future plans. "You'll enjoy the Tommy McDowell clinic. As for the rest, just keep riding and studying when you can. You can write that Level Two on short notice so long as you are ready and you should not worry about a deadline too much for that. It will just suddenly be time and that keeps the pressure off."

Given a quiet moment to think about it all, I was all for keeping the pressure off. I had bitten off a fair bit to chew for the summer of 2015. Only two years prior I'd been standing on the mounting block at Caberfeidh Stables, Adrienne's and Scott's barn in Dundee, thrilled to look down on a golden fairytale mare, but wondering how on earth to get myself into the saddle to ride her, and now I was anticipating a summer of steady lessons, a clinic with a distinguished horseman from Oklahoma, and competing in two horse shows. Some days I simply couldn't believe the facts of my own life. Gratitude put quicksilver in my steps.

In reviewing the year to date, I felt nostalgic for the

winter beauty of January and February, when I rode regularly. March brought one hellish weather system after another; I only rode twice, Winnie, both times. The awful weather also meant hard and lumpy footing in the ring, which in turn was brutal for my back. In April, the weather still poor and often rainy, I alternated riding Shania and Winnie. April continued to be a bad month for my back, which puffed up and ached no matter what the weather was doing, what we did in the lesson, and who I rode. Epsom salt baths were a constant for me, as was feeling disheartened that my back was so reliably unreliable. The creakiness made everything hard, and enervating, both in body and spirit.

It's a good thing I didn't know then that May and June would make bad weather and a complaining back seem the most minor of problems.

20
BECOMING A SHOW TEAM

Throughout May, Helen had me alternately riding Lex and Winnie. (Shania had a number of juniors and other, returning riders taking lessons with her, so I didn't ride her often.) I felt resistant to riding Lex at first, mostly because he is 15.2 hands high, almost a full hand taller than Winnie, which makes it a bit harder for me to work around him on the ground, and due to his bigger build overall, he is a very different "ride" than compact Winnie is. Adding to the challenge, Lex, although a fast and powerful reining horse, can be very difficult to "move along" for a new or returning rider with still-developing leg muscles. No doubt this was part of Helen's plan, to improve my overall strength, as was her hope that my confidence would increase, riding a gelding who is touchingly amiable and rock-solid dependable. He is a teddy bear.

The truth was, Winnie and I had been arguing some of late. I had finally come to understand why the Smith family referred to her as a diva; I thought it was just because of her good looks. But, in fact, it's hard to be a superstar. And Winnie is one. In addition to being exceedingly well-bred, of legendary American quarter-horse stock, Winnie has won championships of all sorts since her youngest days of show-ing. Showmanship, Reining, Western Pleasure, Horseman-ship, Trail, Halter, and English classes of all sorts, too. The golden gal has done it all to high levels, with trophies and boxes of ribbons to show for it. When a horse is as well-schooled as Winnie is, and has had such a close and long-standing riding partnership as Winnie has had with Helen, and secondly Adrienne, they don't always connect with oth-er riders, who can't possibly communicate as correctly with them.

That said, Helen had told me months ago that Winnie was a "bonder," and I was certain from her bright and fol-lowing eyes that Winnie noted my now regular comings and goings to and from the barn with interest, even some mild pleasure. I certainly enjoyed her company. It was when I was aboard her that we sometimes figuratively shouted over one another.

"Why is she so twisty today, Helen? I don't under-stand," I'd say, dismayed at the whine in my voice and the tension in my shoulders. When I haven't gotten something clear in my mind when it comes to riding, the frustration expresses itself in my body and tone of voice. It's common for most people, of course – with new or complex ideas of any kind.

"She's only going where you're telling her to go," Helen would say blandly – spiking my frustration further. Uncomprehending *and* inept I was, apparently – and likely to stay that way, from the silence that followed.

But it was only a second or two of silence, and I was overreacting, as I (Irish-often) do. Self-criticism runs ram-pant in the horse world, and I am no exception. Again and fortunately, I had very little time to stew. Unlike some of the instructors of my youth, Helen does not leave you hanging if you're having trouble understanding a riding concept. She is articulate and eager for light bulbs to go on in her stu-dents' minds. As important, she won't just keep repeating a phrase; instead, she'll rephrase several times over, until your actions or words show her you've caught on. She might even illustrate the point on the horse she's riding, or hop on yours, and show you that way. As I've told my family and friends, Helen teaches the way I learn – thank goodness.

So why was Winnie so "twisty" with me that month and other times?

Going straight. No, it's got nothing to do with leaving a life of crime. Going straight in the horse world is a large concept that some of us need to keep relearning, especially if we spend too much time out of the saddle. When you ride in a ring or an arena, you often use the wall or fence to guide yourself. You haven't actually made the decision to ride straight. This is where the coach or instructor comes in, and asks you to do exercises related to going in straight lines. (Circles are a whole other complicated matter, and yes, they'd better be round, not egg-shaped or any other shape.) So you might be asked to ride away from the wall or fence, in a straight line down the "quarter" or "centre-line" of the ring. At some point, your horse will surely "drift," back towards the side fence or wall. Your job is to focus straight ahead, on a point on the far wall or fence that you can aim for, and to keep your eyes on this point. The focus acts as a magnet. When you feel a drift commence, you use your leg and seat aids to encourage the horse to re-establish a straight line. Rein aids, meanwhile, control the shoulders, while leg and seat control the horse's body. To combat a drift towards the centre of the ring, you use your inside leg to push the horse back. For a drift towards the side, you use your outside leg to push back.

Then there are your hands. When I get frustrated (legs aren't doing their job effectively), I fuss with my hands. Similar to speedy grooming, horses don't like this. Slow and steady is the order of both the groom and ride. I swear Winnie would stick her hooves in her ears and hum, *la-la-la-la-la*, when my hands busied above her. I'd shorten the reins, lengthen the reins, pull one long end or the other out from where they stick under the saddle pad. "Ignore that when it happens," said Helen; *la-la-la-la-la*, hummed the yellow mare. For lovely straight transport your hands have to be even, level, and quiet. You "carry" them above your horse's withers, and at the width of your hips. Next, the reins have to be even, the hand position consistent, low, and just ahead of the saddle horn.

Helen has ferreted out an ancient habit of mine, and that's keeping the inside rein shorter than the outside rein – going to both the left and right reins. I had no clue I did this consistently, and for the life of me on some days, I cannot see the unevenness. But it is there, and it confuses and misdirects whatever horse I might be sitting on. While I do this regularly on both reins, you can bank on me doing it on the right rein.

"Did you have a horse that went badly on the right rein?" asked Helen recently. "Winnie prefers the left rein, too, but there's no need to haul her around on that right rein."

Well, yes, that was Coqeyn, actually, he was much more agile on the left rein – but surely to God after all these years –

"Muscle memory is a funny thing," she mused. "Now lengthen that right rein." I shook out the rein, only to hear my favourite Helen-saying: "Lift that inside hand – no, your *other* inside hand" – which always cracks me up and gets me lifting the correct hand. Amazing how often you can get your hands confused, when you're lost in the process of listening hard and trying to do as you're told.

A final note on reins: you really have to be able to turn rein pressure off and on without pulling. This means closing your fingers on the reins to create boundaries when your horse needs guidance and opening your fingers when the horse relaxes into the proper head-to-tail alignment (straight carriage), and is tracking in a straight line.

Going straight. A simple concept, easily mastered and retained – I wish!

By now, I hope, you can see why I am short-tempered some days – and you can really see how patient my coach is, to run through these points and correct my position. She does this again and again, too, until she sees a light bulb go on in my eyes, for that day, at least.

So we worked on all these points and more throughout May. My "leg yields" (lateral movement by the horse, in response to leg pressure) got better and I had some "ah ha!" moments. For example, I don't remember any instructor of my youth saying, "Point your belly button where you want to go." This was in relation to another unfortunate habit of mine (and a fair number of other English-started riders), and that is (back to frustration and twists again) pulling hard on the rein to make a horse turn left or right. This can work to turn the horse sometimes, but in general, horses are not cars. They're not at all bothered going straight ahead with their necks bent to one side. The more you use the inside rein to pull the horse left or right, the more they set their jaws against that pressure, and "pop" their opposite shoulder out. Without the straightening effect of the outside rein, used in tandem with pressure from the inside leg, the "twisting game" just keeps on going.

I have known this – countless times over. And I have lost the muscle memory for it, as often. When you use the outside rein correctly, without thinking, it is deeply satisfying.

Horses as well-trained as Adrienne's and Helen's don't actually need to be ridden with bridles and reins; they can be guided perfectly well using only seat and legs. Even with neck-reining, the movement of the reins against the neck is discreet enough to be invisible to most observers. (No wonder Western riders use a kissing sound as a canter aid; you can't get much more discreet than that. You also drop your hip and graze your leg behind the girth for a canter strike-off. But when you and the horse are "on," all you need is the kiss. (Just don't kiss or cluck to your horse in the show ring – you'll be disqualified.) When I learned to point my belly button where I wanted to go and, additionally, learned to swivel my shoulders to turn where I wanted to go – well, Westinghouse stock rose higher at that moment.

Troubles with Winnie aside, there no denying I was learning a lot on Lex, progressing each lesson, feeling more and more comfortable on a big horse and yet, unlike my rides on Winnie, I felt I was riding "someone else's horse" – a very nice stranger. His size, to be truthful, had ceased to be an issue. I have, after all, ridden a fair number of big horses over a lifetime. The memory-switch goes on – *oh right, I remember this* – and all of a "sudden," you start to feel fine and look right up there. Part of this was due to my "longer" leg, which, due to muscle development and overall seat improvement, was able to stretch down further. I no longer resembled a rather old child, with very short legs, perched ineffectively on the gelding's back.

"I like the way you look on him," Helen started saying. "I really do. Maybe you should take Lex in the shows, instead of Winnie. That could work well."

Oh, nonononono, I'd think, smiling innocuously at Helen, perhaps even nodding in presumed agreement. I might be looking good on Lex, but I need my lucky golden mare for the clinic and the shows.

The head-butting with Winnie persisted. She may have babysat me while I was weak – truly childlike – but she had no interest in "obeying" or responding with alacrity as I got stronger and more assertive, and yet was still imprecise or jerky in my actions. Forget about hooves in her well-shaped ears, blocking out the sounds of my requests – by now she had a full leg in both of those receptacles.

"She's only doing what you're asking her to do," Helen repeated time and again, as one thing after another went "wrong" during our lessons. I would feel a surge of frustration, which would never improve matters.

"You've got that look on your face, Marjorie," Helen would say. "Not your serious thinking look – I know that one now. The other look, the 'I'm getting mad look.' Relax – breathe. And stop wiggling your seat."

Had I been holding my breath again? Yes, I had. Had I been wiggling again? Yes – blush – I had. When I am not applying enough leg (squeeze, release, squeeze, release), and I tilt forward even a smidge, Winnie simply quits her canter/trot and starts trotting/walking (in effect, decreasing her gait), as a good reining horse, listening to its rider, should do – and there's Marjorie, wiggling her backside, in the vain hope of restarting the lost impulsion. It doesn't work. Nor does banging on her sides with my upturned heels. *Squeeze, release, sit deep, look to where you're going, let the mare do her work.* That works a charm.

On Friday, June 5, on a pearly summer morning at 8:00 a.m., Winnie and I had our worst lesson ever. As far as I could tell, I couldn't do a single thing correctly. I was probably blinking badly. Helen was endlessly patient, but she may as well have been trying to impart knowledge to a fence post. *Thick as a board plank* – isn't that how the late Princess Diana once unkindly referred to herself, when queried about her academic smarts? That was me that day and an angry piece of wood, as well. If I didn't get my act together, then I would not be showing Winnie, and I would have no one but myself to blame. *You're not good enough to ride this horse,* said mocking me. *Yes, I am, I have to be,* said the me who got back on this very horse the summer of 2013 and rode again.

Don't misunderstand – Lex is a talented, flashy reining horse, who will surely have a long and distinguished show career ahead of him, with Helen. But that's Helen. She's already an established Western rider and knows how to ride an emerging equine talent of Lex's calibre. I am well aware how lucky I am to come within ten feet of these horses of

Helen's, let alone ride them. And maybe, I could do a better job on Lex later on, but not now – not for my first clinic ever, and my first horse show in over forty years. Winnie is my magic mare, the one who brought me back from no hope of ever riding again, the one who said, when I stared down at the saddle, unable to imagine sitting in it, "Take your time, I'm not going anywhere. We can stand here all day, if you like." Her calmness gave me courage. Her beauty gave me the will.

Saturday, the day after my worst ride ever on Winnie, I did a lot of walking in circles. If banging my head against a wall would have banged some sense into my cranium, I would have done it in a flash. Instead, I circled between my downstairs office and the kitchen, walked up and down the house stairs on the flimsiest of excuses, and finally, took the two bemused dogs out for a real walk, along the seawall near our home in Halifax.

I had to do better.

And better meant head in the right place from the moment I got in my truck the following morning for my next lesson, to when I walked into the barn and first laid eyes on all the horses, with Winnie at the far end.

I would have to breathe, and I would have to listen with my body and heart, as much as my head. I'd almost forgotten how to feel the connection between Winnie and me, one living creature to another, because too many *I must be perfects* were ricocheting around my mind. When those words in turn gathered up the steady stream of corrective words from coach Helen, a mental maelstrom ensued.

Sunday arrived. On the drive to the barn I listened to classical music on CBC Radio, not the especially chatty hosts and jangly music favoured by "pop" stations in the morning, even the usually sleepy country stations I enjoy later on in the day. I thought of my last yoga class and how we had practised "yoga breathing," or Pranayama. First I focused on slowing and deepening my breathing. I gently drew air deep into my nostrils and exhaled as slowly through my mouth. Next I did "three-part breathing," pulling my breath up from my abdomen, then the mid-chest, then the upper chest, and finally, exhaling for what seemed like a mile's worth of countryside. I took one more rib-expanding breath and –

– parked the truck beside the barn. I floated down the wide aisle of the hay-sugared barn. Hello, Annie, hello, Lex, hello, Shania, Phoebe, and Bart, and hello May, baby of Winnie, born the previous spring and already a "looker," just like your mama.

Hello, Winnie, here you are at last.

I entered her stall. Combing her mane with my fingers, I talked to her, low-pitched chatter-talk *It's a beautiful day ... a good one for grazing in those wide fields all around us ... you're lucky to have such great stablemates, and caring owners ... and all the students who groom and fuss over you ... who, like me, can scarcely believe their good fortune to be riding you.*

Idly, her lips grazed my hip and she attempted to bite me – no doubt affirming that last point, but also because hey, she's a horse – sometimes they just want to lock their teeth onto something other than hay or grain. Another horse will do, or a human, though they tend to holler.

I stepped back just fast enough that I didn't have to holler – she didn't latch onto my skin. I did sputter and laugh, though, and gave her nose a hard rap. "Winnie! Enough of that!" She blinked her toffee-gold eyes, then dropped her head to resume eating her hay.

Horses, they're not dogs, that's for sure. They have their own, more mysterious ways.

I led Winnie out of her stall, connected the cross-ties to her halter, found her brushes and hoof-pick, moving quietly all the while. I groomed her thoroughly and well, and slowly. No more chatter-talk now. I still felt more relaxed than usual, despite her distracted nibble, but my mind was moving onto the lesson ahead.

Trust – remember that first lesson with Helen and riding with your eyes closed on the lunge line? Remember how floaty and great that felt? I want you to ride that way today. I want you to enjoy each moment, to be aware of every moment. I want you to ride like David Esworthy, crisp and soft at the same time. Ride tall, ride warrior-well. Ride as though you never had those gap years, never had the tumbles, never looked down on a saddle as though it were *terra incognita* – perhaps not even a land you never knew, but a distant solar system you never expected to see again.

And remember who you are riding. Ride that mare like the champion she is. Are you two going to be a show team or not? I say yes, let's go build a team.

We're in the ring now and even at four-fifteen, it's still a warm summer day. Before I mount, I pull a few stray hairs from Winnie's forelock that have gone astray under the earpiece of the bridle. Winnie doesn't have a thick forelock, so it's literally a few hairs I join up with the others, but it will still look better tidied up. Perfect presentation for a perfect mare. That's who you are lucky enough to ride.

Our walk has energy, but is not too fast. As far as I can tell, we are "tracking up" nicely, with Winnie's hind feet fitting perfectly into the space the forefeet have just left. A great start.

Then comes our jog. It, too, has impulsion – we are going forward with controlled power – but for the first time in many lessons for Winnie and me, I trust her to keep that measured, slow pace, and she does, because I sit back and stay back, and choose the way forward with upraised eyes.

Lope time. And it is a lope, not a canter, though both words describe the same three-beat gait, and canters can be as slow and collected as this lope of ours is, right now. It may be slow, but it is correct, too. A horse's centre of balance is, in general, directly over their withers, or just behind this area. With the slow, collected lope, the horse must elevate the withers, round the back, and bring the haunches more under itself. This brings the hocks under as well, and allows the rear end of the horse to support its own weight, and the rider's, lightening the shoulders and front end. The upshot of all this is what I am experiencing: a light, maneuverable horse. Technicalities aside, it's forward-moving heaven, as though you're sitting on a tennis ball that Serena Williams just whacked over the net.

The lesson goes on. Our leg yields are excellent. My hands are still, but effective. My chin stays up, and my eyes stay focused straight ahead. I even have lots of "weight" in my heel, with the leg position consistently good, and still.

Winnie, meanwhile, is having a fine day. Finally, that person aboard is riding her as she should be ridden. She feels only sunny energy coming to her, and responds in kind. I really am exceptionally well-trained and giving, she tells me, if you make a good effort yourself.

I do.

Every horse person knows, there's hardly anything sweeter than hearing "Yes, well done!" from your coach. For an "Excellent!" most riders would crawl over a field of broken glass on their hands and knees. For a steady hour of audibly happy responses to the way you're riding – make that two fields of broken glass.

"You look great on Winnie today. Maybe you should ride her at the shows. What do you think?" asked Helen.

I couldn't even pretend to think it over. "Yes," I said. "I want to ride Winnie. I can't imagine not riding her."

Long pause, then, "All right," said Helen. "It's you and Winnie for the shows. Just keep riding her the way you did today, and you'll do super well at my show and Sherry's."

I don't remember the drive home from Ardoise to Halifax. I don't remember what I said to Don, or when I started crying and when I stopped. I probably said, *Don, I was almost the rider I used to be yesterday – but potentially so much better. I am going to get that goddamned outside rein clear in my head and hands if it kills me. I rode well today! Winnie said – I mean she actually said it, with her body and spirit – Well, all right! Let's be a team then. She picked me for her team, Don, and I picked her for mine. It was a real, conscious decision that two creatures made, one after the other, both of them serious, genuine. Star-dust magic – that's what it was. All over me, all over her.*

And Don, bless him, listened to me, nodded, listened more, handed me endless Kleenexes, and tried to understand the source of my copious tears, which didn't seem to have pain as their root cause, but did pummel at my heart, all the same.

I think horse magic can do that to you. Hearts are tender, mostly, and horse magic is so universe-vast at times that hearts become rivers of feelings, fast-flowing and powerful, threatening chaos. I and my river-heart didn't mind the tumult. Look what I'd been given.

Down from the clouds again, it was less than a month until the Roseway Summer Show, Helen's first show at her new home and property. Teamwork with Winnie aside, we had lots of regular work ahead of us, to prepare. Showmanship, Western Pleasure and Trail – I had only the sketchiest understandings of these Western disciplines. I would be showing in each, at both shows. I would be entered in three classes at Helen's show, and six at Sherry's two-day Heritage Championships Show, for a total of nine classes at the two events. This was far less than most of the seasoned entrants would do, and some, Helen and Adrienne among them, would compete in a blizzard of English and Western classes – and place or win in both as well. But Helen and I were in accord that nine classes for me would be quite enough, after a four-decade hiatus from the show ring.

As if becoming a real team with Winnie wasn't enough to raise my spirits and drive, the month of June just kept on flowering with good luck and fun. Mid-month, I entered the early-bird draw for Helen's July 4 show. The winner would win their show fees back. I figured fifty dollars would feel better in my pocket than out of it.

Helen found a hat for the draw. In went my name and the names of other show entrants, who had signed up early for the Roseway Summer Show. Helen asked the veterinarian who was at the barn that day to "float" or file the horses' teeth, to improve their dentition, to make the draw. I was in Winnie's stall, untacking her, after a hard but satisfying lesson.

"Marjorie Simmins?" said the vet, from the opposite end of the barn from where I stood, saddle in arms, en route to the tack room. "Do you know a Marjorie Simmins, Helen?" Helen and I burst out laughing. "Yes," I said. "She sure does."

Then, a few days later, after a lesson where I rode in the pouring rain, an unaccountably cheerful Helen giving me one of our best lessons yet – I took a very large breath and said yes to buying my own Western saddle.

"Why would you buy a saddle," asked Don, when I told him what I'd done, later that day, "when you don't have a horse to put it on?"

"But I do have a horse to put it on," I shot back. "Winnie!"

"But she's not yours," he insisted, still not following my logic.

"No, she's not – but she's mine to take lessons on, and to show this year," I womanfully continued, well aware all logic was lacking from my decision. "And besides, wait 'til you see the bling." Me and magpies – love all those shiny bits, we do.

"The bling?" Don asked, sounding quite lost at this point. "How does this connect to the saddle?"

"It's *on* the saddle," I said dreamily, of the gorgeous brown leather Showman-brand saddle, with a black suede seat. "The back of the seat, the skirt, the pommel. They're all detailed in silver bling, tooled silver. The leather's tooled and beautiful, too. I just love it."

"That's apparent," he said, his voice softer now, the smile widening. "And from what you tell me, you did get a great price on it, so what the hell, enjoy it. It was your hard-earned teaching loot, anyway."

It was Helen who'd found the saddle for me second-hand, taking my request for "$650, and no more. I'll wait if I have to" seriously, and then jumping when she saw the advertisement for the Showman, at exactly that price. The saddle was only a couple of years old and would have cost in the vicinity of $1,500 new.

"It's a steal," she said. "You won't regret it, and if you do, I'll buy it from you myself."

One of those win-win's, I decided, and sent off the e-transfer to the (now ex-) owner. After all, if you're aiming to win – and I'll certainly try my best at the upcoming shows – then looking like a winner doesn't hurt.

It wasn't the shows coming up next, though. It was the Tommy McDowell Clinic, held at the Windsor Exhibition Grounds on July 4 and 5th. Here we come, Windsor-town – Helen and Lex, and me and Winnie – and a new, bling-covered saddle.

21

THE "TOMMY CLINIC"

Judique's on the floor! Who'll put 'er off?

Isn't that what the men from the village of Judique, Cape Breton, used to say when they got all liquored up at the dance hall on a Saturday night, and challenged the men from the surrounding villages one-on-one to "put 'em up"? I am sure that's what Don told me, about the yesteryears of that tough little village along Route 19, overlooking the yet tougher Atlantic Ocean.

Well, it's not the men of Judique saying it now. It's a golden mare originally from Dundee, Cape Breton, latterly from Ardoise, Nova Scotia, and today, standing erect and battle-ready at the far western end of the Windsor Exhibition Grounds' biggest arena.

Winnie's on the floor! Who'll put 'er off? Cue the bugling neigh and the forelegs slicing the air, like "hi-ho, Silver," the white horse the Lone Ranger rode. I can just see the golden steed rising up –

All right, Winnie's not that worked up, but damn close. What I really want to know is, where in the hell did this enormous, puffing horse come from, and why in the name of all that's holy and self-preserving am I aboard her?

The short, trim man near this end of the arena is looking directly at Winnie and me. He has tall, stitch-embroidered, white cowboy boots on, their height, detailing, and colour revealed because his jeans are tidily tucked into them. His cowboy hat and shirt are light-coloured, too, and contrast nicely against the dark-wash jeans. Western clinicians and judges dress smartly, I have come to realize, and Tommy McDowell from Oklahoma is no exception. Winnie realigns herself on the rail, switching her backside right, left, then settling, her spine now perfectly straight; I think suddenly of a grasshopper preparing to jump improbably high and far, as they so often do. I shake the disquieting notion aside, look back to Mr. McDowell, who has a headset on with a boom microphone by the side of his mouth. He has a pleasantly laconic speaking style and a flat Midwest American accent.

"Let's see her go again," he says. "Are you ready?"

Only twenty minutes earlier I'd said to one of my clinic-mates, Charlene Smith, as we stood side by side on our horses, a longer line of horses and riders stretching out beside us, that I was "relieved I don't have to do *that* maneuver." I didn't realize there isn't a lot of choice at clinics such as this. When Mr. McDowell invites you to do a training exercise, you do it. And so I would soon be trying my hand at "fencing," or pre-sliding stops.

"Helen," I'd squeaked to my coach, who flanked my other side, just moments before my turn came around, "I've never done anything like this! And I've hardly ever ridden one-handed!"

Helen smiled. "That's why we come to events like this, to try new things!" No sympathy from that corner, I found – horse people aren't big on mollycoddling – only a brisk nod to indicate I should now walk out from the lineup and get started.

The first day of the clinic had been relaxed and undemanding. We focused primarily on "ground work," meaning working with your horse on the ground, not mounted. We executed a variety of tasks with our horses, many of these asking them to move with us and away from us, all with ease and acquiescence. The only ground work I'd ever formally done was with a halter and a lunge line, asking the horse to walk, trot, canter, and halt. This is certainly a big part of ground work, and lungeing itself, choreographed down to the last detail, for safety and best training effect, is more difficult than it seems.

The exercises we did yesterday, however, were done using a halter and the much shorter lead line. I'd basically received a crash course in the many iterations of ground work: leading, back-ups, forehand turns, haunch turns, side-passes, respect for the rider's space, manners, and touching the horse all over, to eliminate any "no-go" or spook zones. Yesterday, then, had been a meaty learning experience, but for me and most of the others had not included much riding. A couple of individuals had asked to work on certain maneuvers such as sliding stops, or the work that precedes them, and this is where we had picked up again, on day two.

The idea of fencing, or galloping alongside the arena wall, stopping just before you reach the far wall, is to work toward executing a perfect and flashy "sliding stop." Fencing, then, aids horse and rider to gallop straight and true. This is the "approach," and without it, your horse won't be balanced, which means he won't stop with power and relaxation. Fencing builds trust and coordination between horse and rider. Unlike a true sliding stop, a signature move of the reining horse, fencing does not require the horse to round his back and engage his hindquarters into the ground – that photo-op moment when the horse's hind hooves have churned up pluming mountains of dirt and dust, and the horse's front legs are still "walking." This is generally followed by a rapid, sometimes extended back-up, which completes the maneuver. For the fencing exercise we're doing today, Winnie will halt smartly at the fence, her back straight and legs four-square, and then I'll ask her for a short back-up. We then turn, and repeat the exercise. Until I'm told to stop.

Stock still, Winnie is listening with all her pores for my next cue.

"Are you ready?" asks Mr. McDowell asks again, tone kindly. I nod, realizing that the obvious addition to that question would be – *Your horse sure is.* I think *canter* and Winnie strikes off on the correct lead. I encourage her with my legs to extend the canter, which she does. We're rockin' now.

And the wall's getting closer.

"Hand forward! More, more!"

I put the hand what I think is well ahead of the horn.

"More! Put that hand further ahead."

Now I feel unbalanced. I plaster my free, right hand against my thigh; not the best form, but it will have to do. Yes, that's better. I feel more anchored. Good thing, as here's our wall. I swear I can hear the sound effects of a car's tires screeching on the pavement, here in this dusty agricultural arena. Winnie has stopped, on the proverbial dime. I think *turn* and one breath later, we're facing the opposite direction. Each movement neat, each moment tidy. All this cleverness has nothing to do with me, but I'll take the credit all the same. We roar down to the end of the arena again. The used-to-be-a-reiner is galloping now.

"That yellow horse just remembered she used to have a job," says the amplified voice that is Mr. McDowell, his smile riding the airwaves, too. "Go again. And get those legs forward. More, more!"

Winnie and I do a half-dozen fencing runs, with the last one being the best, as far as I am concerned. I swear, my legs were so far forward, they reached the wall before Winnie's nose did. I shake my head; it all felt so strange. *And fun.*

"You're the English rider, right?" asks Mr. McDowell.

"Yes, sir," I say. "Transitioning to Western now."

He pauses, then purses his mouth in sympathy. "It's hard to go against muscle memory, for sure, pushing those hands and legs forward. But you're coming along. You enjoying yourself?"

"Yes, sir. I certainly am."

"Good. Thanks, and good luck. Who's next?"

There's little time for relief or recuperation. In what surely is only one long and hard heartbeat, Winnie and I are back "on the floor," having a go at a second exercise. At Helen's suggestion – I thought my coach *liked* me! – Mr. McDowell has Winnie and me practising large and small canter circles at one end of the arena. Jokes aside, Helen's right to ask this for me. I'll need to do these neatly executed true circles – not egg or oval shapes, as sometimes happens – demonstrating variations of speed at the lope, when it comes time for my Level Two Western rider. Helen wants me to get as much as I can from the clinic; she also knows I might not know how to speak up in these new circumstances. I never was good at pushing myself to the head of the line.

My clinic-mates are lined up mid-ring, watching us – as, of course, Winnie and I watched everyone else, when they did similar or different exercises. Observing then practising is a great way to learn. They're a whole-hearted, fun group, young, middle, and older, mostly women, but stalwart men among them, but oh, they must have eight burning eyes each.

And here's Winnie and I gallop-cantering. I don't know how else to explain it. If I thought she was animated for the fencing exercise – "I was worried she'd do a huge sliding stop on you," said Helen, after we'd wrapped up that session – then it's hard to comprehend how tightly strung she is now. As required for the exercise, Winnie's definitely cantering. I can count the three-beat strides easily. But the gait and the small horse both feel giant. The pace isn't actually fast, as a gallop is, but it feels that way, and mythic-horse big, too. It's the first time in decades – since Boo, perhaps? – I have felt a horse this "under herself." This is the way jumpers look, appearing to gallop "in place" in order to come at a big fence safely. It's also the way top-level dressage horses look, with a truck-load of power under their haunches, as they cleanly perform one impossibly strenuous movement after another. Her hind legs are well engaged and feel like a coiled spring.

Her head and neck are elevated without being stretched out, losing the curve. She is in fact "collected," her hindquarters lower and producing more flexion in the haunches. Her movements feel light, and look fluid and beautiful, I am sure. For me, aboard her, the increased impulsion and energy are breathtaking not for their beauty, but for the excitement of it all, and the physical demands on me, of balance and wind. *Please, God, tell me I am not riding with my mouth open, gasping like a dying guppie. And while you're listening, please keep me in this beautiful new saddle.*

I swear I can channel Winnie's thoughts. *Do you have any idea how many times I've performed in this arena, and others? Remember what Helen said? Sixty times easy. And that's only at the Windsor arena. I've been shown all around this province. I really know how to do this. Just hang on. No one's putting this show horse off the floor, and Winnie-girl is always in the ribbons.*

"Hand ahead of the horn," says Mr. McDowell. "No, more – more yet!" Here we go again. Every time I breathe in, or lean into the circle, I seem to pull that left hand back toward my stomach, to rebalance. Helen and I have done so little one-handed riding in our training time together; we just haven't needed to yet, and I am not good at it. Nor have we done any galloping or exercises such as fencing, which require legs and arms in such a forward position. Western Horsemanship, this ain't. If it were, my hands and legs would be positioned much as they would be for an English Equitation class. When viewed from the side, your shoulders, hips, and heels should be in a straight line. If you look down and see your foot past your knee, your foot is too far forward. English, Western – same body position for the majority of the time.

Once again I plant my right arm and hand on my thigh, basically to keep them out of my way. There, that will do. It's not distracting me, and doesn't look too dorky, I hope. *Concentrate on your circles.*

"Better," he says. "Another, go again."

Excuse me, sir, but I think I may be croaking. I really don't know if I –

"Sit up, shoulders back – yes, looking better."

I'd look a lot better if you'd let me do some two-point. Any chance of letting me stand up in the stirrups, just for a few gulps of air, and less contact on my spine –

"You're tipped forward. Sit back. Let the mare do her job."

I sit back and Winnie peels ahead, three horses for the price of one. We canter some respectable, smaller circles on the right rein, and when asked, come down to a walk, and then turn to the left. I am trying not to allow anxiety make me inch up on my reins too much. I am trying not to interfere in any way with this impressively competent horse. *Let the mare do her job* – says Mr. McDowell, time and again. Or, as Helen always says, *She's a champion. Ride her that way.* Even as Winnie herself said, a moment ago, with a wink, *Just hang on tight.*

I guide us to a perfect spot on the rail, the one that says *canter*, to me, and Winnie strikes off without any aids. All I did was ease my hands and think the word. It's small torture, mostly mental, not to stand in my stirrups, just to ease the intensity of the driving gait off my lower back for a few strides – and to somehow *see* further ahead, to make my circle plump and round. Instead, I sit back, sit down, and for the first time since this exercise began, smile. I'm thinking of how much I enjoy watching Helen ride – how straight-backed she is, and how bold her style seems. I always think, *Celtic warrior, that one*, no matter what horse she rides. We have lots of laughs these days during our lessons, especially when she's working on my posture. *Think snooty,* she says often, *and sit up as much as you can – stick those boobs out.* Somehow my writer's brain has shortened this to "snooty boobs." When she tells me I'm not sitting up enough, I say to myself, Come on, snooty boobs, sit taller. I am usually rewarded with, *That's better,* from Helen.

All right, snooty boobs, I say to myself now, this is no time to do a fold over: sit tall!

We do one more circle I am genuinely pleased with and then come the blessed words: "Thanks very much. You did well, especially that last go-round."

The fire-breathing dragon and I return to our place in the lineup, watch someone else take our place on the rail. To my astonishment, Winnie shrinks and becomes her regular size once we're back in the lineup. She's quiet as a field mouse now.

So am I. I am also tired enough to fall asleep in this saddle. Two early and demanding days in a row, and this one won't finish for some hours yet. Once the clinic concludes, we have to untack, brush, feed, and water the horses; clean and strip to the floorboards the stalls we used in the Windsor Exhibition barn; load up all our tack and belongings, and the hay, bedding, wheelbarrow, broom, pitchforks, feed, brushes, and buckets in Helen's trailer; load the horses; and carefully, slowly, drive humans and horses back down the highway and back-roads to Roseway Stables – where the process is repeated, in reverse order. Then for me, the forty-five-minute drive back to the city.

Oh, God, I can't –

Oh, yes you will – says the memory-of-me standing again for the first time, after months of being unable to, and then relearning to walk, one weaving, wobbly step at a time. And you'll keep your whingeing to yourself, too. Helen's day is far longer and harder than yours – every day. You never hear her complain. You just completed your first clinic, an experience you never thought you'd have in this life. You did everything you were asked to do, and ably enough. You did that. You and Winnie. Sitting tall.

Snooty boobs. I smile, then lift my chin, shoulders, and chest, and watch the next rider start his canter circles.

22

SUMMER CAMP
JULY 8, 9, AND 10, 2015

"Just so you guys know – I've decided I am twelve years old for this week," I say, stepping into Roseway Stables on a peach of a summer morning. "Everyone else here is around twelve, so why can't I be?"

Three sets of young eyes fasten on me, not entirely sure what I am on about. Then three faces smile. If you have to have an adult for your camp-mate, at least a goofy one is all right.

L'Rhya Cranidge, Avery McLean, and Jenna Morley, who is Neil's older daughter, are the trio of amiable adolescents with whom I will be going to "summer camp," here at Helen's stable. I've known them all since the top of the year, when, in one configuration or another, we took lessons together now and again. I waffled about coming to the camp, though, uncertain what I'd take away from it, or if the youngsters would feel comfortable with me. I also wondered if this is what I should be doing the week before Helen's show.

"Of course it is!" said Helen with her usual enthusiasm. "We'll be practising for the show every day. And besides, we're going to have a lot of fun. You should come!"

* * *

In the end, the camp fees were affordable and I did see the sense of three solid days of barn time and show prep, which would support my efforts at the show, only four days away. The "two rides a day" was the deal-maker for me. So for the next three days I'd be at the barn by 8:30 and staying on until 4:30. We'd clean tack and tack boxes, muck out stalls, bathe and trim horses, tidy the tack room and main aisle of the barn, ride two different horses a day, and when the heat just got too much, we'd break for a barbecue lunch, then hop in the pool, which Helen and Neil just managed to get cleaned and operational.

As it turned out, fun was an inadequate word for all the friendly chatter, activities, and learning that went on for those three days in early July at that big old country barn and property in Ardoise. My anxiety about the disciplines I'd be showing in, Trail, Showmanship, and Western Pleasure, settled down and, for the most part, stayed down, as I gained understanding and competency. I also learned from watching my young camp-mates, who were smart and determined. Jenna and I shared the riding of and ground work with Winnie, as we would share the showing of the mare all summer long. I also rode the ever-generous Shania, who built up my confidence nicely, especially with the delicate and precise tasks such as opening and closing rope gates, and backing through groupings of barrels or pylons in the Trail courses Helen set up for us.

On the more sensitive Winnie, I sometimes had trouble, when, for example, my aids to her were overly emphatic or simply incorrect. Winnie was still my teammate, but similarly, she still wasn't cutting me slack for gross corrections or hustling her through tasks she could do upside down, blindfolded, and hobbled – *at her own measured pace.*

The slower I went, the better Winnie went. The more regularly I breathed, the happier she was. The more I *thought* requests, rather than demanding them with boot heels and jerky hands, the more comfortable and successful our rides became. Similarly, the less contact I had on her face, which was addressed by lengthening my reins, and keeping them even, the more the experienced yellow horse simply got the job done. Finally, when I rode with "snooty boobs," shoulders back and spine and legs elongated, I was rewarded with a more rhythmic ride, and graceful transitions, one gait from the other.

And the sun beat down. We all drank gallons of water, on and off the horses, and stood in the shade of the biggest trees that overarched one section of the ring, whenever Helen was focused on only one of us riding or doing a trail course. *Listen, watch, take your own turn.* For me, this triumvirate of auditory, visual, and tactile/active is the most effective way to learn. We also peppered Helen with questions and were peppered with answers, often accompanied with demonstrations, either by one of us or by Helen showing us herself.

When I think of those three days, there are many snippets of dialogue and curled ribbons of girlish laughter that come to mind. Perhaps the most telling line was one all the camp-mates voiced, numerous times over: "Can I go again?" Three girls and one woman, an honourary twelve-year-old, were determined to practise everything they needed to, to build belief in themselves for the upcoming show. "Yes, go again," our coach always replied – until it was obvious we were over-focused, even grumpy and tired. Then Helen would declare it was lunchtime, or swim-time, or even "Take a break in the shade" time. It was *summer camp*, after all. Have a laugh, have some fun. *Balance.* And so we worked hard, in and out of the saddles. Then we jumped in the pool, ate with gusto the hamburgers, hotdogs, and chicken Helen barbecued for our lunches, and savoured the fresh strawberry shortcake she'd made us for dessert.

Dirt, grass, sky, and fields. Profusions of wild roses, their petals rouging the ground. Horses in their stalls, the barn doors open at either end, horses grazing with switching tails in the wide acres around us. Barn cats rolling in the dusty driveway and ring; house cats shooting in and out of the house as we came in and out to use the bathroom. Grasshoppers buzzing and levitating when gravel-scuffing feet come too close. Morning suns that rise gold and pink in the east, and set hard yellow in the west. Our hands stink of horse-sweat, and our own bodies perspire through our cotton T-shirts and socks, make our riding helmets stick to our foreheads. Now and then a blessed breeze comes along, both in the ring and through the barn. We stop when the breeze-tendrils touch our faces, tell ourselves we are cooled by the circulating warmth.

The end of one day came, then the next, then Friday, the day before the show.

"I want you all here early," said Helen. "We have a lot to do. Go home, get a good night's sleep, and be back at 7:00. Don't forget any of your gear and clothing."

Three chattering girls departed the barn, their excitement about the following day evident in their high-spirited jostling and jokes. Unlike after the "Tommy Clinic," the honourary twelve-year-old stayed a little later to help Helen with end-of-the-day tasks. Yet again, in this miraculous year(s) of the horse, the camp exceeded all I hoped for. The happy experiences didn't just appear out of thin air, either. Helen worked her guts out for us. I couldn't say too much then about all she did for us without getting choked up. Level-headed Helen wouldn't feel comfortable with that, I knew. So I thanked her briefly, hoping my tone conveyed my deep gratitude.

"See you first thing in the morning," she smiled. "It's gonna be a great day."

23

The Roseway Stables Summer Show
July 11, 2015, 6:40 a.m.

"We're late." I've kept up this terse refrain for most of the trip from Halifax to Ardoise. Don is driving, the Shelties are in the back seat.

"We're not." Don has responded with the same rebuttal for an equally long period. My genial husband is only now starting to sound frayed.

"How's my makeup?" I pose this question to the mirror on the sun visor, not to Don, though the beleaguered man glances over. I mutter my own answer: "As good as it's going to get." A deep sigh, then, "I'm really not sure about this show bow." I pat the small bun at the back of my head for the twentieth time since Don affixed the bow and the attached hairnet below it at 5:30 this morning. Some of the Western women riders use these "show bows," and I liked the feminine look of them. The bun we fashioned for me is tidy, but the hair within the net is more droopy than nicely rounded. My husband has countless skills, but hairdressing for women doesn't count among them. For all my fretting, my heart kept contracting with humour, and then opening with love for him, as he manfully worked on that bun, gently pushing bobby pins in to anchor it in place. Then came the *pat-pat* with those beloved man-hands – and I knew he was done. I have never in my life worn such a headpiece, though I may have used a simple hairnet when Karin and I showed in English classes, four decades and three years ago, but who's counting?

I've already asked myself, silently but several times over, if I have my new Western hat and boots, show jacket, makeup bag (should my efforts all melt away in the heat), and second show shirt with me – and my boiled eggs, in the cooler, for protein snacks – and answered myself that yes, I do have them all gathered together in a cloth bag in the back of the truck. My head nods as this interior checklist is once again repeated.

"When you've finished talking to yourself, let me know," teases Don, blessedly adding some humour to this fraught morning. In return, I manage a weak smile, the inner dialogue relentless. *Don't let them down, don't let them down –*

I look out my window, hoping to settle my pulse as I always do, by touching green with my eyes, this time in the rolling rural acres around us. Then my heart lifts, as it does every single time, when we come to the elevated bend in the road where you can first spot Helen's and Neil's house. I can't help this. I just feel happy when I see that house, and know I am nearly at the barn. Best Valium ever. No, best natural *stabil*izer ever – yes, I mean that *stable* pun – for this girl, anyway.

We're here. The front field is full of cars, trucks, trailers, campers, and motorhomes. *Show people* are here. There's going to be a *horse show*, and *I* am going to be a part of it. Yoga-breathe, I must remember to yoga-breathe.

"What's my job?" This, too, I've asked myself silently numerous times, and now, aloud. Don parks the truck, turns to me, and we chant together, "Show up, stay on, cheer on your new friends and camp-mates."

"You can do all that and more, Marjorie," says Don. "I know you can."

"I'll stick with those three," I reply.

I'll be there for you, too – comes the voice I thought I might hear, at some point this day. My eyes instantly fill with fear-and-love tears. *Bekindbekindbekind,* I ask – and Karin answers, *That's all I can be, now.*

For one contained moment, I remember the sound of her laugh, a flute in the distance, on this summer day. Then I bump back to the moment. "Showtime," I say, and open the truck door.

* * *

I've never seen so many people in Helen's barn; the space is full of human whirlwinds of all shapes and sizes, all chattering at high volume. My three camp-mates are here, of course, and so are numerous members of their families – mothers, fathers, and aunts, along with friends and neighbours of all assembled, I come to learn. Helen's boarders, one of whom teaches and has students of her own, are here today, too. People from one end of the barn to the other are brushing horses, braiding manes and tails. Others carefully manipulate wheelbarrows under cross-ties after they "pick out" the stalls, which have already been fully mucked out at 5:00 this morning. Stalls only ever look clean for the shortest of times.

I am the only one already dressed in my show clothes; everyone else has work clothes on, their show clothes safely stored in dry-cleaning bags, hanging in the tack room or their vehicles. My show shirt is *white*, for heaven's sakes, and there's work to be done to get the horses and ourselves ready for the show's start at 9:30. *Novice*, indeed. Guts tight, I pull a grey hoodie out of my gear bag and slip it on over my shirt.

"What do you want me to do?" I ask Helen. She will not only be looking after her students today, but showing in both Western and English classes herself, on Lex. Along with Neil and some volunteers, she'll also be overseeing the running of the show. Multi-tasking and capable, Helen is in her element. "It's not my first rodeo," she said, when, hour after hour, we prepared ourselves and the horses for the Tommy clinic. She said it again last evening, laughing, as we finished off the chores from the summer camp and bathed and scrubbed the horses for the second time that day. *Not my first rodeo.*

No, it's not. But for me, it may as well be.

"What do you want me to do?" I'd asked my coach. I don't remember her reply. She suggested something, and I did something. There were all sorts of requests, from Helen and other people, and I did whatever I could to push our readiness ahead – and not get my black show jeans too dirty in the process. Almost everyone in that barn got painted: girls, women, and horses, their faces, nails, and hooves coloured/shined/makeup'd/oiled/sprinkled with glitter. The men and the barn cats were spared, but only, I am thinking, because they didn't come within arm's reach of the women's octopus arms, suction cups pulling in the objects of their desires, all of whom must be improved and beautified, made "show-ready."

This isn't a horse show, I remember thinking. *It's pure theatre.*

And the second I thought that, I knew what I had to do. There are uses for a minor in theatre from university.

Today's schedule offers thirty-two classes, starting at 9:30 and ending when it ends, late in the afternoon. There are eight divisions, senior and youth novice among them. Those last two cover me and my camp-mates. I see lots of seniors here – that's anyone over eighteen – and a fair number of "select," or over-fifties, people who have generally been riding and showing their own horses for many years.

This includes Adrienne, who has trucked down from Cape Breton with her primary show horse, Boo, a bay quarter horse, initially trained for reining by Helen, though Adrienne shows him in all disciplines now. Adrienne will be riding Boo in the select classes, and one of her stellar young students, Janine Lock, will be riding him in the youth classes, the same way Jenna and I will be sharing Winnie in ours. The Youth Novice classes come directly before Senior Novice, so Jenna will be handing off Winnie to me. As our patterns in Showmanship and Trail will be the same, I get the advantage of seeing Winnie do the pattern that she and I will repeat only minutes later. Jenna is also an effective, quiet rider. Winnie will come to me calm and biddable. Our first class, Showmanship, Senior and Youth Novice, is number four and five on the schedule. Not too long to go now.

I put on my black show jacket and light, mesh gloves (the latter being optional and no longer popular, I find out later). I am ready to take Winnie from Jenna, who, to my surprise, did not place first, as I thought she might. Her face is flushed as she hands me the supple leather lead line, attached to the dazzling, close-fitting show halter, embellished with silver.

"I missed the back-up," she says miserably. I feel badly for this bright-eyed young girl, who had her heart set on a win. I don't actually understand what occurred, but I have no time to wonder. I'm up next. "Sorry, Jenna," I say. "But you did well, all the same."

The thirteen-year-old bites her lip, then gamely lifts her chin. "Good luck in your class."

In a quiet moment with Winnie by my side, I close my eyes and, like water darkening a dry cloth, my showmanship pattern appears at the forefront of memory:

1. Walk to the judge and stand square.
2. Back up two steps.
3. Stand for inspection.
4. 180-degree turn over haunches.

5. Trot back through the line.
6. 180-degree turn over haunches.
7. Stand square in line.

Oh, that's what Jenna meant! *Number two, back up two steps.* With so many tips and prompts yesterday, for each of our three different classes – Showmanship, Trail, and Western Pleasure – it was hard to remember everything. Paper-obsessed me hadn't noticed, because I memorized the pattern that had been posted online days ago, and then checked again, a half hour ago, when it was posted on the bulletin board by the side of the barn.

It's moments away from the start of my class and I still don't know how many senior novice riders – if any – I'll be competing against. Then, happy day! I see a woman enter the ring leading her petite bay Morgan mare. The woman herself is dressed smartly in embellished black. We both wear black hats. I walk in after her. Then, happier day, another taller, equally smartly dressed woman, also leading a bay, follows me in, making the class a trio of contenders. It is one of the best moments of the day thus far: I won't be competing against myself! Let the showmanship class for senior novice begin.

Showmanship is a component of 4-H competition for young people. 4-H is a grassroots organization "of leaders building leaders," they say. Showmanship taught youth how to present a horse "in-hand," with only a halter and lead line. Over time, and now a popular part of Western shows, showmanship has become a highly competitive event with exacting standards at the highest level. In those lofty circles, it is a test of footwork, elegance and concentration, and seamless teamwork. Type A's need apply.

And senior novice me? I just want to keep smiling, and nail the pattern as best I can.

"Remember," Helen repeated to me and my camp-mates this past week, "it's all about your *confidence*. You can win a class practically with that alone. So smile the whole time you're in the ring. And don't just walk to the judge and stand there – set up and *present* that horse to the judge!" Her hands would rise up with the word "present," mimicking how the leather lead-shank would look, with the close end and chain held near to the horse's cheek, and the bottom end looped and tidy. "Keep your elbows in," she'd add. "And don't forget to quarter your judge!"

Right, quartering – had some trouble with that. The quarter method of showing essentially ensures that the judge always has an unobstructed view of the horse in the ring. When moving forward, the handler is always on the left or "off" side of the horse. However, when standing still, the horse is to be between the handler and the judge. The quartering system divides the horse into quarters, with a line from muzzle to tail, and a line crossing at the withers.

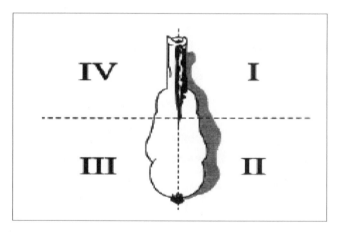

I can visualize this now – but what I really remember is Helen saying, "You switch over sides when the judge is at the girth, and at the tail." The handler never stands in the II or III quadrants, but moves from I and IV as the judge inspects the horse, a process that literally goes from stem to stern, and takes into account the horse's appearance, grooming, position, and behaviour in the most minute detail.

Here's how it goes: Every time the judge crosses an

imaginary line, the handler switches positions. Let's say the judge is in I and you are in IV. When she crosses the "wither line," or girth area, as Helen said, into II, you step from IV into I. Then, when the judge passes the tail line, you step back from I into IV. When the judge crosses from III into IV, you go back to I. Finally, when the judge crosses directly in front of the horse, you cross in front of her back to IV. At no point should you ever have your back to the judge, even in the lineup.

It seems foreign and graceless (those are big, even steps you're taking, as you switch back and forth) – until it becomes natural and graceful. Myself, I'll aim for not tripping on the extra long hem of my jeans, which is necessary, so they don't inch up my boots when I ride.

In the lineup on the rail, Winnie's the light-coloured cheese in the dark-rye sandwich of the two bays. Beyond that contrast, I believe she is standing out by her stunning appearance and stock-still behaviour. Exactly as she knew at the Tommy clinic that she was at an "event," she seems to know now that today, in the same ring as our summer camp, it is not summer camp, it's a show.

I stand as tall as I can, my feet angled to Winnie, as they are supposed to be. Jenna braided her mane this week, then we took out the tiny round elastics this morning. The tresses are platinum blonde and wavy. She's holding her head high, watching, in turn, the crowd of onlookers and participants at the end of the ring, and across the ring, another immaculately dressed Western judge. Summertime bounty: Winnie has shining golden dapples all over her body, coins of the seasonal realm, pressed into that soft coat of hers. What a regal mare ...

The handler who came in ahead of me goes first. She did an excellent job. *Keep smiling*, I tell myself. Again, I minutely adjust the angle of my feet.

The judge nods to me. *It's theatre*, I tell myself. *This dusty ring's a stage, and you're literally and figuratively centre stage, right now. Use that diaphragm to breathe and remember that an audience enjoys seeing things done right, with panache.* The pattern done, Winnie and I returned to the line. I think we did all right. Winnie did, for sure.

The third handler does her pattern. That looked good, too. Or what I saw of it. I am mostly trying to concentrate on our position in line, and on watching the judge. *That is your job,* Helen told all of us last week. *To watch the judge. Keep your eyes pinned on her.*

"Please line up in the centre of the ring," says the announcer, from the nearby tent that also houses the canteen and a few fold-out chairs for those seeking shade. The announcer is actually another new horse friend, Marion Crosby. She and her husband Sean are good friends of Helen's and Neil's, and close neighbours. An experienced horsewoman who's done a good deal of showing herself, Marion is doing an excellent job today of keeping the classes moving along at a steady pace. She also has a mellow but clear voice, well suited for the job at hand and pleasant for the atmosphere of the show.

She announces the third-place winner, which is the first handler who came into the ring. *Oh, I think, then I'm not third.* The woman accepts her ribbon with the same lovely warm smile she wore the entire class, and exits the ring.

Marion announces the second-place winner. *Oh, oh,* I think, *then I am not second.* The willowy woman accepts her ribbon graciously, and exits the ring.

"Your class winner is ring number 264, Marjorie Simmins and Juanawinsome." Winnie's registered show name: Juanawinsome (wanna win some). Yes, thank you, I do.

A red ribbon is proffered to me, along with a small trophy and a generous basket of gifts from Avon. I hope to heavens I said *thank you.* I feel stunned, completely unable to take in the moment beneath my skin. If I do, I'll shriek. It's a goddamned red ribbon, and a fancy one, a rosette. I didn't let them down – not Adrienne, not Helen, not Karin or my sweet Don, who looked after me for so long, after the accident, and still looks after my heart and soul, now. He of all people knows the before, during, and after of this story.

The ringmaster – a woman – asks if I need a hand carrying out the basket. "Oh, yes, please," I hear myself answer. "That would be great." I walk two more steps toward the gate, left hand holding my red ribbon and trophy in a death-grip.

"Hey, can you stop there, say cheese?" asks another warm voice, and this turns out to be yet another new horse friend, and photographer, Dawn Josey – who is also coming back to riding from an accident and with whom I share lessons at Helen's some days. She points her expensive camera at me. *Click.* "There, got a nice one." When I spoke with Dawn earlier today, having noted the serious camera, I had asked her to take a photo or two. I think she's taken a bunch. And Don, bless him, has been using our camera to video the whole showmanship class. I will learn so much from watching it. I'll treasure having it, and the photos.

Some sweltering hours later, it is time for my Trail class. I somehow thought the first-place win in the Showmanship class might bolster my confidence. Instead, I am guppy-breathing again, though with my show smile tacked in place. *Claim the stage,* I tell myself. Again, I've had the good fortune to see Jenna and Winnie – who had a terrific round – and others do the Trail pattern ahead of me. I don't have to close my eyes to see this one. It's right in front of me.

Here's the course, for Senior and Junior Novice Trail, as set up in the ring:

> Enter arena/ring at walk; walk over bridge.
> Walk to mailbox – deliver mail.
> Jog.
> Walk; open and close gate.
> Walk over poles.

Walk into box (made of log poles); turn 360
degrees; walk out.
Back through markers.
Exit under direction of the ringmaster.

Jenna did her course slowly. I do mine slowly, too. I almost knock over the mailbox because I shorten my reins too much, and put too much right leg on, causing Winnie to swing her haunches left. I *freeze* in the saddle, hands lighter, legs off, and the dangerous moment passes. In freeze-mode still, I go on to do my favourite part – mailing the letter and putting up the plastic delivery arm that says (to us older people), "You have mail."

All the other maneuvers go well, including the challenging 360-degree turn in the "box," where you must not touch the logs with the horse's hooves, or step outside of the box. We even sail through the opening and closing the rope gate, which we had trouble with days earlier. We back through the markers a tad on the fast side, but the gods smile and no mishaps occur. Winnie has a lovely insouciant swagger as she exits the ring – *Yes,* it says, *you were expecting less than perfect from the golden diva?*

Not from you, Winnie, but from me, perhaps ...

Don't sweat it, you guys, Helen had said to her young and not-so-young charges. *This is your first time for all these classes. Enjoy yourselves. It doesn't matter if you're not perfect. It doesn't even matter if you make lots of mistakes, or knock things over. It's all about the experience.*

We'd all nodded, agreed she had a point. And all my camp-mates rode like champs. Even the honourary twelve-year-old. It seemed like the best "thank you" we could give to Helen.

"Dear Big Sibs," I texted Zoë, in British Columbia, and Geoffrey, in Alberta, "I seem to have won my second class, Trail. Shocked, happy."

When it comes time for my third and final class, Western Pleasure, which came at the end of the day, I am stone-faced euphoric. It seems rude to be jumping up and down about how happy I am with the first two wins, when the other two senior novice riders are still very much on-site and competing. Some people may even wonder if I am pleased at all with how the day has unfolded so far. But I just can't take it in. I've sneaked in some happy kisses and hugs with Don, and sent some other texts to West Coast horse friends, but mostly, I thank all the kind people at the show who congratulate me, and keep quiet. I think even Helen is surprised at how contained I am.

"Good for you! Are you happy?" she asks when I come out of my Trail class, another red ribbon, trophy, and booty in hand.

"Amazing," I answer/non-answer. "Can't quite believe it." Now that is an understatement. Helen smiles, and whirls away.

Now it's time for Western Pleasure, walk and jog. No canter for the senior and junior novices, and no "patterns," either, which all the other divisions must do for most of their classes. I inhale deeply through my nose, fill my chest with fragrant if dusty summer air, and think about making my modest walk and jog look as comfortable and attractive as I can. Western *Pleasure* – that's right, watching my ride and the other riders', you the spectator should be thinking, *That looks so smooth and nice. I should just hop aboard. Bet we could cover the continent, just like that ...*

"And your class winner is ring number 264, Marjorie Simmins and Juanawinsome."

Another gorgeous crimson rosette, another small trophy, and yet more wonderful loot, in the form of a certificate for a trail ride at a nearby stable and a finely wrought metal votive candle holder.

I am out-of-body at this point, still determined not to make a fuss over myself, or make anyone else feel "less than," because of my wins. Hardly anyone here knows that it's been more than forty years since my last show, and they certainly can't guess about all the pain and despair that preceded this astonishing day. I do take another bear hug from my husband, who'd slipped away from the show for a bit and had then come back in time to see me collecting up my third ribbon. He even wahooed and clapped, bless him.

"Congratulations!" says my young friend Kendra Samson from Cape Breton, who is attending the show today, but not showing her graceful, small mare, Carlie. She'll be at Sherry's show, though.

"Thank you," I reply. "I couldn't have done any of this without my coaches, and Winnie."

"It's OK to take some credit for yourself," says the doe-eyed eighteen-year-old, suddenly serious. "Really, you worked for this, too."

Feeling embarrassed, I duck my head and nod. "Such a great day," is all I can manage.

And it is. Not long after my third class, I find out that the splendid black and white rosettes I've been admiring all day are for the divisional wins.

"Divisional wins?" I ask someone in the announcer's tent, where the ribbons have been displayed.

"You know," they say, "Youth English, Youth Western, Youth Novice, Senior English, Senior Western –"

"Senior Novice?" I interrupt.

A nod, then, "Select English, Select Western – and that's it."

"Ahhh," I say.

A few minutes later, a tired Don asks if I can't collect up my gear and we can go home.

"Don," I say, "I don't want to sound conceited, or make you wait too much longer, but I think one of those beautiful ribbons there –" I point at the tent wall, where they're hanging in an impressive row – "I think one of those might be mine, for the divisional win."

It was, along with an impressive black and white-trimmed "cooler," which is a light cooling-out blanket for a horse. Its side was boldly emblazoned with the words, "Avondale Sky Senior Novice Divisional Champion." The Avondale Sky winery had generously provided the cooler.

"But I don't have a horse," I laughed to Helen.

"I know a horse who needs one," she answered. "Winnie!"

Which was perfect, of course. Finally, after all she'd given me, I could do something for the golden steed.

"Has it sunken in yet, all those wins?" Don asks gently on the drive home to Halifax in the darkening twilight. I am so grateful he is driving. I can barely think or speak for the fatigue that presses down on me. It's as much psychic and emotional as physical. What a long road to get here.

"No," I say. "Not at all." Not just my wins, either. Helen, Adrienne, Janine Lock, Katie Giles, Jen MacNeil, and other new horse friends did wonderfully well, as did Jenna, and all our camp-mates. Long gone were the noodle-legs and other signs of new riders. Instead, Jenna, L'Rhya, and Avery rode legs still, shoulders back, and eyes up, testament to Helen's dedication to her students, and their own grit and hard work. Ribbons fluttered down. Little rock stars, I called the girls, swelling with as much pride as if I had been their coach, not Helen.

"Ready for some supper – and a glass of wine?"

Never more ready in recent or long history. The boiled eggs and small bits of food I managed to eat at the show were consumed a long time ago. "Yes," I say. "I'm ready." We drive on towards the city, my left hand on his jean-clad leg, my right hand resting on my lap. Two tired Shelties are stretched out on the back seat. I can completely relax now, with my pack all around me. The joy about the day is so expansive and yet hidden away, I can't share it yet. I focus instead on the steady hum of the truck and the solidity of Don's leg under my hand. Above us, a broad country sky escorts us home.

24

THE HERITAGE CHAMPIONSHIPS

Five days after Helen's show, I wrote her a Facebook message.

"Listen – could I try out an idea with you? As far as my riding goals are concerned, I have everything I wanted, and more, right now. I could not possibly do better at Sherry's show, and might not place at all. I just happened to do a tiny bit better than the two other women in my classes at your show. And I am thrilled it worked out that way, obviously. But what this writer needs right now is to write. If I didn't compete at Sherry's show, I could really get my teeth into my work. So again, if I skipped the big show, and just carried on training with you and your mum for Level Two – frankly, I'd be delighted. If, on the other hand, you think it's a good idea for whatever reasons that I do the big show, I will. What do you think? It could make your life easier, too."

Helen responded immediately – with evident disappointment. "We are going to the show regardless. And right now you are leading the province by a long shot for high point novice senior champion. So I do suggest you go. And we have been working towards Level Two [in recent lessons]. I think we should keep on and let the show be a relaxing experience. Also: Sherry needs the support for the show if you can swing it. And we will all be there. Good times!"

I took time to blink rapidly, smack aside my shame for trying to weasel out of a commitment, and then wrote her back. "OMG – you see I don't understand the big picture at all! I forgot all about the point system, and that I was ahead there. My heart went BUMP when I read that part. Good bump! And yes, of course, I do want to support Sherry. And yes again, we will have fun, like we always do. Right, we're on for the show!"

When Simminses get flustered and excited, or have good news to share – they generally write a letter or email. This Simmins wrote a letter that day to sibs and friends, describing my correspondence with Helen. "It's hard to comprehend my life these days. The stakes just go higher and higher, and wonderful things just keep happening. I am thrilled, with a kajillion butterflies in my stomach."

While I did feel ashamed about trying to deke out of Sherry's show, the feelings behind it were valid. Writing chose me as a vocation, when I was a teenager. I then chose it, when I turned thirty, as a way to make a modest and difficult living as a freelance journalist and teacher. It's hard to explain to anyone who doesn't have writing at the centre of their lives and psyches how unsettled writers get, when they don't put in long hours at their desks. No matter how outgoing I can be at times, writers are often equally unsettled when they've had a lot of "public time" and not enough quiet time, just in the company of words.

To deal with all of this, and after discussion with Don, I decided shortly after Helen's show that I would maintain my teaching commitments, but take a break from freelance writing and slot that time into my own book writing. The author of seventeen books, Don was all for it. He completely understood that with the time I was giving over to riding and training, and, secondarily, to magazine work, my own book writing was taking the hit. This unease, then, essentially explained my message to Helen, with its request to back out of Sherry's show.

Essentially, but not entirely. The other points still stood. I had recommitted to training for and going to the Heritage Championships, but I was still worried that I couldn't do nearly as well at the bigger show as I had at Helen's smaller show. Selfishly, I didn't want to lose the glow of victory I was finally permitting myself to feel in the aftermath of Helen's show. With horse shows, you can go from top-of-the-pile to out-with-the-trash in no time at all. If you train and show all your life, I believe you develop some resiliency in this regard: you know for an empirical fact that the equation works both ways. You also know that showing is actually about *community* – showing up, staying on, and cheering on your friends, just as I had told myself and done at the clinic and at the Roseway Summer Show. Which is why Helen stressed how everyone supported Sherry's show, and that newcomer or not, I should, too. The time and work that goes into putting on a two-day yearly horse show is considerable. It takes months. In ways small or large, I wouldn't be surprised if Sherry started on the work for next year's show the day after the previous one. You thank someone for this by – yes, *showing up*.

No one denies that showing is competitive. It is part of the thrill. You do your best on your own mount and hope to show the world what favoured equines they are, if only in your heart. Showing of any sort is "my baby's the cutest" writ large, and everyone knows that, and laughs and teases about that. It's also an opportunity to see which horse and rider team has been working and training hard, and to recognize those efforts with a cheerful word.

For the rider, there's no getting around it: everyone loves to win. Failing that, then doing well is just dandy. It's the "you are excused" that you don't want to hear, and certainly will, now and again, over a lifetime of showing.

I just don't want that to happen on August 8 or 9.

No promises.

And for once, I really have no idea who said that. I'll presume it was the voice of worry again. In which case, and again – *bugger off.*

* * *

Nearly an hour from Halifax, Windsor is the oldest of many "gracious little Valley towns," as my husband says, which lead into the heart of the Annapolis Valley, one of the Maritime region's most fecund agricultural areas, now filled with vineyards and wineries, too. Originally known as Pesaquid, a Mi'kmaq term meaning "junction of waters," the town is sited at the confluence of the Avon and St. Croix rivers, which flow into the Bay of Fundy. Residents of Nova Scotia claim the bay has the highest tides in the world. Residents of the town of Windsor claim it as the birthplace of hockey (other Canadian towns also claim hockey as their own). Facts more widely accepted are that French settlement began in the area around 1685 – that would be one hundred years before Marie Antoinette was discussing the merits of cake over bread – with permanent British settlement beginning in 1749, the same year Halifax was founded. In 1764, The Township of Windsor was created; one year later, the first annual Hants County Exhibition was held. This September, the exhibition would celebrate its 250th anniversary, making it the oldest, continuously run agricultural fair in North America.

The exhibition has always been held at the Windsor Fairgrounds. This is where I went for Tommy McDowell's Clinic, and this is where I am going this morning, August 8, to take part in Sherry Clark's Heritage Championship 2015. Imagine how many boot prints, current and historic, I'll be walking over and around in coming days, so many cowgirls and cowboys among them.

Last night, Don and I stayed at the Downeast Motel, only a kilometre from the fairgrounds. So there was no long drive in from Halifax in the dawn light, the truck loaded down with gear for the show, me endlessly intoning, "We're late." Instead, we drove our two vehicles down to Windsor yesterday and were comfortably snugged away in our motel by the late afternoon. Don, the Shelties, and I then had a quiet evening and a relatively easy start to the day. My nerves are already the better for it. It is typical of thoughtful Don to arrange this for us.

Now in the truck, en route to the fairgrounds, the pack of four together again, I check my makeup in the visor mirror, am content with what I see, and say nothing. I already know, unquestionably, that my Western hat, show jacket, makeup bag, and two show shirts are all with me, along with snacks and water. I am wearing an old T-shirt that I can work in, and my show jeans are tucked into my boots, to keep them clean. My show bow looks a tad odd again, with a lumpy bun, but I don't care. I'm even breathing like a yogi.

Gee, I am getting better at this.

If I thought Helen's barn on show day was a frothing cauldron of industry and femininity, then Sherry's show was all that – and a Himalayan mountain more. A few brave men were competing, often as part of a family show-contingent, and another few loyal, non-competing ones, my Don, Neil Morley, and Scott Smith included, were there to support their sweethearts and/or keep home properties running. Once again Adrienne had trucked horses down from Cape Breton, accompanied by Janine, Kendra, and also Jen Mac-Neil, from Sydney Mines, whose horse Harley is a "brother by a different mother," as Jen likes to joke, to both Boo and Winnie. While not a palomino, chestnut Harley's overall resemblance to Winnie, added to his own sweet, slightly comical nature, has fanned a crush-flame in my heart. I love watching the easy camaraderie Jen and Harley share and they are a team to be reckoned with in the show ring. In spite of trailer troubles on the way to Windsor, all the Cape Breton crew have now arrived safely. I heartily disliked the idea of crew and horses stuck by the side of the highway and was relieved to see them finally arrive. I am sure Helen, who has a uniquely close tie with her mother and has known most of the rest of the crew for many years, was very relieved.

We set up at the eastern end of the large main barn. Once again, my camp-mates' families are bubbling in and out of stalls and under cross-ties, grooming horses and girls alike, and generally creating a Mardi Gras atmosphere. Some of the women change their clothes in the bathrooms or in nearby empty stalls. Others simply cross their arms and whip off their T-shirts, replacing them with show shirts and jackets, in the middle of the aisle. Sequins, bold colours, and rhinestones are everywhere. As there was at Helen's show, there is talk of "lucky bras," red ones in particular, and lots of giddy laughter.

You couldn't dream up a more committed show family that L'Rhya's mother Michelle, grandmother Margo, aunt Ravyn, and Michelle's cousin, Sherry Tooke. Stalls are cleaned – once, twice, even thrice in a day – along with aisleways swept, boots polished, errands run, and lost items found. Sherry, a professional hair stylist, is much in demand. Ravyn had helped to re-anchor my show bow at Helen's show, when by mid-afternoon the droop had gotten droopier yet. Today Sherry tells me she would be happy to style my hair without the show bow, suggesting instead a fancy braided style that, once in place, won't budge until the start of the next millennium. Yes, please, I smile, that would be great. We hustle off to an empty stall, where Sherry has set up a folding camp chair and on top of a cooler has placed all her lotions, potions, makeup, and brushes. In short order I have a dazzling and secured hairdo, and feel as Blanche DuBois did in *A Streetcar Named Desire*, greatly touched by this kindness from a stranger.

I am enjoying seeing familiar faces of young women and men I met first at the clinic and then some of whom I saw again at Helen's show. Also in attendance are some of the boarders I know from Helen's barn. There's the always genial Wendy Glenham and her tall, chestnut mare, Annie. Nearby, the pert, all-things-horses teenager, Mary Solway-Ferguson, who is openly dotty about her multi-talented Fjord Horse, Cookie B. Nibblin. That girl is gratitude on two long legs, and loads of fun.

Nice to see Katie Giles, too. I was so impressed when I first met her at Helen's barn a few days before the clinic. She'd come striding into the barn, looking for Helen, who was out in the ring. Seeing me instead, Katie resumed her leggy gait with her right hand stretched out before her. "Hi, I'm Katie Giles," she said, and then related the nature of her business, which concerned trucking her horse. Her self-assurance and good manners were delightful. I found out later from Helen that eighteen-year-old Katie runs her own business as a barn manager, leasing a nearby barn, then renting out the stalls to other horse owners, overseeing all aspects of the boarding operation. Fair and freckled, strong but feminine, Katie was among the first people to greet us when we arrived for the clinic, over a month ago now. We'd barely parked the truck and trailer before she (once again) came striding out of the main barn saying, "Need a hand?" and then proceeded to start hauling in our supplies and gear. She halved our set-up time. What a gift.

Sherry's show has thirty-six classes, four more than Helen's show. A couple more English classes, a couple more Western. With forty-five entrants, there's a good turnout for the event, with some showing English and Western, and everyone going in a fair number of classes overall. Some of the classes, such as English Equitation and Showmanship, will be large, with fifteen or more entrants.

I am still congratulating myself on feeling calmer than I did at the first show, when I wander over to the smaller of the two indoor arenas and see the course for my first class, Trail.

"Helen? Is there a mistake? Is this actually the course for the novice riders?" My eyes are wide as I take in the long bridge, surrounded by horse-distracting greenery, with a horses-hate-it tarp underneath, the tight log "L" into which we will trot and back out of, the tightly spaced logs, over which we'll trot and try not to hit or bump out of place, and the profusion of potted flowers and small evergreens, all intended more to divert horses' attention than to beautify the course. Some horses even try to eat the greenery, or bite and lift the plants by their centre stalks and wave them around. If they do this, they will receive a penalty, for "disturbing the course."

I've already looked at the pattern for the class, and it, too, is more demanding than I've done before. Included are a half-pass – in this case, a lateral movement along a pole – and a turn on the forehand, another lateral movement that involves moving the horse's hindquarters around his front legs. Fortunately, I have experience with these movements, and Winnie is excellent at them. Not so sure about the –

"Winnie might not like that tarp," muses Helen. "But not to worry. We'll get through this."

It is Jenna who will "get through it" first, as once again the Junior Novice Trail class precedes the Senior Novice. Jenna, like all of us novices, is concerned about the course. But up comes that chin again. As always, she's ready to give it her best shot.

Seasoned, willing, smart, and generous Winnie wants absolutely no part of crossing the bridge, with a *blue* tarp under it, of all the nasty and alarming things. She is pleasantly, stoically immovable. Jenna keeps her cool, but despite some good thumps with her heels cannot get the mare to move. She negotiates with Winnie for some minutes, but it's obvious to all, including the judge, that the first obstacle is an obstacle indeed to the horse's and rider's progress around the course. Jenna is permitted to go around the bridge, complete another element, and is then excused.

"You can do this," says Helen, when my Trail class starts and I am next up. "Pound her with your legs if you have to, but get across that bridge. You'll be fine with the rest of it."

For the first time since my return to riding in the summer of 2013, I am *certain* I can do this. If there's one thing a start in the hunter-jumper discipline gives you, it's a knowledge of "pounding" with your feet and legs. *This horse ain't'a gonna quit on me* is mother's milk to those who ride hunter and jumper courses. It's just too *dangerous* for horses to quit on a jump-course. Long before you feel the horse *thinking* about hesitating, you've been driving them on. And if that first thought does get formed, you drive even harder, looking up and ahead to the *next* fence, if you please. Yeah, I can do this.

Which doesn't mean I have much control over my hammering heart. Jenna tried hard, too.

We approach the bridge walking out nicely. There is impulsion to this gait. I settle deeper into the saddle, hands light, legs ready to do what they have to do. *We will do this.* One stride, two strides, and I can feel her just starting to think. I mash on my leg – and Winnie stops. Bang, bang, bang, bang, bang, go my heels. Nothing. Not one yellow hair moves forward. The mare doesn't go sideways, she doesn't back up. She simply doesn't move. I am not upset, but I am in a state of disbelief. *Winnie, no! We can do this – come on!* My heels keep on drumming, even harder now. She takes one step forward – *we've got it!* – and slams on the brakes again.

The ring master is waving me on. I, too, am allowed to complete another element, for the sake of schooling, and finishing on a good note, and then ... *I am excused from the class ...*

"I tried, Helen, I really, really tried." I remain shocked, more than upset, as I dismount. "She wouldn't budge."

"It's not a problem," she says briskly. "Mum will ride her in Senior Trail tomorrow, and we'll take care of this. We just have to get her over the bridge once, and she'll be fine. She doesn't like that tarp."

Which is the whole idea of Trail classes, which originally mimicked elements a horse and rider might find on a trail ride and need to deal with, and later incorporated all sorts of elements, many of which a horse would find perturbing. When I was growing up, I once saw a Trail class at the Pacific National Exhibition that included a pen full of pigs, which many horses detest. Some horses didn't walk by that, either. The best trail horses are calm by nature, and calmer by intensive training. They will literally take anything that's thrown at or over them. Champion Winnie was just feeling stubborn today – and had novices riding her.

I've been so busy with my small crisis that I haven't paid full attention to "the horse on course," as they say in jumper circles. This is another senior novice, and she is having an awesome round, steady and successful. It's Marilyn MacKay, one of the senior novices who competed in the same classes I did, at Helen's show! I'd seen her earlier on, and we'd hugged, delighted to see one another again, and to be competing side by side again. "I don't know if I am happy to see you or not," she'd laughed, that elfin smile I'd remembered once again dimpling her face. "You kicked my butt last time!" "Ah, but it's a whole new day," I'd laughed in return. "We'll just see what goes on today and tomorrow."

Indeed. We are seeing it now. Marilyn and Jigs, a black and white Paint, just aced the Trail class. It was a treat to watch, from start to finish. Her husband, Claude, and their daughter, Meg, an accomplished young rider who's been helping prepare her mother for the shows, must be thrilled. As Marilyn is the only other competitor, she is the class winner, and I come second. I know this is how shows can work sometimes – that you get a second-place ribbon and don't really "deserve" it – but even still, I feel peculiar reaching out to take my blue ribbon. Conversely, Marilyn deserved her first-place ribbon, twice over. Perversely and thoroughly, I am enjoying losing to such a great round. But once is enough. I'll try to do better tomorrow.

The day continues unevenly for me. Jenna's on fire now and does a beautiful Showmanship class. Mine, in the same big arena where we rode in the clinic, was odd. I could blame the Trail class for disturbing my equanimity, which in turn meant I wasn't paying full attention when I did my next class, but that wouldn't be the whole truth. I was distracted by nerves, all right, but mostly I hadn't correctly memorized the pattern.

"You'll need to work on your pivots and turns on the haunches," said the attractive, brown- and cream-clad judge from Ontario, as the three senior novices waited in line for the results.

Pivot? I was supposed to do a pivot? I smiled at her, nodded, was dumbfounded.

A pivot is a forward-motion maneuver where the horse plants one leg and walks around that leg. Done precisely, the hoofprint and circle done with the hoof should be visible in the dirt or sand. I'd simply done a circle, with all four legs moving.

Do not howl, I tell myself. A mistake is only a mistake, not a Greek tragedy. But I feel desolate. The judging proceeds and a few minutes later I am picking up my second, blue, undeserved ribbon of the day, having once again been trounced by Marilyn, though coming ahead, apparently, of the third handler, who I do not know.

The class finishes, and horses and humans exit the ring. I find Helen.

"When the judge said, 'You'll have to work on your pivot,' I just kept blinking at her, and smiling like a fool. Pivot? What bloody pivot? I completely gapped on that!"

Without skipping a beat Helen, ever the coach, says, "You'll have to work on them, and before tomorrow, too. Remember, this is a two-day show and you'll be doing the exact same classes in the same order tomorrow."

Oh, yes, I hadn't forgotten …

Not to worry, says the suggestion of a voice, a dragon-fly's whirr by my ear, *You're gonna win your Western Pleasure class …*

I am?

I did. It was an exhilarating end to the day, with renewed hope for more red ribbons the following one.

Don and I pick up some ready-made food from a near-by grocery store, make a stop at the liquor store for wine, and return to our modest motel, the "air-conditioning" in our room provided by a stand-up fan. I am relieved we aren't back on the highway heading to Halifax, and then coming back again tomorrow, for the last day of the show. We eat, sip, talk, and laugh. I am feeling much better than I did after Helen's show – not as tired, not as tightly held together – and I've decided I am thrilled with blue ribbons, however haphazardly they may come into my life, and the prizes that came with them, too. I riffle through the gift certificates, think about the fun I'll have later on, spending them. Gotta say, Western shows rock the prizes.

Middle-aged me doesn't sleep through the night, but has had enough rest to be getting on with. Soon enough we're back in the truck again, heading for the fairgrounds and the final day of the Heritage Championships. I'm not really sure who this woman is, the one who's quietly sitting here, alongside her husband, but she seems to be a new, im-proved version of me. Composed.

It won't last.

Senior Trail, the class that Adrienne takes Winnie in,

before Jenna's class and mine, doesn't go as any of us expects. To my surprise, once Winnie has made it clear she is not walking over the bridge, Adrienne does not try to force her. I watch with interest as she confers with the judge – one seasoned professional to another – and asks to lead Winnie across, on foot. This she does, calmly leading the now non-resistant palomino across the wooden bridge.

"Now that's she's gone across once, she'll be fine," says Helen.

And so she is. It helps that the course has been changed and is now to be done in the exact reverse order. The bridge was the first obstacle yesterday, and the last today. The other elements aren't easy, by any means, but they all come before the bridge, so we'll have momentum on our side. I watch with admiration as Jenna does a calm, clean round. It should help to give me a boost, emotionally speaking. Instead, I feel worried off the scale of measurement. Yesterday I was confident – and look what happened. I think my superstitious Celtic mind wants to low-key the expectations today. I manage to keep my worries mostly to myself and listen to Helen, once again coaching me by the starting gate. I mount Winnie, wait for number 264 to be called.

Helen steps up beside us. I smile when she sets my reins at the right length, just as she does for the young girls. I think she may even have said, *There, now leave them be.* But no sooner does she send me on my way into the ring than I shorten the reins – because I'm *in a show ring, you fool, and I need to be in control!* I just can't help it. Western reins always feel too long to me. Responsive Winnie reacts instantly with two back-up steps, just as we come alongside the pole we're supposed to be half-passing along. She had been in the perfect position to start the lateral movement, and I blew it. Feeling a bit sick, I slacken the reins and the most forgiving mare ever stops her backing, corrects her position, and commences the half-pass. It feels graceful and good, if a bit speedy.

We move right into the turn on the forehand, which was smartly executed, and are then ready to trot over the poles leading into the log box. Bingo, nice and tidy on that, too. Now's the part I've been dreading: backing through the narrow log "L." *Ride her like the champion she is, and go slowly,* says the voice of dozens of lessons at Roseway Stables. I do these things, and Winnie backs the L picture-perfect. I am so buoyed by the last maneuver I am barely conscious that we are heading straight for the big, bad bridge, complete with trolls beneath the tarp, surely. Bridge, what bridge? I sit up and back, slack the reins a whisker, put full leg on, and Winnie gently clumps across it. We are done.

My heart is hot with joy. This time, I can't tamp down my feelings. I don't say or do anything much, just sit there in the saddle feeling the world around me edgeless and welcoming. Every heartbeat is a yes in my chest and in my life and in my eyes, as I look for a silver-haired scribe and two orange dogs in the crowds. Yes, they are coming towards me.

Later, and with an immense grin, I accept the red first-place ribbon the judge hands me. Now *this* is a win, and finally, I permit myself to feel ecstatic. I used head, heart, and spirit for this ribbon, and all settled right in the world, like a great blue heron swooping down for water from a creek, his wings folding in as he lands, exactly where he aimed to.

No rest for the wicked or weary. It's after lunch now, and I am about to enter the arena for my second Showman-ship class. I have the pattern burned into my brain, and am once again following an excellent round by Jenna. That girl does such good pivots with Winnie! Marilyn is in my class again, along with a third entrant I do not know. Winnie and I begin the pattern. Don is videoing us from the right side of the arena and even thinking about this makes me pull back my shoulders and straighten my spine. We trot to the judge and then walk, and halt. I step back from Winnie and prepare to set her up for inspection.

And I can't. She is already standing one hundred percent square. I don't actually trust my eyes. Is this possible, or should I move her one tiny inch left, right, forwards or backwards?

"Don't see that often," says the judge drily. "Take it."

Flabbergasted, I manage to say, "I can barely believe my eyes – and yes, I'll take it." The rest of the pattern is one hundred and one percent perfect, and I take that, too, pivot and all. *Winnie's on the floor! Who'll put 'er off?* No one. Not this day, and not with this entrant. I float to the judge again, Winnie loose-limbed, her finely etched face smug, and accept my first-place ribbon.

And just as I knew at Helen's show that I was going to win high-point for my division that day, I know now that I will win all three of my classes today, and the high-point for my division this day. I lost high-point to Marilyn yesterday and was happy to do so. She rocked her classes yesterday. But behind Winnie and me are Don and my family, and Helen and Adrienne, and all my new and old horse friends, who said, "Enjoy – go out there and enjoy." And so we do, the yellow mare and me.

The class seems far too short and I'd love to do a rocking-horse lope for the judge, not just a walk and jog, just to show her how well Winnie and I do that now. We do a bunch of things not too badly now. Could I interest you in seeing our counter-canter, a balanced lope or canter on one lead while the horse is travelling in a curve in the opposite direction, or maybe a few "fencing runs"? Perhaps some large and small canter circles, with collections and extensions? I know, we can't really do that latter bit consistently yet, but we're working on it. That will come next year, I hope, when Winnie and I show in the Senior or Select divisions, both of which are open to over fifties. *Can't wait.*

I accept the third red ribbon of the day with reverberating happiness. And then feel exhilarated as hell.

The last hour of a show is comparable to the last hour of a circus's stay in town. Everything is done at fast-forward speed. The next "town" – regular nine-to-five work-life, resettling horses at home barns – awaits. The "tents," or small tent cities, more like, inside the barns, come down. Stalls are stripped. Water and feed buckets are stowed in the back of trailers, along with tack, lunge lines, halters, and rolling, three-tier tack boxes. Garbage is collected up. Lawn chairs are folded, coolers collected. Show clothes are placed back on hangers, covered by dry cleaner bags, hung on hooks in cars, trucks, and motorhomes. Purses and car keys with heavy fobs are lost, for the twelfth time that day, and found with eager cries, for the thirteenth time. Horses are led into trailers; hay nets are secured above their heads. Extra hay and grain is stored back in the vehicles. Barn aisleways are swept. Jokes are traded, congratulations or commiserations exchanged.

All this goes on as the warm Valley skies decide to open and torrents of rain come down. We had taken both vehicles to the hotel during our two-day stay, so we could come and go independently, as needed. I have our car now and will be driving myself home; Don and the dogs left for Halifax in the truck some time ago. I check with Helen that all is done that needs to be done, here at the show grounds. She is in her truck now, the horses and gear loaded, Kendra in the passenger's seat beside her, about to leave for Ardoise. Adrienne and her crew, meanwhile, have accepted the invitation to stay at Sherry's place in Brooklyn tonight, as the highways aren't fit to drive, certainly not the long way back to Cape Breton. I stand beside Helen's rumbling diesel truck, the rain sluicing down, waiting to make the sprint to my car, a good ways off in the main parking lot. "Are we good to go?" I ask. "We're good to go!" says Helen. I nod, see the electric window start to draw upwards.

Then I am running alongside the truck as Helen pulls away. Me, *running*, the woman who used to feel the base of her back was full of broken marbles, clicking and resetting every time I ran a few steps. The back is leaden and swollen from two days of riding and standing, but it does not hurt, and I can run and I want to run and I do run, arms pumping and water from the puddles smacking upwards, soaking my jeans. There's also something in my throat, something fluttery I can't seem to swallow away. It's a circular song, a tumbleweed of thrumming emotion and vitality.

WAHOOOOO!

I lift my face to the black, wet sky, shout it again –

WAHOOOOO!

Helen and Kendra laugh as they pass me in the truck. I keep running, my boots splashing through the horizontal line of puddles that take me to my car.

Sonuva gun, that was a fairly decent wahoo, by me, for me, and no one else.

Inside the car I turn on the ignition and resist the urge to shake my sopping raincoat like a Labrador retriever at the beach. Instead, I pull off the coat, scrunch it on the floor beside me. It's still warm outside, just riotously rainy. As I wait for the windshield to defog, I start shivering. Warm or not, I am weary, and my jeans are soaked. I turn the heater dial, cranking it up. I am poised to leave when I suddenly realize I am not going anywhere, not stuck as I am in a loose-pebble and water-slooshy rut. Car won't go forward, car won't go back. It just settles deeper in the muck.

The parking lot is damn near empty now, but I manage to bolt from my car and ask two men who are just leaving the grounds to help me out. They are brawny country men, and efficient problem-solvers. Quicker than you can say, "Horse on the loose!" the fellows attach a hauling chain underneath my car and pull it out of the deep rut with one of their big diesel trucks.

All of this means that I am almost the last person to

Winnie and me, accepting a first-place ribbon for Showmanship, Roseway Stables Summer Show, July 2015. (Photo by Dawn Josey)

Winnie and me, Shania and Avery McLean. One of many bitter-cold rides at Roseway Stables during the winter of 2015. (Photo by Helen Morley)

leave the Windsor fairgrounds. Even Sherry, having first ascertained that I was "rescued," is on her way home. No cars, trucks, trailers, or motorhomes anywhere around me. The circus has definitely left town.

After the many companionable times with Don and the dogs in the truck of late, I feel a twinge of loneliness here in the car by myself. There's a darkening stretch of highway between me and home. When I get there, I'll take a deep bubble bath and make myself a hot rum, with lemon and honey. The thought cheers me. I turn off the heat, open the driver's window, make myself uncomfortable enough, wide-awake enough, to drive home safely. Beside me on the seat, my gear bag, stuffed with water bottles and uneaten snacks. In the far corner of it I see a small detail of shiny crimson, peeking out from under my grey hoodie. That's all the company I need.

25

COUNTRY WEDDING
BROOKLYN, NOVA SCOTIA, AUGUST 29, 2015

The small square church with its high ceiling is full of people who love Helen Smith and Neil Morley. Among these, luckily, are both sets of parents – all in good health, with durable marriages of their own. The atmosphere is softly romantic, as summer weddings are supposed to be. The room is filled with filtered summer light; roses, lavender, and horseshoe pew-bows; colourful bouquets set in vases on each window ledge, and by the pulpit; well-dressed family and friends from near and far; and at the front, on the left, Wendy MacIsaac, a Cape Breton fiddler and guitar-accompanist of the finest order. Soon, we'll all turn our heads to see a radiant young horsewoman enter this sacred space, walking down the aisle on the arm of her father. She has come to marry a man who shares her dreams for a future full of love, laughter, work, and horses. Lots of horses. They are both ready for whatever adventures pull them forward.

Neil, looking every inch the tall, wide-shouldered football player that he was in university, is resplendent in a well-cut grey suit and stands beside his groomsman, a friend of some years, and his best man, whom he has known since childhood and with whom – the height and heft are a dead giveaway – he played football. Neil looks all the things you'd expect: nervous, excited, happy, eager. I look at him, and tears fill my eyes. Those are all the feelings any man or woman should feel on such a day. It takes me straight back to March 14, 1998, the day of my own wedding, in a cherry-blossom-filled Vancouver.

Neil's two beautiful daughters, Kaitlyn and Jenna, along with tiny Olivia Potvin, are Helen's flower girls. The bridesmaids, Jennifer MacNeil and Sandi Powell, and Maid of Honour, Natalie Joan MacLellan, are long-time friends. Jen and Sandi are horsewomen, through and through; it's been a pleasure to spend time with them over the re-cent show period. To Jen's amusement, my crush on Har-ley continues unabated. And I sure smiled to find out it was Jen's sweetheart Scott Roberts who helped me the last day of Sherry's show, when my car got stuck in the mud in the parking lot. Horsewomen and -men, they won't let you down. The bridal party here assembled is "show-groomed," and beaming. There is a palpable feeling of What a great idea! Let's do this!

Helen and her father Scott enter the church. Helen's el-egant, embellished wedding dress is strapless. I think of the riding lessons we had earlier in the summer, how she'd stand in the centre of the hot riding ring to teach, calling out this and that instruction, all the while pulling the straps on her tank top over the caps of her shoulders, and lathering on sunscreen, "because I don't want to have strap marks on my wedding day," she'd say. Sure enough, her shoulders are gen-tly rosy, without strap marks, her carriage erect as a danc-er's, or rather, the proud equestrienne she is, in the saddle on her own since she was three. A sparkling necklace is set against her throat, and her long auburn hair is pulled away from her smiling face. Her bouquet is made up of white and pink roses, lavender, and round-leafed greenery; the stems are gathered in a wrap of green and blue MacKenzie tartan, and against this, a vertical line of pearls, surrounded by a Celtic horseshoe. There is also a wee bit of lace trim on the bouquet, taken from Adrienne's veil.

Something old, something new, something borrowed, something blue, a sixpence in your shoe – the latter item might not be in evidence, but I am guessing the four other objects are, as per the old English rhyme. If I remember correctly, something old represents continuity; something new offers optimism for the future; something borrowed symbolizes borrowing happiness from other happily married couples; something blue stands for purity, love, and fidelity. And the sixpence in your shoe? A wish for good fortune and prosperity.

The wedding ceremony begins. And not so far in, one of my favourite Biblical passages, Corinthians 13:1-13 ...

... *When I was a child, I spake as a child, I understood as a child, I thought as a child: but when I became a [wo]man, I put away childish things.*

For now we see through a glass, darkly; but then face to face: now I know in part; but then shall I know even as also I am known.

And now abideth faith, hope, charity, these three; but the greatest of these is charity.

Charity, a synonym for love. The greatest of these is love.

26

THEN, NOW, AND ALWAYS
SEPTEMBER 2015

A day on my own, no lessons, shows or barn time, no desk or deadlines, not even the company of Don or the dogs. Just rambling around Halifax on my own, with a short list of errands to keep my feet moving and my thoughts free to roam.

I want to be better. I might have said that once or twice before.

If you really care about an endeavour that comes with its own complex universe, such as riding and the horse world, you will always want to be better and learn more. You can as easily be inspired by an excellent rider, as you can be discouraged. Maybe one day, you think, I will be able to ride that gracefully, or even have a single ride that stirringly beautiful. Just as fast comes the other voice, the one that, for most of us, tempers unrealistic dreams: Don't be silly, you'll never be that good – that's inborn talent and life-long drive you're looking at. Sometimes it seems like a daily choice in choosing positive or negative thought, as to how you assess your progress, and how you feel when you walk in a barn for a lesson or a ride. You do your best to be positive, of course. Other times your emotions are insubordinate. Your job then is to breathe deeply and shake off the jitters, before the horse does some shaking of his own.

Keeping steady emotionally and physically when you're healing from a serious accident is tough. Over the course of three focused years of coming back to riding, I've had days of stony depression and bounding joy. That last day of the Tommy Clinic was one of the harder times. I remember thinking that after seven months of training, I should have been further along than I was. Helen seemed pleased with me, and Tommy McDowell himself had said to her, "She's coming along all right," so I felt good about that. I was also aware that my exhaustion didn't help. Fatigue is a joy-killer. But at that point and others in my life, I have felt that riding is a never-ending battle between small victories and endless self-criticisms.

By the end of this year's showing season, my head was also buzzing with information overload. The number of new concepts related to riding and horsemanship that I'd crammed in my noggin since the previous summer was … considerable. I felt very much as though I were a Jill of new concepts, and a mistress of none. I don't know how many times I'd thought to myself, "And you used to be a horse owner?"

The horse world changes all the time, incorporating new disciplines and technologies. New fads and philosophies rule the day, too. My time away from the sport didn't do me any favours. Beyond that, I seemed to be rusty at everything connected to horses – because, I was. I burned with embarrassment at times, when I made simple mistakes in front of either of my coaches. Other days it saddened me that neither Adrienne nor Helen ever saw me young, fit, and capable. They never will.

Only older and determined. And that will have to do. I feel blue sometimes.

Gee, it's not that bad, giggles Karin. *No one died.*

What the hell – Karin! I did not hear you say that!

Oh, yes, you did! Come on, have a little laugh. No one died.

It's the black joke the Simmins family has used ever since December 25, 1974, when we learned that Karin had died from an overdose. How was your Christmas? people ask each other each year. Oh, fine, we'd say for many years after the unrelenting horror and pain that was most of the second decade of Karin's life, and then, her "sudden" death, ruled a suicide, No one died. If you don't laugh through the pain sometimes, you'd just keep howling, and never heal.

My point exactly, says Karin.

I gather you're still here.

For a while, she says. *But then I have to go … soon …*

She always did love a good laugh, and had a wicked-keen sense of humour and mimicry.

Hello, I haven't left yet. And what do you mean, did? I still do love to laugh. Besides, buck up and fly right, as Mum used to tell us. Remember when I told you that you were gonna win that Western Pleasure class at Sherry's show?

That was you? I ask. That dragonfly sound?

Yeah, I thought for sure you'd know it was me. I was there the day you said goodbye to Coqeyn, too – remember all those dragonflies? What a gorgeous summer day …

Why were you there? I am not sure I like this version of my story.

To keep you from falling.

But I wasn't going to fall that day. Of that I remain positive. I think she's still waiting for more of an answer, so I say: Even then, Karin, I was getting stronger. You must know that.

Well, hell, no credit for that, eh? She sounds so cheery, I hate to dash her mood.

Can't do, I say.

No reply from Wherever-She-Is. I hear nothing. Then a tiny sigh, the saddest ever. Suddenly, I feel a shared, scalding pain that makes me gasp.

You came to say goodbye, too ... you came to say you were sor –

Something like that, she mumbles. *Don't get maud –*

– lin, I finish for her. Maudlin – that sounds like the sister I know, I think to myself with a smile. She wasn't big on tearful moments, though she tolerated mine. Be fair. She loved Coqeyn. She loved you. Until she couldn't love anyone anymore, especially herself. I am not used to thinking about her with a knowing love, the kind you have when someone is living, not gone, long gone. It hurts.

Anyway, look, I just wanted to tell you –

No, I think, with a wash of unexpected stubbornness, I don't want her to tell me anything. I can't manage this.

Karin, let's get real – or whatever the hell this is. You can't tell me anything. That's not logical or possible.

Some things aren't logical, she says. She aims for black humour again: *My life would be one of those things. This conversation, too, but it's as real as I can do.* A short pause, then she pushes on. *I just wanted to tell you – keep riding. You have some bad days. So what? Keep on. You were right all along. It's the way ahead. You're "better" every day horses are in your heart.*

Thanks for believing, I say. And I do not cry, or feel sad. I just feel ... supported, by someone who really knows how hard the journey's been.

I always did believe, she says firmly. A geologically long pause. *I just didn't know how to see, or believe in my own future ...*

I know I should feel sorry for her. But I don't. Instead, the never-lost anger surges, riptide strong.

Karin, it was so hard, for all of us. Mum, Dad, us kids. When you lied and cheated and stole from us, and then hurt us, physically. When you hurt Mum!

I know. It was me, and it wasn't – do you understand?

No, I never did. I mean, we all understood the facts.

290 - Marjorie Simmins

It was the day-to-day horrors that tore at our hearts, beat us down to our knees. Your betrayals were staggering. The sister I loved would never have hurt us that way – even poor Coqeyn. In the end, you were a stranger.

To myself, too.

Another Precambrian pause. I need a little time to feel all right with her again, or all right with the one she is now – who – say it – came in peace. I breathe to the sky and back, settle myself just the same way I do at the barn, on a day of messy emotions. What's the important thing to ask now? Easy, comes the answer. Keep in the present.

And so I ask, But it's better now, much better, right?

Right, she agrees. A third weighted pause, this one full of mirth. *But you won't know about that for a while yet.*

We are laughing. I am, anyway, and I know she must be because my laugh feels so twinned, with high and low notes of hers, mine, both.

Won't know about that for a while yet, I repeat, deadpan ... best news of the day, that. But I need to tell her one more thing. For the then, now, and always of our lives ...

Karin? Let's really, really put it all behind us, can we?

Maggie, what do you think I've been trying to do? I could only stay long enough to see you strong again, to help make that happen by sharing the good memories, muting the others, even having a laugh. Can't stay much longer ...

And that, I decide, is good. Certainly for today; I need my private reality now. I am not worried about finalities. Really, are there such things? No matter what Karin says, I am sure I'll hear her voice again, but on my terms now, adult to adult, and here-and-now, me opening the door to Over There, where-she-travelled-to, and only now and then, when I wish to. I am not only stronger physically at this point, the best yet since the accident, I am also much stronger psychically, at fifty-six, than I was as a fourteen-year-old.

Karin's laughing again. *That was so adorable, when Hel-*

en set your reins at the right length for you.

Yeah, cute, huh? I really was just "one of the girls" at Roseway Stables.

Think of it, Maggie – Karin's voice is fading – *for all those instructors of ours who didn't care the way this one does, and Adrienne does – don't you feel lucky now?*

Lucky for most of them, Karin, when you think back – but outright blessed for these ones.

Ride. Ride for yourself, no one else. Those easy, off-the-clock times with horses you yearn for will come, from what I see.

See?

The air molecules around me are shimmering. The brightest ones pull me forward, determinedly, a fresh horse on a windy autumn day.

I have to go, I say. And I do. It's the end of the day now, and I need to be with Don, MacTavish and Franki, the Shelties, not here in Another Place of Thought, far from them.

I'm so happy for those three in your life, says Karin, the quietest yet.

Yes, I say. Blessings.

For all, she whispers.

For all, I whisper back.

Afterword
November 2015

Changes ahead, for Don and me. After two long years of trying to sell our house in Halifax, we finally have a sale looming. It is time to downsize and simplify our lives. Owning one home in Cape Breton is the right choice for us.

I'll miss Halifax. It's been good to me. But lucky me, I have Caberfeidh Stables to go to in Cape Breton, and my first coach, Adrienne, with whom to train. Don and I also hope to skip some Maritime winters by overwintering in B.C. again, as we did for several years when we first married. It was a good system then, and it will be good again. We might even go to Florida for some of the worst winter months.

And yet, so many changes. Whenever I feel overwhelmed, Don takes my hand, squeezes it, and says, "Vancouver." My hometown. Where I learned to ride.

Riding. I can't lose what I've gained in the past two years – I just can't. I swear, it would hurt as much as the riding accident to spend over two years training, striving, and succeeding, only to allow changing circumstances to take it all away again. Continuity, commitment – like marriage, it's all part of the equation.

So use your head, I've told myself. You have horse friends on the West Coast, too. Tash, Letsa, Edie, in Langley, and Nancy at the Pony Barn at Southlands – these are people you've known for decades, all of whom are still connected to the horse world, still own or ride horses, and all of whom you know how to contact again, or have already been in recent contact with. You like them, they like you. And if that doesn't work out, for whatever reason, something else will. Keep your focus and drive, to get what you need. If the last two years haven't taught you that, nothing will. Honestly, as our Australian sailor friend Trevor Robertson is fond of saying, give your head a shake.

Or, as Adrienne told me earlier this year, "This is a journey. There will be detours. You just have to go along as best you can and when things change or get delayed, you go along with that, too. The most important thing is to keep on riding."

Funny, I've heard that phrase a lot over the years ...

Incredibly, after a year of much change and endeavour for Helen, the full-time-working, newly wed, new "esquire" or landowner, and for me, the senior novice Western rider and lifelong writer, she and I were able to schedule and do my Equine Canada Level Two Western Rider exams on November 1, 2015. On that day, I "exceeded expectations" on the written and oral exams, and "met expectations" on the riding exam – which unexpectedly, I took on Shania, the mare with the spine of "pure kindness," because Winnie was in need of a shoeing that week and it couldn't be arranged. Considering how tired I was physically from nearly a year of training and effort, and how distracted I was with our complicated and protracted house sale, and the upcoming move to Cape Breton, and how nervous I was generally – a test, you fool, it was a test! – and particularly, because I wasn't riding Winnie, all in all, I'd have to say that "jubilant" wouldn't half cover the aftermath of that day.

So, Level Two is done now, and even though Level

Three is apparently three times as hard as the first two, I'd still like to try for it. I just don't know when, or how, or who I might be riding. For someone who loves continuity and predictability ...

You know, says the voice of riding confidence I haven't heard in years, you rode without Helen and Winnie for decades – remember?

Yes, of course, but that was before.

And this is after. Your healing is almost done, or as manageable as it ever will be. Helen can still be your coach, you can still have time in Ardoise, and still ride Winnie, just not as much of all three as you did this past year. And as you've said, you're going back to Cape Breton to ride with Adrienne again. Without Adrienne, you'd still be dreaming about riding, not actually doing it. There now, feel better?

Yes, I do.

And I feel really good about how the provincial standing for my division worked out. Neither Helen nor I knew it, but the Nova Scotia Equestrian Federation puts the youth and senior novice in the same division – even though we don't compete in the same classes. Points are accumulated in a variety of ways, including how many other entrants compete in the same classes you do. So I might have won the majority of my senior novice classes, but my classes were small. A youth novice rider – one of my great camp-mates, L'Rhya Cranidge – who rode so well all year, won Champion for the Novice Division in our district. All this meant I was the Reserve Champion for the Novice Division. Our third, most excellent camp-mate, Avery McLean, only competed at Helen's show, not Sherry's, as L'Rhya, Jenna, and I did, which gave us an opportunity to collect more points. Avery rode shoulders back and head high all through 2015, and did a great job on Lex.

Best news of all, for all our hard-driving crew, was that Jenna, who worked so hard on Winnie and had by far the longest and most successful show year of all of us, won overall Novice Champion for the whole province!

Year of the Horse, years of the horse ... what an astonishing period of renewal and learning, along with the privilege of meeting so many people I like and admire. Every time I made mention of "coming back" from an accident, to resume riding in a thoughtful but stimulating new way, the person I was speaking to would invariably say, "Me, too." And then I'd hear a story that would humble me into silence. I had one set of physical and emotional challenges I was dealing with; most often, the friends and acquaintances I spoke with dealt with much more serious and complex ones. Their courage and determination deeply touched me, helped me stay resolute.

And so I return to the horse world grateful for goals both achieved and in planning stages. More important than these, I think about all the people in my personal horse worlds and the larger equestrian world beyond who have been unable to return to riding after an injury, or lost their lives due to accidents while riding. I ride with them in my heart, and I pray they ride in mine, even guide my hands, on difficult days, keeping me from harm's way. Riders on the wind, riders of nova-bright skies, we remember your names, and how you, just as the horse you rode, made the landscape more beautiful.

You are in the arms of love, Karin said, all those years ago.

May you be as well, I'll say in return, the next time it seems right to see her. For now, sister, if ever you find a horse who smells of marigolds and sea salt, tell him to wait for me. You know where to look for him – under the shadows of summer-lush trees, where the grass is bluest, and silver and turquoise dragonflies pass above his handsome head, riding the air currents of yesterday and tomorrow.

Horse and Pony Cheat-Sheet

The evolution of the horse, a mammal of the family *Equidae*, occurred over a geologic time scale of 50 million years, beginning with the small, dog-sized, forest-dwelling *Eohippus*.

There are hundreds of different **breeds** of horses and ponies that have lived on every continent (including the North and South Poles), mostly domesticated, and with domestic ancestries. **Wild horses** also exist around the world (Sable Island, Nova Scotia; Alberta; British Columbia; the Bahamas; Virginia, South Carolina, and Maryland; Colorado; Wyoming; Montana; Idaho; Australia; Portugal; India; the Camargue in France; etc.) The Przewalski's horse, or Dzungarian horse, is a rare and endangered subspecies of wild horse (*Equus ferus*) native to the steppes of central Asia.

A **feral horse** is a free-roaming horse of domesticated ancestry. The horses that people commonly refer to as "wild" still have/had domesticated ancestors. Feral horses managed as wildlife are often called wild, too. Feral horses descended from domestic horses that strayed, escaped from farms or shipwrecks, or were deliberately released into the wild, and managed to survive and reproduce there.

Horse families consist of stallions, mares, and their young, which are called foals. Young males are colts, young females are fillies. A gelding is a stallion that has been gelded (testicles removed).

Horses are **primarily herbivores**, and eat diets of grass, hay (dried grass), and grains. There are instances around the world of **meat- or fish-eating, or omnivorous** horses.

Among the most **commonly known horse breed is the Thoroughbred**. This should not be confused with the adjective "thoroughbred," which denotes careful breeding, usually but not always of horses, but of other animals, too. Thoroughbreds are often used as racehorses, or as hunters and jumpers on the show circuits and in other disciplines. All registered Thoroughbreds (whose breeding histories have been carefully recorded) can trace their lineage to three founding Arabian stallions. **The elegant, short-backed Arabian** (which has one vertebra less than other horse breeds) is also commonly recognized, and popular for use in many different disciplines, from endurance riding to the full gamut of Western riding disciplines.

There are dozens of different **horse colours**. Among the most common are chestnut (the colour can range from light brown or blonde, to reddish tan to red, to simple brown, or "liver"); black; bay (light reddish brown to very dark brown, with black "points," which are the mane, tail, and lower legs); greys (the horse has black skin, but white or mixed dark and white hairs); and white, which most often are greys with fully white coats. Grey horses lighten as they age.

"Colour breeds" include the **buckskin** (tan or gold-coloured coat, with black "points" (mane, tail, and lower legs); the **palomino** (gold coat, white mane and tail); and the **pinto** (dark background colouring, with random patches of white). All these colours can appear in different genetic breeds, or genetic half-breeds (i.e. quarter horses; Thoroughbreds; etc.).

"True or Genetic Breeds" with preferred colours include the **Friesian** (very dark brown to true black); the

Cleveland Bay (bays have reddish brown body colour, with a black mane, tail, ear edges, and lower legs); the **Appaloosa** (which has "spots" all over its body, making it a **leopard Appaloosa**, or spots only on the back half of their bodies, or their rumps, called a **blanket Appaloosa**); and the **American Paint Horse**, or Paint, which has a wide variety of coat patterns. The Paint's different colours, markings, and patterns, combined with the stock-type conformation (horses used to work "stock," or cattle), athletic ability, and agreeable disposition have made the breed popular in recent years. Paints can also be roans (red or bay), which means their coats have white hairs mixed in with darker hairs.

Horses and ponies are primarily differentiated by breeds and size. Some pony breeds are tiny. The Shetland pony, from the Shetland Islands, ranges between 7 hands high (HH), or 28 inches from the hoof to the withers or top of the shoulder, to 11 HH, or 44 inches. The measurement of a hand is a literal man's hand, approximately four inches across, and placed sideways, one atop the other from the ground to the horse's withers, to measure the horse's height.

Ponies are not miniature horses, though **Miniature Horses** exist as a breed, and are measured in inches only, commonly ranging from 34 to 38 inches. Ponies have their own unique qualities and characteristics. The "pony-ness" of ponies is hard to explain, and much more fun to experience. They can be more playful and mischievous than horses, are often uncommonly strong for their size, and are gifted with a work ethic similar to **Draft (U.S.) or Draught (U.K. and Commonwealth) Horses** (Percherons, Belgians, Clydesdales, Shire, and others), which are the largest and heaviest of all horse breeds, often used to pull carriages and wagons, or to work on farms. "Pit-ponies" were used to work in the coal mines in Britain, North America and elsewhere around the globe, and were great favourites of the crews. Ponies can also be epically stubborn and immovable, despite their mostly affectionate hearts and nimble feet and minds.

Estimates suggest that there are around 60 million horses in the world.

Horses and Ponies sleep both lying down and standing up and run shortly after birth. They live around twenty-five years, though with luck and good health, can live to twenty-five or forty years. The oldest horse on record was Old Billy, a working barge horse in England. He was sixty-two years old when he died on November 27, 1822. Born in Woolston, Lancashire, in 1760, Old Billy spent his life pulling barges along canals. Horses have around 205 bones in their skeleton; have been domesticated for over 5,000 years; are capable of seeing about 350 degrees at one time, because their eyes are on the side of their head; and can gallop at around 44 k.p.h. (27 m.p.h.).

ONE HORSEWOMAN'S LIBRARY

The following list represents books either in my personal library, or that I have read many times, or that I plan to read (*). There are, of course, countless books about horses for people of all ages, many of these related to particular disciplines or horse breeds. For anyone starting out or starting back to riding, I also recommend the English and Western rider's handbooks published by Equine Canada as part of their Learn to Ride Program. I have the first three levels in the Western rider series and even after passing Levels One and Two, I find myself referring to the first two books often. I have only just begun to study for Level Three.

For information about studying for your rider's levels, contact your provincial equestrian federation. In Nova Scotia, contact the Nova Scotia Equestrian Federation at www.horsenovascotia.ca. In British Columbia, contact Horse Council BC at http://www.hcbc.ca.

Canada's national sport and equine organization is Equine Canada, which "fulfills a broad range of governance, advocacy, and development functions, all of which focus, in one way or another, on the horse and draw on the enthusiasm it arouses." Further, it is "recognized by Sport Canada and the Féderation Equestre Internationale (FEI) as the national governing body for equestrian sport and recreation in Canada. It is the industry sector leader and as such is recognized and supported by Agriculture and Agri-food Canada. In particular, its leadership in improving both the quality and condition of horses is lauded at home and abroad." For more information: www.equinecanada.ca

Adams, Richard. *Traveller*. New York: Alfred A. Knopf, 1988.

Armstrong, Luanne. *Sand*. Vancouver, British Columbia: Ronsdale Press, 2016.

Farley, Walter. *The Black Stallion*. New York: Random House, 1941.

Fraser, Andrew F. *The Newfoundland Pony*. St. John's, Newfoundland: Creative Publishers, 1992.

German National Equestrian Federation. *The Principles of Riding*. New York: Arco Publishing, 1985.

Gloss, Molly. *The Hearts of Horses*. New York: Houghton, Mifflin, 2007.

Hanauer, Elsie V. *The Horse Owner's Concise Guide*. South Brunswick and New York: A.S. Barnes & Co., 1969.

Hawcroft, Tim. *A-Z of Horse Diseases & Health Problems*. Sydney, Australia: Landsdowne Publishing, 1990.

Hawthorne, Nathaniel. *Pegasus, The Winged Horse – A Greek Legend Retold by Nathaniel Hawthorne*. New York: The Macmillan Company, 1963.

Henry, Marguerite. *Justin Morgan Had a Horse*. Chicago: Wilcox & Follett, 1945.

Henry, Marguerite. *King of the Wind*. Chicago: Rand McNally & Co., 1948.

Henry, Marguerite. *Misty the Wonder Pony*. Chicago: Rand McNally & Co., 1961.

Hillenbrand, Lauren. *Seabiscuit*. New York: Random House Publishing Group, 2002.

*Hutton, Robin. *Sgt. Reckless: America's War Horse*. Washington, D.C.: Regnery History, 2014.

Lehmann, Arthur-Heinz. *The Noble Stallion – The Love Story of Two People and a Great Horse*. London: Jarrolds Publishers, 1954.

Letts, Elizabeth. *The Eighty-Dollar Champion*. New York: Ballantine Books, 2011.

Lewis, C.S. *The Horse and His Boy*. London: Geoffrey Bles Book Publisher, 1954.

Mitchell, Elayne. *The Silver Brumby*. London: Hutchinson, 1958.

Scanlan, Lawrence. *Big Ben*. Markham, Ontario: Scholastic Canada Ltd., 1994.

Scanlan, Lawrence. *Little Horse of Iron – A Quest for the Canadian Horse*. Toronto: Vintage Canada Edition, 2002.

Scanlan, Lawrence. *The Horse God Built – Secretariat, His Groom, Their Legacy*. Toronto: HarperCollins, 2006.

Scanlan, Lawrence. *Wild About Horses*. Toronto: Random House of Canada, 1998.

Sewell, Anna. *Black Beauty, The Autobiography of a Horse*. (First printed by Jarrolds: Norwich, U.K., 1877.)

Silver, Caroline. *Guide to Horses of the World*. London: Treasure Press, 1976. (First printed in Great Britain by Elsevier Phaidon.)

Smiley, Jane. *Horse Heaven*. New York: Alfred A. Knopf, 2000.

The British Horse Society and The Pony Club. *The Manual of Horsemanship*. Lewes, Sussex, England: W.E. Baxter Ltd., 1972.

Whitaker, Julie. *The Horse – A Miscellany of Equine Knowledge*. New York: Ivy Press Ltd., St. Martin's Press, 2007.

Also by Marjorie Simmins

Non-Fiction:

Coastal Lives: A Memoir. Pottersfield Press: Lawrencetown Beach, Nova Scotia, 2014.

Anthologies:

Nova Scotia Love Stories. Pottersfield Press: Lawrencetown Beach, Nova Scotia, 2015. ("Forever Worlds")

Untying the Apron: Daughters Remember Mothers of the 1950s. Edited by Lorri Neilsen Glenn. Guernica Editions: Toronto, 2013. ("The House With Many Doors")

Saltlines. Edited by Lorri Neilsen Glenn and Carsten Knox. Backalong Books: Big Tancook Island, N.S., 2012. ("The Rowdy Lot")

Essays from Contemporary Culture. Second Edition. Edited by Katherine Anne Achley. Harcourt Brace College Publishers: Toronto, O.N., 1995. ("Trips From Here to There")

Essays from Contemporary Culture. Third Edition. Edited by Katherine Anne Achley. Harcourt Brace College Publishers: Toronto, 1998. ("Trips From Here to There")

Essays from Contemporary Culture. Fourth Edition. Edited by Katherine Anne Achley. Harcourt Brace College Publishers: Toronto, 2001. ("Trips From Here to There")

Journeys Through Our World. Third Edition. Compiled by the Developmental English Department at Santa Fe Community College. Pearson Custom Publishing: Boston, M.A., 2007. ("Trips From Here to There")

Working the Tides: A Portrait of Canada's West Coast Fishery. Edited by Peter A. Robson and Michael Skog. Harbour Publishing: Pender Harbour, B.C., 1996. ("Three Generations of Annieville Fishermen")

For more information about Marjorie Simmins, please go to her website: www.marjoriesimmins.ca